Truly Blessed and Highly Favored

Truly Blessed and Highly Favored

A Memoir

H. Carl McCall

with Paul Grondahl

excelsior editions
AN IMPRINT OF STATE UNIVERSITY OF NEW YORK PRESS

Published by State University of New York Press, Albany

Excelsior Editions is an imprint of State Universty of New York Press

For information, contact State University of New York Press, Albany, NY
www.sunypress.edu

Library of Congress Cataloging-in-Publication Data

Name: McCall, H. Carl, author. | With assistance from Paul Grondahl.
Title: Truly blessed and highly favored : a memoir / H. Carl McCall with
   Paul Grondahl.
Description: Albany : State University of New York Press, [2022] | Includes
   index.
Identifiers: ISBN 9781438489650 (hardcover : alk. paper) | ISBN 9781438489643
   (ebook)
Further information is available at the Library of Congress.

10 9 8 7 6 5 4 3 2 1

*This book is dedicated to the women who loved me,
inspired me, supported me, and enriched my life:
my mother, my wife, and my daughter*

Contents

A photo gallery follows chapter 10

Prologue
Controlling My Exit

It has been a strange and humbling experience to write this memoir. I am not by nature a reflective person. I am more of a doer than a contemplative. My tense is active rather than passive. I am someone who is forever looking forward, moving ahead, strategizing for the future, planning for a better tomorrow. This exercise of slowing down, looking back, of sorting through the past and trying to unpack the full range of my rich and rewarding life experiences took some getting used to, but it has also taught me many important lessons.

I am very disciplined and methodical, but my narrative has been marked, like all of our lives, by things outside my control. We do not get to choose our parents or the circumstances of our upbringing, for instance. It has been often quoted that "the best-laid plans of mice and men often go awry," and so I have come to understand this truism, often by painful and disappointing setbacks and challenges. On the other side of the equation, there is the matter of fate or divine providence or whatever you choose to call it. So much of my most valuable personal experiences and professional successes have been a matter of good fortune and the hand of fate. Call it luck. I prefer to think of them as blessings.

My life has been blessed, even when I experienced failure or setbacks. One of the most fortunate elements of my life has been the love, support, and kindness shown to me by my family and by important mentors throughout my life. So much of what I have achieved is a result of guidance and advice imparted from the time I was a youngster by teachers, camp counselors, ministers, political leaders, professors, bosses, and professional colleagues.

One such lesson came to mind as I have tried to put my life in perspective in this memoir and to provide something of interest and value to readers. I am going to begin at the end, as it were, and to start at the conclusion of my long professional career in public service, politics, and business.

My friend Vernon Jordan, whom we recently lost, once gave me some advice that I have followed and that I am putting into practice now. Vernon told me: "You should control your exit." He went on to suggest that I should make plans for when to step down, leave on my own terms and at a time of my own choosing. Based on his long and illustrious career in politics, he drove home one point in particular, gained from his own experience across a varied career as a prominent civil rights activist, successful business executive, and influential adviser to President Bill Clinton. His main takeaway was this: Do not allow someone else or circumstances decide my exit for me.

That always stuck with me and I have heeded Vernon's advice. I also learned that controlling my exit is easier said than done.

I turned eighty-three years old in October 2018 and I was preparing to downshift and to begin a new phase of my life, otherwise known as retirement, which is something many of my friends and colleagues had done one or two decades earlier. But again, I am a doer and I had resisted making that decision because I like being active, making a useful contribution, and because I was working in a job I enjoyed.

My major activity at this time was my position as chairman of the Board of Trustees of the State University of New York, the nation's largest comprehensive system of public higher education in the United States. It serves more than one million students annually, employs more than ninety thousand faculty and staff, and connects with more than three million alumni around the world. It is a vast and complex system that includes sixty-four colleges and universities throughout New York State. Although it was an unpaid appointment, I never considered it a volunteer position to be shrugged off. For me, it was a full-time position that I approached with the fullest measure of commitment, energy, and my full skill set. I believe passionately in the value of higher education, particularly as a pathway for opportunity and advancement for young people from minority and underserved communities. I knew firsthand how a college education could provide the foundation for upward mobility and achieving heights not possible without it.

As chairman of SUNY, I maintained an office in New York City and in Albany, the state capital, where I had spent several years at various stages of my public service career. I spent a lot of time on the road, which I felt was essential to do my job to the best of my ability. I frequently traveled all around the state in order to make site visits and meet with administrators at our sixty-four institutions. At that point, in the fall of 2018, I had been chairman for twelve years, beginning when I was seventy-one years old. Now I was in my eighties and the drain of the frequent travel and full-time demands of the position were wearing me down physically and taking a toll in other ways. I was hearing Vernon's voice in my head. It was time to start planning how I could control my exit.

It was time to move on. The vast and enormously challenging SUNY system was stable. The SUNY chancellor, Dr. Kristina M. Johnson, the thirteenth chancellor, began her tenure in September 2017 and was about to begin her third year on the job. She was demonstrating remarkable energy, intellect, and vision. The SUNY Board of Trustees was composed of a group of eighteen cooperative and committed members. At that time, the vice chair, Dr. Merryl Tisch, a professional educator and former chancellor of the state's Board of Regents, seemed likely to become my successor. I considered her a good choice.

For myself, personally, it seemed like the right time for a transition. My personal life was very good and gave me pleasure. My wife, Joyce Brown, and I had an apartment in Manhattan and our country home in the Hudson Valley. My close friends described it as my promised forty acres and a pool. We always had a good chuckle out of their quip. Joyce and I spent weekends and long stretches in the summer there, savoring the country life. I had a pond on our property stocked with bass and fishing was my new pastime as a gentleman of leisure.

Meanwhile, my wife Joyce was entering her twentieth productive year as president of the Fashion Institute of Technology, known as FIT, which is one of the most acclaimed institutions of higher education in the SUNY system. Joyce had worked tirelessly for years and had raised the remarkable sum of $190 million to build a new academic building on FIT's Manhattan campus. But the ongoing real estate boom and robust new construction activity had escalated construction costs considerably and Joyce was understandably upset when revised bids for building the facility came in at $20 million over the original estimate and her budget. The bottom line is that she will have to raise an additional $20 million or scale back the building's design. It's the challenge of doing business in New York, she has been told. That's small consolation for President Brown's efforts to elevate FIT's campus in a brutal construction landscape, made even more challenging due to the coronavirus pandemic.

As I was making plans for my transition and working on controlling my exit, in December 2018, I experienced troubling health issues. I was having mobility problems. Walking was becoming difficult. I attributed it to the two hip replacements I had several years ago. My physician wanted me to come in for testing right away. Examinations at the Hospital for Special Surgery in Manhattan, one of the nation's top-ranked orthopedic hospitals, diagnosed my problem as spinal stenosis. Surgery was not advised. I would be treated with medication and physical therapy.

A more concerning development was noticed by my primary care physician during a routine semi-annual physical exam. She indicated that I had lost eighteen pounds since my last exam six months earlier. I had noticed that my pants were not fitting as well, but the gradual weight loss went unnoticed by me and others.

My doctor ordered a chest X-ray. It was mid-December. Usually, Joyce and I spend the Christmas holiday in St. Thomas in the Virgin Islands. We have a time-share unit that we use over the holiday season each winter. Yet due to major damage left in the wake of two hurricanes that devastated the island, the recovery and rebuilding was slow and we decided it would not be a good time to travel there.

As an alternative, we planned a major travel adventure to Southeast Asia, with Vietnam, Cambodia, and Thailand included in our itinerary.

I did not delude myself. I understood that I might be in the early stages of a serious health condition, but we both needed a break from the stress and demands of work, so I postponed the X-ray and Joyce and I began our much-anticipated journey to Asia.

The trip was wonderful. We had hired experienced, knowledgeable guides; we had booked excellent accommodations; and we enjoyed delightful and memorable meals. My overall impression was that Vietnam and Thailand are bustling, hyper-developing countries—benefiting from significant support, investment, and presence of Chinese officials and experts.

On the other hand, Cambodia's development was far less robust. The people were warm and welcoming and we enjoyed visiting the vibrant marketplaces, the glittering National Palace, and the impressive temples at Angkor Wat. All things considered, Joyce and I decided that Cambodia was our favorite destination on the trip. We both agreed we would like to return to explore Cambodia in even greater depth.

As soon as we returned in January 2019, I had my chest X-ray. The results felt like a sucker-punch in the stomach. A growth was detected. My physician then ordered a CAT scan, an MRI, a biopsy of tissue from my lung, and a host of other diagnostic exams. The diagnosis hit me hard. I had stage-four lung cancer. It was spreading to other parts of my body. Joyce was with me for all of the exams. She asked tough questions and provided great support. It was great to have a loving partner for this ordeal. We were devastated by the outcome.

I went through the stages of grief and I had to confront hard truths. I thought a lot about three people in particular who became my closest longtime friends in New York: Leon Watts, Jim McGraw, and Calvin Pressley. All four of us landed in Brooklyn in June 1963 and we each began our careers as ministers: Leon as an assistant at First AME Zion Church, Jim as youth minister at Warren Street United Methodist Church, and Calvin at the Church of the Open Door of the New York City Mission Society in Fort Greene, Brooklyn. I was assigned by the New York City Mission Society to serve as a community organizer for a number of Black churches in the Bedford-Stuyvesant neighborhood of Brooklyn.

My mind flashed back to 1963 when these three wonderful friends, as close as I had to brothers, advised and assisted me in organizing a demonstration at the construction site for a new Downstate Medical Center Hospital after Governor Nelson A. Rockefeller refused to hire minority construction workers. By the time the demonstration had been broken up by the police, more than two hundred people were arrested, including thirty of Brooklyn's most prominent ministers. We were locked up in the basement of a precinct on Empire Boulevard that served as a makeshift jail. We spent hours there and we passed the time by singing hymns and freedom songs. The four of us bonded during those hours and our friendship began. It was one of the most amazing experiences of my life. We were a band of brothers from that night onward.

Calvin was perhaps the most special of the three. He became the inseparable big brother I never had. Our families connected, we took vacations together, collaborated on a variety of projects, bought houses and shared time at Martha's Vineyard. Calvin joined in as an active volunteer who participated in all of my political campaigns. We also began an annual tradition of attending the Penn Relays in Philadelphia for forty consecutive years. They are all gone now; each died of cancer. I struggled through long sleepless nights of the soul and had to confront my own mortality. Was it now my time?

I was angry. I never smoked. I paid attention to my health and maintained good medical care. I always got regular checkups. Why was this happening to me?

After my anger and depression passed, I experienced a period of quiet reflection. I stopped focusing on this terrible disease that was happening to me now and focused on all the incredible and even miraculous things that happened to me during my life's journey.

I started out with very little in a poor, fractured family, abandoned by my father. Fortunately, I had a wonderful, loving mother who raised me and instilled in me the value of education. I received a solid public school education and an outstanding experience at one of America's most prestigious colleges and one of Europe's best theological schools, both essentially free due to scholarships and the financial support of Black ministers who mentored me. I was also proud of the fact that as a young man I established a unique community service center, boosted by church support, in my hometown of Roxbury, Massachusetts. I was also fortunate that I was given an opportunity to launch a career in New York City in community empowerment, politics, government, and the private sector.

I was elected and appointed to important public offices. I received more than 1.5 million votes from New Yorkers when I ran for governor. There is a landmark building in Albany named for me. It also happened that I found in Joyce an extraordinary, supportive, and understanding wife and best friend. I was blessed with a wonderful daughter and five sisters who were always there for me, along with a large group of wonderful friends who were always supportive and in my corner.

As I looked back on all I had experienced and accomplished in my life, I found the most telling description of my life in a greeting from Sister Harris that she offered on the Sunday mornings when I occasionally preached at Metropolitan Community Methodist Church in Harlem. She would greet me by saying, "Good morning Brother McCall, how are you?"

I replied, "I am fine, Sister Harris, how are you?"

She responded with a phrase that churchgoing folks from the South are familiar with: "I am truly blessed and highly favored," Sister Harris would tell me.

Truly blessed and highly favored. That was what has happened to me. Sister Harris summed it up so beautifully. Yes, indeed, I have been truly blessed and highly favored.

Still, the minister in me compelled me to affirm the source of my blessings. Blessed by whom and favored by whom?

The answer came as I remembered these words from the doxology that we sing in our Christian service.

> *Praise God, from whom all blessings flow;*
> *Praise Him, all creatures here below;*
> *Praise Him above, ye heav'nly host;*
> *Praise Father, Son, and Holy Ghost!*

I have always believed that God has guided me through all of the triumphs and disappointments of my life. And I have tried to serve Him by serving His people through my ministry and public service. I have faith that He will be with me with whatever lies ahead. I am ready to accept whatever is to come.

This book is about the blessings that happened to me.

Chapter 1

Roots

I was born in 1935 and like many African Americans of my generation—particularly those who, like me, are descended from slaves—I lack
concrete details about my early family history. Our origin story is muted,
often intentionally so. There is too much pain in a past marked by bond-
age and subjugation at the hands of white masters. Thus, the narrative
remains opaque, or missing key elements.

Many people want to know how my family's history and my own
beginnings informed or defined my sense of identity as an African American. Essentially, they are inquiring about my inherent understanding of
my blackness. I try to tell them that I have mostly a void where so many
of my friends have a rich and detailed family history. There are gaps
and unanswered questions and so much I do not know about my ancestors. My friends who are Irish American or Italian American or Greek
American tell wonderfully detailed and heartwarming stories about their
heritage passed down from great-grandparents, grandparents, and parents.
Many have traced out the branches of their family trees and have written
extensive genealogies. As these stories were being told and shared, I sat
silently and listened. I wished I had stories like theirs to contribute. I felt
a dull ache in my heart and I always wanted to know more about my
family history. I had a longing for a firm foundation and wished that I,
too, could describe all the branches in my family tree.

Instead, I had a sense of rootlessness, of not knowing much about my family's earliest history. Although I did not know the term growing up, I would come to understand that I am part of the African Diaspora. Large-scale enslavement dispersed millions of people from Western and Central Africa on slave ships to regions throughout the Caribbean, the Americas, and the United States. These slaves served as indentured servants on plantations, in factories, as servants in the homes of wealthy homeowners, and anywhere that slave labor was deemed necessary and accepted.

I have since come to know and understand the term African Diaspora. I am descended from slaves and I am part of the African Diaspora. It was a rootless, nomadic existence for my ancestors. For countless people like myself, a deep understanding and knowledge of my family's history going back generations was, for all practical purposes, unattainable.

Therefore, what I know about where I came from fills only a few short sentences. My grandparents chose not to talk much about their past because it was generally not a positive experience. Like all children, I was curious, of course, and I remember when I was young asking my grandmother and grandfather about the South, which they had fled in order to migrate to the North.

About the South I can remember my grandfather saying only this: "It was a place you had to get away from."

Period. Nothing more. I did not get to ask a follow-up question or, even if I did, he declined to tell me anything more.

I do not even know the names of my forebearers.

What I was told by my mother and grandmother and managed to piece together is that my great-grandmother was a slave. Her name was never spoken to me and even my grandmother, the daughter of a slave, knew very little about her family history.

My consciousness of race and a deeper understanding of my past began with my maternal grandfather, Calvin Ray. He grew up in North Carolina and he was the one who often voiced the sentiment that the South was a place he wanted to leave. He offered few details, but he did talk about migrating from North Carolina to Boston around 1905.

Calvin Ray was ahead of his time. Without strictly fitting its historical parameters, he was part of the Great Migration, at least in spirit. The

Great Migration involved the voluntary relocation of six million African Americans from the rural South to cities in the industrial North, Midwest, and West beginning around 1916 and continuing through 1970. Although Calvin Ray was more than a decade early, his exodus fit the paradigm of the Great Migration. These huge numbers of Black people were driven northward out of the Southern states due to the harsh reality of Jim Crow laws that enforced racial segregation and fueled discrimination in many forms. This racial caste system was rigorously enforced until 1965.

My grandfather never explained to me the motivations for his migration, or why he chose to settle in Boston. He suggested in oblique ways that he left North Carolina both to escape discrimination and overt racism but also to find better economic opportunities.

The few details I managed to glean from my grandfather Calvin was that he had three brothers. The brothers all left the South in the same era, the early 1900s, but took different paths in their journey from the oppression they experienced in the South. One brother ended up in Washington, DC, and worked for the United States Postal Service. One of the brothers settled in New Hampshire, but I was not told what he did for a living. And one other brother came to Boston along with Calvin, but, once again, my knowledge of these great-uncles of mine was extremely limited.

Around the same time, the early 1900s, my maternal grandmother, Mamie Brooks, relocated from Richmond, Virginia, to the Boston area. She said her mother was born after slavery, but her grandmother, who would be my great-great-grandmother, was born into slavery and she was owned by a plantation owner in the South. She told me that her grandmother was assigned to work as a domestic servant for the wife of a wealthy plantation owner. The story passed down to me noted that she slept on the hardwood floor at the foot of the bed and, among her other duties, she looked after the personal needs of the plantation owner's wife, cooked and cleaned their large house, and was also responsible for raising their children. She said she was one of several enslaved females who were assigned various domestic duties on the Virginia plantation.

Again, she either did not know her enslaved grandmother's name or she chose not to share it at family gatherings, because I was an astute and inquisitive child and I am sure I asked what it was. But I have no recollection of ever being told her name.

Mamie Brooks and Calvin Ray migrated to Boston, where they met, four decades after the end of the Civil War and the abolition of slavery. Calvin worked as a janitor who maintained and repaired coal-burning furnaces and was put in charge of maintenance of commercial buildings in downtown Boston. They married in 1909 and their first child, Calvin Jr., was born in 1910. Their second child, Caroleasa, my mother, was born in 1912. They had a son, Donald, who died as a toddler of a childhood disease. Mamie Brooks Ray gave birth without complication to three more baby girls—my aunts Inez, Eunice, and Hazel.

I have fond memories of my grandfather Calvin. He was a tall, dark-skinned Black man with thick, gray hair. He spoke softly and with only the trace of a Southern drawl. He was reserved in his demeanor and very quiet, a man of few words. I remember he'd come home from his job as a maintenance worker and furnace technician and he decompressed from his long work day by listening to the radio. We understood intuitively that he did not want to be interrupted, especially not by a young grandson. I remember hearing his heavy sighs and he would confide to me, in a low voice, what grinding toil it was to shovel coal into the furnace and to make sure the boiler and the other parts were functioning properly through the long, cold New England winters. I did not know who his friends were, because he did not socialize much and they rarely invited visitors into their apartment.

I wondered about their education, but neither my grandfather Calvin nor my grandmother Mamie ever told me how far they got with their formal schooling. I had the sense that both of them dropped out of school at a young age to work full-time to help support their families.

Mamie was aided by a force of personality. She was short of stature but large in other ways. She was very sociable, a big talker in contrast to her husband's long silences. Whatever Southern drawl they might have once possessed was worn away by their years in Boston, although neither of my grandparents developed the elongated flatness and lack of the *r* sound that characterized Boston natives. Mamie occupied the center of our extended multigenerational family. She was deeply involved in the rearing of all her grandchildren and also our babysitter when our parents went out at night to socialize or when my mother entered the workforce full-time.

My Grandma Mamie and Grandpa Calvin lived in a rented brownstone on Hammond Street in the South End of Boston, an African American enclave. The streets were cobblestone and the nineteenth-century brownstones were well maintained. It was a haven for Black people, where they felt comfortable and where their culture flourished. Boston's South End was one of the only places in the city that had not been racially redlined, a rare locale where Blacks were welcome and encouraged to rent or buy homes. In essence, it was a ghetto, but it was also a place of pride and solidarity. If Mamie and Calvin were victims of overt racism, I never heard about it, although I have no doubt that once they left the confines of Hammond Street they faced issues of the institutional prejudice and discrimination embedded in the nation at that time, including in New England.

One of my earliest, strongest memories of my grandmother Mamie was her fascination with a form of numerology, particularly when it came to playing the numbers, and her role in the underground gambling culture among Black residents in her South End neighborhood.

Mamie was a devoted player of the numbers, a form of gambling that involved picking three random numerals. Players picked their three digits in the morning and when they picked up a copy of the evening paper, the *Boston Record*, and they would find out if they had the winning numbers by looking at horse racing results buried deep in the sports pages from Suffolk Downs, a racetrack in East Boston that opened in 1935. The first three numbers of the previous day's parimutuel betting handle at Suffolk Downs—which were completely random and could not be manipulated—were the winning numbers for thousands of small daily wagers on the numbers that ranged from a dime to $1 or more.

Playing the numbers was a staple in working-class neighborhoods in Boston and cities across the Northeast and the nation, long before Massachusetts and other states created state-sanctioned lottery games of chance.

At least in her telling, Mamie was especially adept at picking the winning numbers. She had an elaborate system of picking her numbers that bordered on religious devotion. Her "Bible" of gambling on the numbers was a dog-eared copy of *Dr. Buzzard's Dream Book*, a thin pamphlet that assigned numbers to interpretations of dreams. This book was widely sold at the five-and-dime, at drugstores, or corner stores. It looked like Mamie had owned hers for many decades and she preserved it like a talisman. The *Dream Book* was a kind of glossary of dreams, arranged alphabetically, with numbers assigned to each category of dream. A dream about being caught in floodwaters, for instance, might carry the number thirty-six, and Mamie would play the numbers three and six and find another single-digit number in the *Dream Book* or by some other method to come up with the three numbers she would play for that day. She also liked to use combinations of the birthdays of her grandchildren, but she swore by the power of her dreams. Nobody, myself included, ever expressed skepticism or questioned the scientific efficacy of *Dr. Buzzard's Dream Book* or, for that matter, what branch of medicine this sketchy author and numerologist claimed to represent. No matter. For Mamie, recalled dreams and consulting her ever-present *Dream Book* formed the foundation of her gambling tools.

Mamie did not have a large amount of discretionary income, but she wagered a dime or a quarter each day, hoping to win a six-to-one payout. She hit her share of winning numbers, but she also made herself an indispensable part of the daily numbers landscape in the South End of Boston. Her brownstone on Hammond Street became a drop-off point for neighbors who wanted to play the numbers on their way to work in the morning. In her living room, she had a tidy stack of slips of paper with names and numbers scrawled on them. Various runners would stop by, Mamie would hand over the stack of paper slips, and the person would hustle off with that day's entries. If one of the players hit the three-digit number, the runner would return to Mamie's house with the winnings.

At some point, our family lore goes, Mamie's brownstone was raided by Boston police. Mamie's son, Calvin Jr., was arrested for serving as a Hammond Street runner and for playing a central role in the numbers game. Although he never implicated his mother and refused to cooperate with the investigation, the scandal and the time he had to serve derailed a promising academic career. He had been an excellent student up to that point, but his arrest led to his expulsion from high school. The damage had been done and Calvin Jr. never fully recovered.

"Moving up the hill" is what we called it in my family, this relocation from the South End, which in reality was only a slightly more upwardly mobile locale from where we had lived before. We moved to the Boston neighborhood of Roxbury, which was known as the heart of Black culture in the city, and the numbers operation established a foothold there as well. The numbers game centered on Humboldt Avenue, the main commercial thoroughfare, which is where we lived and where the life and action was. I got to know Mr. Wright, who was an usher at Mamie's church and who owned a corner store on Humboldt Avenue that was primarily a newsstand that sold a few sundry items and also stocked a selection of magazines and newspapers. My limited involvement was to drop off Mamie's numbers at his store as a favor to my grandmother.

This was gambling on a small scale, a dollar-and-a-dream respite for poor, Black working-class families like mine. It was grassroots and benign as far as I knew—based upon the little nuggets of incomplete information I gathered when I asked Mamie about it in later years. She didn't like to delve too deeply into the past and never offered me much detail, whether I wanted to know about our family's connection to slavery or how she had gotten involved in the numbers and how the operation worked. She did concede she did not read much, but she purchased the *Boston Record* each evening because she wanted to look at the horse racing track's parimutuel betting handle in order to find the three digits that determined who hit the number that day. She also confided she was not much of a churchgoer, but when she did attend Sunday service, she memorized the row of three digits on the board near the choir. Those numbers corresponded to that Sunday's hymn selection and Mamie believed strongly in using the hymn numbers because she thought it brought her divine luck when she played them for money in the game.

I never saw Mamie work outside the house, which is why she needed me to serve as her runner. She raised me and my five siblings and she also took care of five additional grandchildren. I remember that Mamie was in charge and we young ones dared not challenge her authority. Even though she was low-key and never raised her voice to us in anger or frustration, she had a firm sense of rules and decorum and we learned to follow what she laid down without argument or complaint. For us youngsters, it was

Mamie's world. We just lived in it. She was a cross between a field marshal and den mother, whose daily attire consisted of a house dress and slippers. She just had little need to dress otherwise. Mamie occasionally yielded the kitchen, where she also ruled, to her husband. He loved to reconnect himself and his family members to their native North Carolina by serving a dinner of Southern-fried chicken, smoked ribs, and collard greens.

Calvin Jr. never bounced back from his downward spiral after being expelled from high school. He married and had four children. They moved off Hammond Street so he could put the difficult episode behind him. He never seemed to be able to outrun his past. He worked in the upholstery business until the company shut down for lack of customers and he was forced to do domestic work—the only steady job he could find. Several female members of our family had made their living cleaning up after wealthy white families, including my aunt Inez who worked for an heiress to the Pabst Blue Ribbon fortune and lived in Westchester County. She seemed to enjoy her work. But I think it grated on Calvin Jr. that this was the only kind of employment he could find. Unfortunately, he was not highly skilled and lacked the kind of employment history that would lift him out of domestic work. That was what was available and the need to feed, house, and clothe his family took precedence over his ego.

My family put down roots at 27 Harold Street in Roxbury. Multiple generations of family members lived in two connected buildings. My grandmother and aunts lived on the second floor and my parents and my sisters and I lived on the third floor. It was north of Fenway Park and near the Franklin Park Zoo. It was a neighborhood in transition during the 1940s. It had been a predominantly Jewish neighborhood, but many of the Jewish families had moved out and relocated to more affluent areas outside the city. Despite the exodus, most of the small businesses and the daily economy of Roxbury were controlled by Jewish merchants. That's just the way it was. I did not sense any racial tensions between Jews and the Black community. Everyone seemed to get along fairly well.

My aunt Inez was an influence on me in many ways, particularly in how she taught me about proper deportment and protocol and how to feel confident and comfortable in the world of wealthy white families—lessons I would draw upon throughout my adult professional and personal life.

Inez married the butler at the Purchase estate, where they both worked. His name was Luther and he was a kind man. After their marriage, Inez moved with her new husband to Washington, DC, but he died tragically in an automobile accident shortly after the newlyweds settled in the nation's capital. She grieved his loss but eventually remarried a few years later to the postal carrier who delivered mail to her home in DC. His name was Richard. They struck up a friendship that led to a courtship and a marriage proposal. They were happy together, they had a strong union, and they had an influence on me.

I can still picture Aunt Inez running me and my siblings through our paces about how to function at formal dinners. She taught us etiquette and proper manners, such as how to set a table formally; which forks to use for salad, entrée, and dessert; where to place one's napkin and how to act during dinner. She had great references and work experience as a maid and she never had trouble finding work with wealthy white families. She was a wonderfully positive influence and she also encouraged us to work hard and to strive to get ahead. In practical terms, she also helped out her sister, our mother, when we struggled financially in later years. Aunt Inez was our rock during turbulent times. My mother relied on her generosity and kindness and, by extension, so did we children.

Chapter 2

A Father I Hardly Knew

M y mother, Caroleasa McCall, was a tall and stately woman who considered nurturing and raising her children to be her life's most important work. After her parents relocated from North Carolina and settled in Boston, Caroleasa was born and raised in the city. She graduated from Commercial High School in Boston, where she took courses in cooking and sewing and domestic duties that came to be known as home economics. In the late 1920s, in the era that she graduated, there were very few jobs available to African American women besides domestic work. As a result, she became a domestic worker and was hired as a maid for a white family in Boston. But my mother was not willing to simply accept her limited lot in life. She aspired to be something more than someone who did the scut work for rich white folks.

In 1931, she earned a job with the New Haven Railroad. She worked at the Dover Street Terminal, where trains were prepared to be put into service. Although her job still involved cleaning, she washed windows, vacuumed the coaches, and made those coaches gleam. She was part of a force of Black women who were hired to clean the cars. In my mother's mind, it was a promotion and she was pleased to no longer be called part of "the help." She made more money and worked for a large employer. It also was more convenient because she only had a short walk each day from her family's apartment in the South End to the nearby Dover Street Terminal.

After she had been working as a cleaner with the New Haven Railroad for some months, she met a charming young Black man who was a waiter for the railroad—a position held primarily by Black men. It was an extension of Chicago businessman George Pullman's business model to hire former slaves and thousands of African American men after the Civil War to serve white passengers on his segregated luxury rail sleeper cars. Although journalists and historians would disclose the racism, low pay, and poor working conditions they endured, the vast army of Pullman porters who helped launch the civil rights movement were in the vanguard of creating a new Black middle class.

Although they were not history-shapers in the way of a Pullman porter, the Black men who served as porters on the New Haven Railroad were success stories in their own right, overcoming discrimination and bigotry and the keen competition for those jobs. My mother met several of those men as she was cleaning the cars at the Dover Street Terminal, but one in particular took special notice of her, and she of him. His name was Herman McCall and he was a waiter who started his shift early in the morning and would cross paths with Caroleasa in the terminal. When she got a break from cleaning the coaches, they talked and hit it off. He was assigned as a waiter on trains that traveled from Boston, to Philadelphia and Washington, DC, and all the way to Miami, Florida.

These were the Depression years, too, and the railroad suffered economically like every other business. When business dipped, there were layoffs. Waiters and other railroad workers had fewer trips, which meant less tips and a sharp decline in their income along with periods of unemployment that sapped their meager savings and defeated their spirits.

Herman McCall did not particularly like his given name. He was tall and lean and everybody called him Skinny. That's how he introduced himself to my mother. In fact, none of his coworkers knew his real name. Skinny was the silent type. He didn't talk much about his background or share his story. He grew up in Waycross, Georgia, and still had a slight twang in his voice. He was raised for the most part by his aunt Ida because his parents apparently split up. He lived for several years in Philadelphia. He stood just over six feet tall and had a wiry build. He slicked his hair back with oil, his white dress shirts and dark suits were pressed and neat. He took special care with his appearance and he was always sharply dressed when he went to work or out on the town.

Caroleasa and Skinny married in 1934, after a year or two of courtship. They lived in Roxbury and after I was born on October 17, 1935, they moved "up the hill" to 27 Harold Street because my mother was pregnant with her second child, my sister. They needed help with child care because Skinny was traveling frequently with his job as a railroad waiter. My early memories of Skinny are sporadic because, given his long trips for work, he was not a strong or steady presence in our lives. I remember he liked to dress up on Saturday nights in a nice suit and tie. Sometimes, he'd take my mother out to the movies and Mamie would babysit us. Other times, he got dressed up and went out by himself. His favorite hangout was a South End nightclub that catered to Blacks called Little Dixie. He'd meet his friends there, usually without my mother. I remember he liked to drink Pickwick Ale from the can. It was a popular and cheap Boston beer and he always had cans of it in the refrigerator in our apartment. He never gave me a taste or encouraged me to drink alcohol, which I am thankful for because I saw many of my friends succumb to the addiction of booze. I never acquired much of a taste for alcohol and was not a drinker in college. I just did not like the feeling of being drunk or out of control. Today, I will have an occasional glass of white wine, and I do not drink to excess.

Although it was simply decorated and not luxurious by any means, we had a large apartment, bright and clean, with four bedrooms. On the outside, at least, we looked like a happy and relatively prosperous family. As a youngster, I did not intuit or realize the strains that underpinned my parents' marriage, although I came to realize years later that they were significant. I do not recall any loud arguments and no physical altercations or fighting of any sort. They must have aired their grievances and problems out of earshot of us children.

With frequent furloughs or temporary layoffs for Skinny when railroad ridership slumped, additional work became imperative. My mother applied for a job for the unemployed through the Works Progress Administration, or WPA.

As the only boy alongside five sisters, household chores were divided among us. I had to empty water from the pan under the icebox and set the new block of ice into the icebox. I filled the coal bin, stoked the furnace, and cleaned up the residue of the burned coal. We made the most of the basics in that era before technology and modern conveniences. Since we had a big family and a small icebox, it was my job to put food and beverages out on the open-air back porch in the winter to keep them cool, careful not to let liquids freeze and burst their cans or glass bottles. The Pickwick Ale always went on the back porch in the cold months.

My bedroom was spartan, but I was happy to have my privacy. My mother bought a desk and chair for me so I could do my homework in quiet. The desk had a drop-down lid and I was very proud of that desk. It was something special my mom gave to me. She presented the desk with a lecture on how she expected me to do well in school and that the desk was a down payment on her expectation that I would excel academically. We did not own a television until I went away to college. It's not that TV did not exist at that time. We just could not afford a TV set when they first came out and were considered expensive new gadgets. I chose to get my entertainment by reading comics. *Archie* was my favorite and I also loved the Popeye cartoons shown in the movie theater before the feature film. I was impressed by how spinach made Popeye super-strong and that's how spinach became my favorite vegetable. I wanted to be strong like Popeye.

My favorite thing to do on Saturday afternoons was to go to the movies. It was a glorious outing. We'd watch the cartoons and cheer when Popeye came on. We saw newsreels, a cartoon, and a feature film all for the price of twenty-five cents. I also remember that a big bag of popcorn cost just ten cents. Mamie sometimes had some extra quarters she would give me, but only with the provision that I had to take two of my younger sisters with me. I did not mind the arrangement because I got to see Popeye and enjoyed an entire afternoon of movie magic and my sisters were never any trouble. But I longed to make money of my own so I would not have to be beholden to the largesse of Mamie and to her requirement of taking my sisters along.

Fortune shined on me in the form of an elderly Jewish woman who summoned me from the window of her apartment building, which I passed each day on my way to and from school. She needed help with turning on her gas on Friday evenings in preparation for the Sabbath rituals on Saturday and she gave me a dime for my trouble. She asked me to come back next Friday. I did. I saved those dimes and could anticipate independent movie outings on future Saturdays. Better yet, she introduced me to two other elderly Orthodox Jewish women who also needed me to change their gas control settings in accordance with Orthodox rules for observing the Sabbath. Soon, I had three more weekly customers and I brought home 40 cents each Friday evening. I later learned they called me the Sabbath Goy, which was just fine by me. I suddenly had an income stream that would allow me to go to the movies on Saturdays whenever I chose instead of counting on Mamie to give me the money. The Jewish women lived on Walnut Avenue, just one block over from our place on Harold Street. Their apartments were only marginally nicer than ours. Despite the racial and cultural divide, we were essentially all working class, facing similar struggles and financial strains.

I grew up as a carefree kid for the most part, oblivious to economic disparities and racial inequality because our neighborhood of Roxbury was diverse by all measures and reasonably peaceful. It was not until I reached my teenage years and went off to college that I began to realize how difficult things were for my parents and our extended family. I knew my father was only sporadically employed, given seasonal layoffs by the railroad and the roller-coaster ride of frequent disruptions of paychecks based on ridership levels and the general economy. It was not that we went without adequate food or were on the verge of becoming homeless. Yet there were tangible reminders that struck home with me as a youngster, such as the fact that my father's paychecks had become diminished and I would not get a new pair of winter boots or athletic sneakers that year. I only vaguely remember the impact of the Great Depression, since I was only four years old when the worst economic downturn in US history finally began to wane in 1939. But the damage was deep and lasting, particularly for the families of the thirteen million Americans who were unemployed at the peak of its destructive economic spiral. Following the stock market crash and the failure of nearly half of the nation's banks, consumer spending and investment dropped sharply, in turn causing a catastrophic decline in industrial output and the nation's workforce, as failing companies laid off workers in an attempt to stay afloat.

This was the backdrop of the problems facing our family and millions of others across America during my childhood. Fortunately, we were a tight-knit family; my aunts had steady employment as domestic workers and they helped us out financially to tide us over so that we could make ends meet when my father's work experienced prolonged droughts.

By the time I was seven or eight years old, my mother was working outside the home to bring in supplemental cash because my father could not find steady work and his opportunities at the railroad continued to decline. My mom worked as a night cashier part-time at a small restaurant near our apartment that was owned by Lonnie, a friend of my father who ran the numbers as a side hustle. If my father was away working on the railroad and my mother had to pull a shift at the restaurant, my grandmother would babysit my sisters and me. We were barely surviving as a household, but as a youngster I did not sense or understand the financial and marital strains all this reliance on relatives and my mother's job outside the house was causing.

Eventually, my father's on-again, off-again job as a waiter for the New Haven Railroad ended when he was laid off in a round of downsizing due to diminished ridership and declining patrons in the dining cars. My father was officially unemployed and he turned to the safety net of the Works Progress Administration, or WPA, an agency created as part of President Franklin D. Roosevelt's New Deal. The WPA assisted millions of unemployed workers—primarily unskilled men—by providing them with jobs on public works projects such as constructing roads and public buildings. The pay was often meager, but it beat the alternative. My father got a WPA job at Franklin Park Zoo in Boston, where Skinny, as he was known, became something of a ringleader because he had the gift of gab developed during his years waiting on diners of all social classes on the railroad.

The family story goes that Skinny enjoyed observing the large animals at the Franklin Park Zoo, including lions and tigers, zebras and giraffes, gorillas and wildebeests. He also helped feed them and grew increasingly perturbed by the rich diet of prime meat the big animals received each day at the zoo during a time when he and the other men working for the WPA struggled to put food on the table at home. Skinny started voicing this objection to the other workers and he found a receptive audience. Soon, my father and some of his buddies were skimming off some of the meat they were supposed to be feeding the animals at the zoo and hiding it in their lunch pails or work satchels they carried in and out of the complex each day. What nobody suspected was that the men were stealing meat from the zoo animals to feed their own families at home. They were law breakers, but to my knowledge they were never caught for their Robin Hood–like indiscretions.

Skinny did not extend the lie to his own household. He freely admitted to my mother, his children, and anyone who would listen that he had pulled one over on the government by supplementing his modest WPA pay by pilfering cuts of meat intended for the zoo animals. I remember we shrugged and made a joke about eating the animals' food. As a kid, I was thrilled at this windfall of choice cuts such as steaks, chops, hamburger, and stew meat after we had gone for months without any such luxury food items as my mother tried to stretch a dollar with soups, pastas, and watery stews where nuggets of meat were hard to find. We ate the zoo animals' meat without a pang of conscience, and an utter lack of squeamishness.

Franklin Park Zoo was a sprawling seventy-two-acre site along Franklin Park Road in a historic area of Boston. The park had a lot of other things we liked besides purloined zoo meat. There were large grassy areas, football fields, and baseball diamonds, free and open to the public, where I played sports with my buddies. There was also a municipal golf course adjacent to it. I regret that I never learned to play golf because it might have helped me at college and later in my professional and political career. But I did know a couple of Black men from our church who used to play at the course, so it was integrated—at least in theory. Still, golf was a white man's game in that era, very few Black people had the means or the opportunity to play, and most of the country clubs at that time did not allow Black members.

Regarding matters of race while I was growing up, I didn't feel deprived or denied access and there were no outward signs of racial discrimination that I was aware of as a youngster. It did seem obvious to me as a kid that white people enjoyed more intrinsic advantages and that they seemed to have more upward mobility, at least based on what

I witnessed. As I entered adolescence, I began to be aware of the outmigration of Jewish families leaving our neighborhood for upscale suburbs like Brookline. More working-class Black families moved in. This was long before the term "white flight" had been coined but that is what was occurring, whether it had been given a name or not.

I guess I did not give it much thought when I would go with my mother to the New Haven Railroad and notice that all the men who worked as waiters, like my father, were Black. The railroad car cleaners, like my mother, were mostly Black, too. The jobs that went to white people were the better positions: engineers, track foremen, conductors, and supervisors. I did not have the vocabulary as a boy to give racism a name, but I was living it and experiencing it and being immersed in it. As far as I remember, my parents did not talk about such matters, at least not in front of me. And coming from the Jim Crow South, the racial inequality they experienced in Boston was certainly of a less egregious nature. But it was real and it was present.

I do not remember a lot of details about my father or what life lessons, if any, Skinny imparted to me early on. He was only an infrequent presence in our home, since he traveled so much with the railroad. Even when he was in between jobs or unemployed, he spent a lot of time with his friends at the local watering hole or hanging out with number runners or other men from the neighborhood. Skinny was of the streets, except when he put on his work uniform. I recall I flushed with pride when he suited up at home with the crisp white jacket, white shirt, black bow tie, and starched black slacks—the uniform of the Black waiters on the New Haven Railroad.

One strong memory I have of my father is when he came home from a road trip and took off his uniform. First, he paused to empty his pockets bulging with coins he earned as tips. He made a ritual of counting out all the coins and handing them over to my mother for groceries and incidentals—tips being an important supplement to his paycheck.

Much has been made of my name and reporters who covered my political career always wanted to know what the H stood for. I never told them. It was my secret. I had a saying that any politician had to have at least one secret, and that was mine.

It became an issue as early as my enrollment as a kindergartner at David Ellis Elementary School, where my mother had to provide my birth certificate. I stole a look. In large, black letters it said: Herman Carl McCall. I didn't know what to make of this information at age five. It was the first time I realized my actual name was Herman, since all my friends and my sisters and my parents called me Carl. One day in class, the teacher addressed me as Herman and I paid no attention. I didn't realize she was speaking to me. After that, my mother had a meeting with my teacher and told her that I was to be called Carl and that nobody in our family called me Herman. The teacher changed my records and enrolled me as H. Carl McCall. It stuck. I have stayed with that iteration of my name ever since.

Since my father never liked the name and never used it—preferring his nickname of Skinny instead—I stuck with Carl for informal usage. I'm not aware if my father had a middle name, and it was not clear to me if Carl was from him or just a name chosen because he and my mother liked it.

The years of World War II, 1939 to 1945, were a good time economically for my family because the railroad was busy and there was steady employment. My father received a waiver from the military draft because he had six children, my five sisters and me. I was the oldest of the McCall brood, followed by Judith, Inez, Audrey, Edith, and Cheryl—the youngest. We were all just a year or two apart and we all got along fairly well for such a large group of siblings.

Since I was his only son, my father tried to give me special bonding moments. Since he was Skinny, he wanted to give me a nickname, too. He settled on Boy Friend. He would say it so it sounded cool, though, like "Hey, Boy Friend, how you doing with your homework?" So, that's what he called me and he also encouraged me to do well in school and to participate in sports. When we went to the store to pick up a few sundry items for my mother and a couple cans of Pickwick Ale for him, he would often challenge me to a race to the end of the block. He was thin and quick, but by the time I was ten or eleven and had gone through a growth spurt, I started to beat him in these sprints. One fond memory is when he would bring home containers of chop suey for dinner, picked up on the way from a Chinese restaurant as a peace offering if his train was late or if he stopped off and lingered too long at a tavern.

I do not remember any memorable conversations or quality time spent with my father. I recalled that he liked to tell stories about New York City and a particular rooming house in Harlem where he stayed when laying over on a train run back to Boston, as well as a couple night clubs and restaurants he enjoyed in Harlem. He always promised he was going to take me to Harlem to show me his favorite spots, but he never got around to it.

The only time I remember traveling with my father was when I was about eight and he took me to meet his aunt Ida, who lived in Philadelphia. We took the train and she greeted us warmly and we stayed with Ida, her husband, and daughter in their nice single-family house in South Philly. My strongest memory of that trip was that they did not have indoor plumbing. When I asked to use the bathroom after dinner one night, Ida gave me a flashlight and directed me out in the backyard to the outhouse. I had never encountered anything like that before and it stuck with me. It was somehow very important to my father that I meet his aunt Ida. It was the only time I ever saw her and we never reconnected or stayed in touch.

My father left our family when I was eleven years old. After World War II ended, there were fewer train passengers with the loss of troop transports. Eastern Air Lines eclipsed the New Haven Railroad because it flew the same routes much faster and, in some cases, for less money. By 1946, my father was complaining he could not find work in Boston and he began migrating more to New York City, where he could get occasional work as a rail car waiter. He began spending more and more time in New York. Eventually, he just never returned.

It did not seem like a catastrophic event at first. We had grown accustomed to his long absences. This time, he just drifted away for good. It was the way he did it that really hurt and disrupted our lives. He gave us no warning and no explanation. He just went AWOL. We never heard from him. I remember my mother had a number for the rooming house where he used to stay in Harlem and she kept calling it, trying to reach him, but to no avail. After about two weeks, I remember my father finally calling us. We didn't have a phone so we had to go downstairs to use my grandmother's telephone. He did not apologize or give a reason for why he was not coming back, other than he needed to find work and his best option was to stay in New York City.

By then, there were six mouths to feed and my mother only had her part-time restaurant cashier's job. Occasionally, my father sent a money order from New York, but it was not consistent and it was not enough to sustain us. Eventually, he stopped calling and the rooming house where he had stayed informed my mother that he had vacated the premises. We felt abandoned and a whole range of emotions consumed me.

I was sad and angry, heartbroken and bitter, despondent and confused—all those emotions at once. Mainly, I wanted to know why. Why had he left us? Why did he never return? What had we done wrong? I was only eleven, but old enough to understand a little bit of the ways of the world and I had a lot of questions and wondered about the possible scenarios. Was he too proud and embarrassed to face his wife and children and family at not being able to provide for them? Did he have a woman in New York City, perhaps another family that he cared about more than ours? Had he had a big fight and major falling-out with my mother? I remember waiting and waiting and waiting and feeling depressed when Skinny never came. If he had made a lot of tips, he occasionally took a taxicab home. I remember hearing an occasional taxi pulling up on the street below our apartment and I would rush to the window, press my nose to the glass, and peer down to the street. I was hoping against hope that it was my father, and that he had changed his mind and was coming home to his family. That never happened.

My mother was a woman of iron will. Caroleasa McCall had grit. She was obviously very upset when her husband abandoned her and their children, but she was good at protecting us and holding things together without unduly disturbing us. As the oldest of six, it fell to me to be her protector and supporter and to assist with my sisters since I was the only one old enough to have a sense of the seriousness of the situation. I asked her what happened to Skinny and she said she honestly could not explain it. I accompanied her once or twice down to the Dover Street station, where she went in search of answers. She asked some of the other Black waiters who had been his friends on the New Haven Railroad line what they knew. They had very little information, except that they had seen him occasionally in passing at Pennsylvania Station or Grand Central Terminal in New York City—but never long enough to have an in-depth conversation and to ask him why he left Boston for good and abandoned his family.

When it finally sank in that our father was not returning, it had a profound effect on my younger sisters. They felt the abandonment acutely. They cried and suffered. I could not console them and neither could my mother, no matter how hard she tried. It was an extremely disruptive and stressful time for my family. Luckily, we were supported emotionally and financially by our grandmother and my mother's sisters who lived in the same apartment building as we did. It was a dark and depressing period for all of us.

My mother was a survivor and possessed remarkable resilience. She easily could have fallen into a deep funk, but instead she mobilized and labored to support herself and her six children. She took on domestic work for wealthy white families in Brookline and got a job in the kitchen at Trinity Episcopal Church in Copley Square. She made extra money serving at large church functions. She brought us home leftovers from those church dinners that we ate happily and appreciatively—without the joking tone we reserved for the zoo animal meat our father had stolen. We saw more and more of our grandmother, who babysat us more frequently since our mother had to be away on nights and weekends to earn enough money to support us.

I became my mother's ally in delaying rent payments and putting off the landlord. We regularly fell behind a month or two and we became experts at explaining our delinquency. We always eventually paid, but some months were tougher than others.

Around this same time, our family suffered an additional blow when my grandfather passed away. My sister Audrey moved downstairs to help our widowed grandmother and my sister Judith went to live with my aunt Inez at her domestic position in Purchase, New York. Fewer mouths to feed lessened the burden on my mother, but only slightly. She simply could not earn enough money at her menial jobs to sustain us.

My mother was a proud woman and she did not like to have to ask for public assistance, but becoming a single mother with six children was a shock to the system and she had few options. She applied for Aid to Dependent Children several months after my father left. I remember that we had periodic home visits from a social worker, since single parents like my mother were discouraged from working outside the home because it was felt they could not care for their children adequately. But my mother had no alternative. The social worker asked questions about how often we saw our father and how our mother treated us and about our meals and homework and sanitary habits. We were instructed by our mother not to tell the social worker that two of our sisters had moved out so that we could get the aid allotment for six children instead of the four who actually lived under one roof full-time. My mother was not going down without a fight and she had no qualms about getting as much as possible from the government when it came to feeding her children.

When our father left our family, it changed our household's dynamic in ways large and small. It changed his children's psychology, including my own. I felt abandoned and bereft, yet I had to cover it up. My friends would wonder why they never saw my father anymore and they asked where Skinny had gone. I said he left to go to New York because that's where he could find steady work on the railroad, but I hinted that it was just a temporary situation and that he would be returning. I lied out of shame. I found refuge in athletics and began to play football and basketball for long hours in Franklin Park to cover up my pain.

Chapter 3

The Village That Raised Me

After my father abandoned us, I was confused and caught up in a welter of emotions, shifting from disbelief to anger, bitterness to a sense of self-blame. It has been well documented that there are seven stages of grief and in hindsight I realize I passed through them all, beginning with shock and denial, eventually through bargaining and to the final stage of acceptance. It took a long time to process this family trauma and longer still to come to my own sense of perspective. Adolescence is a difficult time of transition under the best of circumstances, but suddenly being left without a father was a very hard thing for me to come to terms with at that age. I was only eleven years old and still trying to figure out who I was and my place in the world. This sort of catastrophic disruption did not help, to say the least.

The true hero in this turbulent period was my mother. She was a single mother left to raise six children on her own. She was not able to make ends meet and did not want to go on welfare, but eventually that is what she had to do. She only received about $275 per month in Aid to Dependent Children, or about $3,300 in annual household income, plus the small amounts she made as a domestic worker and waitress. At one point several years later, an admissions counselor at a college to which I applied looked over my financial aid statement and inquired if I had left off a couple zeroes because the income total was shockingly low.

I was worried not just for myself and my own well-being, but I was concerned that my mother might fall apart under the weight of this new and unexpected burden. But she was a very strong woman and she made it clear that every fiber of her being would be committed to caring for her children. Her strength and resilience were infectious. We children soldiered on and did what we had to do to confront this difficult set of circumstances. Somehow, we managed. I do not recall ever going to bed hungry or feeling destitute. Our financial situation was certainly precarious and we had our ups and downs as a family run by a single parent. My father's departure strengthened the bond between my mother and me, as the eldest child. She assured me that no matter what, we would get a good education and have the opportunity to attend college. She said that was the promise she made to each of us. In turn, I agreed that I would never intentionally disappoint her and that I would change my behavior if I was doing something that was troubling or not to her liking.

It was due to my mother's influence as a wonderful parent and role model that I was able to avoid the lures of the street and the pitfalls that pulled some of my friends into their undertow. By the time I was twelve or thirteen, some of the kids I knew from our neighborhood were skipping school and had become chronic truants. Several would drop out altogether by the time they turned fifteen or sixteen. They started hanging out on the corners of the mean streets of Roxbury, drinking cheap wine from brown paper bags. Their drink of choice was Thunderbird, a sweet fortified wine with a high alcohol content that could get a person drunk for less than a buck. Thunderbird was so popular on the streets that a call-and-response greeting emerged. I can still hear some of my friends who lost their way calling out: "What's the word?" "Thunderbird," someone else would answer. "What's the price?" "Thirty twice," came the response. In other words, you could buy Thunderbird for sixty cents a pint and it carried nearly twice the potency of regular wine. This made it popular and dangerous in terms of alcohol addiction. It was heartbreaking to see some close friends and gifted athletes became alcoholics, damaging their future prospects and essentially ruining their lives. In college, I remember in one of my sociology textbooks reading about families like mine, with a single mother raising several children in an impoverished neighborhood.

The conclusion of the scholars was that this form of poverty was a terminal condition and resulted in a multigenerational cycle of poverty. There was one problem with their hypothesis. They had not met my mother Caroleasa. She was resolute and she brought out that trait in her children.

Along with my mother's influence, I had some sort of internal moral compass that kept me on a straight path. I saw what was happening to the guys who started abusing alcohol and that was not the direction I wanted my life to take. I refused to allow myself to be pulled down to the level of the streets. Even though it was all around me and there was tremendous peer pressure to experiment, I never drank Thunderbird or any alcohol as a teenager. I think I tried a cigarette once. That was the extent of my rebellion. I also refused to get lured into street fights. Even though I was big and strong and was about six feet tall, reaching six feet three by high school, I never used my physical size and strength to engage in physical altercations or to bully anyone. I was what might be called a mild-mannered young man.

Another important anchor in my life during this troublesome period was my faith. We belonged to the Saint Mark Congregational Church. There were several elders in the church who looked after my mother and helped us out when necessary, including the pastor, the Reverend Samuel Laviscount. He became an important figure in our lives. Our religious affiliation was somewhat unusual. Most of the Black families in our neighborhood were Southern Baptists, while our church was a mainline Protestant denomination. Historically, it dated back to the General Council of Congregational Christian Churches founded under the New England Pilgrims and Puritans. In 1957, the General Council of the Congregational Christian Church united with the Evangelical and Reformed to form the United Church of Christ. This merger created a large national Protestant denomination with nearly a million members in more than five thousand congregations across the United States. The UCC, as it is known, is made up of a predominantly white and highly educated membership. One of the hallmarks of the United Church of Christ is its liberal views on social issues and support of civil rights and women's rights. Perhaps more importantly, the UCC is not beholden to a central ruling body and congregations may exercise considerable independence in terms of doctrine and ministry. One of the core mission statements of the United Church of Christ is that it defines itself as "an extremely pluralistic and diverse denomination."

For us, one of the strengths of St. Mark Congregational Church was that it was led by a Black pastor and had a number of Black congregants, mostly from middle- or upper-middle-class families. My mother became acquainted with the church because it offered youth educational programs, in which she enrolled me, and we later began attending Sunday services there. The church was a short walk from our apartment and my mother wanted her children to have a faith tradition growing up—unlike my father, who rarely if ever attended church—and that was the church she chose.

Another defining aspect of Roxbury and especially Harold Street, where we lived, was that the residents were a mix of middle-class Black families and poor Black families like ours. We all attended the same schools and the same churches, which created an intertwining of socioeconomic groups. The underlying reason was that segregation and discriminatory practices such as redlining made it very difficult for affluent Black families to move out of Roxbury and into the suburbs. Thus, racist policies forced financially successful Black families to remain in our neighborhood, which was why I had so many mentors who were Black lawyers, teachers, successful Black business owners and other professionals because we all lived in close proximity to and supported each other. The experience I had growing up in Roxbury is in stark contrast to today's racial divide, created when increasing numbers of affluent Black families fled Black urban neighborhoods once the possibility of living in predominantly white suburbs became an option for them.

My mom started taking me to Sunday school at St. Mark's when I was in third grade and to summer Bible school and other religious programming later in elementary school. My favorite part was the community center, known as the St. Mark Social Center, which had a full-size basketball court and ping-pong tables. I spent a lot of time there as a teenager. It was a safe and wholesome hangout and kept me away from the bad influences on the street corners. After my dad left, the community center became a second home and Mr. Jarvis who ran it became something of a surrogate father. It was a nurturing environment and I felt good there. It was a place of stability in the turbulent aftermath of Skinny's abandonment.

I tried to put it behind me, but it was always in the back of my mind and, from time to time over my teenage years, it would bother me and gnaw away at my self-confidence. Seeing how hard my mother worked to support us and never wanting to disappoint her, I wanted to model the behavior of several Black men in our Roxbury neighborhood, including a dentist, lawyer, physician, teacher, and postal worker. Just being around them, I recognized that a good education increased the chances of upward mobility.

When I was growing up, the socioeconomic dynamic of the business sector in our community gradually began to shift and a few Black entrepreneurs started their own businesses or took over when Jewish merchants left the neighborhood. I remember one Black family became very successful by starting an ice and coal business, later buying a fleet of trucks to deliver home heating oil. Eventually, they were able to add local and state government agencies as customers. My mother never made a fuss about accepting the welfare check and it kept our household together. She continued to patch together part-time jobs. She never pressured me to find work to help with our family's finances. She encouraged me to focus first and foremost on academics. She also supported my interest in athletics and let me join sports teams. By the time I was a teenager, I got a part-time job at the local drugstore and I felt good about contributing a few dollars to help cover our grocery bill—in addition to spending some of what I made on the movies and other extras.

I also got a firsthand lesson in an unlicensed loan operation. There was a local woman, Mrs. Rosen, and she extended credit like a hometown bank. Only there was no office or license. If a family needed, say, furniture items and could not pay for them, Mrs. Rosen would come around, take down the order, buy the items, and have them delivered. She carried a ledger that had each family's weekly payment plan. This was akin to a bank's line of credit. I remember my mother purchased a few items on credit from Mrs. Rosen and there were a few Saturdays when my mother was short and I had to fib and say my mother had gone out and was not home when the woman came to collect—although my mother was actually hiding silently in the bedroom.

When high school graduation approached, my mother contacted Mrs.

Rosen and made arrangements to get a suit for me since I did not own one. The woman accompanied me to a wholesale clothing outlet, where they fitted me for a suit and she placed the order. When I got home, Mrs. Rosen told my mother what her weekly payment would be even though she never disclosed to my mother or me what the suit actually cost. She controlled a lending enterprise in our neighborhood that took advantage of our financial straits. My mother and other families did not qualify for credit at any bank or store. We could only receive financing through Mrs. Rosen, and we paid every week whatever charges and interest rates she determined.

The driving force in the congregation of St. Mark's was the Reverend Samuel Laviscount, a graduate of Howard University and a native of Antigua, who created the St. Mark Social Center in 1934. It was the first social service agency for children and youth in upper Roxbury. It pioneered community outreach and efforts to get wayward youths off the street and into productive after-school programs and back on track at school. Early on, Laviscount literally made rounds of the neighborhood and, with his lilting West Indies accent, convinced kids to come in off the street and create a future for themselves. For all the delinquents I saw who squandered their lives with alcohol and petty crimes to support their habits, Laviscount probably saved an equal number with his social service program.

I felt at home at the St. Mark Social Center, and another thing I liked about the congregation was its focus on intellectual rigor and improving one's base of knowledge. I was influenced also by a Sunday school teacher I had, Herbert Tucker, who was a lawyer and became a judge and lived in our neighborhood. He encouraged me during my teenage years to attend the church's speaker series, which featured a group of prominent Black intellectuals invited to speak to the congregation. One of the speakers who made an impression on me was Dr. Charles S. Johnson, a notable sociologist. In 1946, he was named the first Black president of Fisk University, a historically Black institution of higher education in Nashville, Tennessee. Johnson grew up in Virginia, the son of a highly regarded Baptist minister. He earned his PhD in sociology from the University of Chicago and settled with his wife in New York City when he took a position in 1920 as director of research and investigation at the National Urban League. He was credited with helping to foster the Harlem Renaissance by editing two journals that published African American writers of the period who often were overlooked by white editors. He also established literary prizes at the National Urban League to recognize young writers of color. His purpose was to elevate the Black experience by bolstering self-image and by celebrating the important cultural contribution of Black writers and artists, many of whom were based in Harlem.

I vividly recall hearing Dr. Johnson speak, even though it was more than seventy years ago, because of his scholarship and erudition rather than a fire-and-brimstone delivery. He spoke calmly yet forcefully about his life's work advocating for racial equality and fighting for the advancement of civil rights for Black people, as well as other minority groups. What struck me most deeply was that he did not vilify white people or the so-called Establishment, as I had heard from several Black preachers. He spoke powerfully about working in collaboration with progressive white leaders and liberal organizations in the Jim Crow South to create incremental change over time. I remember he said his focus was more on winning small victories with incremental success and gradual inroads, rather than trying to overthrow the white power structure. He called himself a "sideline activist" and said he was a pragmatist who preferred to work quietly within the system to foster equality, rather than being an outside rabble-rouser loudly demanding immediate racial justice. Dr. Johnson struck me as a leader who understood how the real world worked and who had carefully studied our social structures. He presented his ideas with a clear-eyed rationalism that engaged me and aligned with my own ideology. I found myself nodding in agreement and concurring with his positions.

I was comfortable in our congregation, which had about four hundred members, and the church was filled with more than two hundred people on any given Sunday. There were plenty of youngsters my age and members ranged from young families to senior citizens. They treated my mother and her children with respect and never looked down on us because we were being raised by a single parent and accepted welfare benefits. What they did was set a quiet example of getting a good education and following a disciplined life of hard work and commitment to attain upward mobility and financial security. They were not classic strivers, who valued wealth and material possessions above all else. Rather, they felt that a comfortable middle- or upper-middle-class lifestyle was something to be valued and worth the hard work it took to achieve it.

Another influential figure I met when I was coming of age in Boston was Edward William Brooke III, a Republican politician who became in 1966 the first African American elected by popular vote to the United States Senate. He represented Massachusetts in the senate from 1967 to 1979. Brooke was raised in Washington, DC, graduated from Howard University, and served as a commissioned officer in the US Army during World War II. After his military service, Brooke earned a law degree from Boston University School of Law, graduating in 1948. I met him in the early 1950s during his two campaigns for a seat in the Massachusetts House of Representatives and for secretary of state. I heard him speak at our church during his campaigns on more than one occasion. Although he lost both races, I was impressed by his commanding presence, by his message, and by his positions on most issues. He was a centrist who represented a more moderate wing of the Republican Party that connected with my values and suited my quiet demeanor and ethos of making gains by working within the system.

To my way of thinking, the most interesting and vital Black leaders in Boston were Republicans and I heard many of them speak at our church and interacted with a few. The Democratic Party as far as I could tell was run by the Irish and Italians and they had their constituency and were not interested at the time in bringing in Black members. It seemed like a closed shop. By contrast, the Republicans were the party of Lincoln and Black citizens had been comfortable with their policies on core issues going back to Reconstruction. In my limited universe of Roxbury and Boston, the overwhelming number of Black professionals and political leaders I admired were Republicans rather than Democrats. Of course, that political affiliation would change drastically for myself and countless other Black voters over the course of coming decades and the advance of the civil rights movement agenda. But Edward Brooke was a Black Republican who supported important causes that impacted Blacks. For instance, after he served as Massachusetts attorney general from 1962 to 1966, he won election to the US Senate, fought housing discrimination against Blacks, and cowrote the Civil Rights Act of 1968 that prohibited such racial injustice. In addition, Brooke broke political ranks and voted his conscience on key issues. For instance, he became a vocal critic of President Richard Nixon during the Watergate scandal and was the first Republican senator to call for Nixon's resignation when details of his dirty deeds came out during an impeachment investigation. After two terms in the senate, Brooke was defeated in 1978 by Democrat Paul Tsongas. He ended his political career, practiced law in the nation's capital, and got involved with a variety of not-for-profit groups there.

I got to know Ed Brooke through his visits to our church and I spoke to him on a couple of occasions when I was a high school student and he passed through Roxbury. I was very impressed with the fact that he was one of the first Blacks to run for elected office as a Republican and that he connected with our community with a message that reso- nated across Roxbury and beyond. In fact, a couple of classmates and I were so inspired by Brooke that we volunteered to work for his early campaign as a state legislator and we handed out flyers on street corners, stuffed envelopes at his campaign headquarters, and I got swept up in the excitement of my first political campaign. It was my initial exposure to electoral politics and it made a strong impression. Even though Brooke lost that first election and the subsequent one, he believed in his core philosophy, he refused to quit, and he went on to national prominence. That lesson of resilience was not lost on me and I sensed that his type of toughness would pay off in the end. The GOP paid close attention to and focused on the Black community in Roxbury and Boston, while the Democrats tended to focus almost exclusively on the large Irish and Italian population. In the end, this concerted effort and focused attention paid off for Republicans with successful Black candidates like Brooke who were on the GOP slate.

I also got an important lesson in identity politics. Brooke ran a good campaign, he worked hard and he was assisted by an energetic team of Black volunteers, including myself and a handful of my buddies. It was a learning process, and I learned that he was in politics for the right reasons and that he was taking the long view. Even though he lost elections, he was not defeated and the relationships and volunteer group he fostered paid off years later when he won his race for Massachusetts Attorney General and was the first Black person elected to statewide office. Many years later, when I purchased property on Martha's Vineyard, I discovered that Brooke was a neighbor who owned a house on the same road as ours and he was part of the historical legacy of Black ownership of summer homes on Martha's Vineyard.

Despite the disruption of my father's abandonment, I was influenced and inspired by St. Mark Congregational Church and dynamic Black leaders such as Ed Brooke, Herbert Tucker, Dr. Charles Johnson, Reverend Michael Haynes, and the Reverend Samuel Laviscount. I was surrounded by positive Black male role models who formed a kind of surrogate fatherhood to bolster my mother's own powerful example of courage and resilience. I experienced stages of grief, to be sure, but I never let the sorrow weigh me down or sidetrack me from focusing on my education, my emerging interest in politics, and becoming the best person I could be.

Chapter 4

College Dreams

My world remained insular and narrowly defined, essentially a small quadrant of a dozen or so urban blocks. I entered Roxbury Memorial High School for Boys, which was within walking distance of our apartment. I was beginning the first tentative steps toward manhood, and I was becoming the de facto male head of the household, an authority figure to my younger siblings. My mother, grandmother, and aunts relied on me to keep the household and my sisters on track. I had come to the realization that my father was not going to come back and I stopped worrying or anticipating his return. There was a sense of freedom in that new reality. My mother helped shape my ambitions and she told me every chance she got that studying hard and getting a good education was going to be the key to my success and moving beyond my small corner of Roxbury.

Roxbury Memorial High was an all-boys school and it was connected to Roxbury Memorial High School for Girls, literally and figuratively. In fact, the two single-gender high schools shared the same building. It was a four-year public high school that served students in ninth through twelfth grade. We had about two hundred students in my incoming freshman class, the Class of 1954. Like our neighborhood, it was a high school in transition, with a predominantly white and Jewish student population. Gradually, the school was becoming more diverse with a rising number of African American students. There were eleven Blacks in my class, but that number was growing each year starting in the 1950s, as our section of Roxbury eventually became home to a majority of Black families.

Roxbury Memorial High was a hulking red-brick building that stretched the length of a city block along Townsend Street, with the boys' and girls' schools each occupying one half of the sprawling structure. It was established in 1926 and the building had distinctive architecture that bore elements of that era's Art Deco movement. One thing we were famous for was being the first school in the city of Boston to feature an indoor swimming pool.

To my mind, what made our high school most distinctive and the feature I loved best was that the Boston Public Library operated the Memorial Branch in our building. In fact, the library served as the buffer, the dividing line, between the raging hormones on either side in the all-boys and all-girls wings of Roxbury Memorial High.

The library became my haven, a home away from home. I did my homework there after school each late afternoon and evening. The librarians recommended books for me to read, encouraged my academic interests, and mentored me. I read a wide range of books, including classic literature, contemporary fiction, history, adventure stories, and a great mix of topics and authors. I spent so much time in the library I felt like I should have had a nameplate on my favorite chair and table in a quiet corner, near a window overlooking Townsend Street.

Roxbury Memorial had three academic tracks in an era where tracking was commonly employed: Manual Arts, for printing trades; Commercial, which was a basic education; and College Prep, which was the highest track and meant for those who were deemed ("tracked") to be college material.

I remember when I went to enroll and, because I was Black, the counselor immediately assumed I was going into the lowest track, Manual Arts, and he told me all about jobs in the printing industry. But when I said that I wanted to be in College Prep, he paused and was silent for a moment. He sighed and sort of hemmed and hawed, but eventually he reluctantly listened to my entreaties and he said he would enroll me in the College Prep track. It was an important moment for me, when I asserted myself as an independent young Black man, pushed back against authority and white establishment expectations, insisted upon being heard, and demanded that my wishes be followed.

I was not alone in demolishing low expectations at Roxbury Memorial High. I am proud to note that among the eleven Black students in my freshman class, five of them, including me, had aspirations of higher education and were admitted to colleges and universities, including two who attended historically Black colleges in the South.

I worked hard inside the classroom and out. I was diligent about spending hours in the library each day after school in order to complete all my homework assignments. I was in the top tier of my class and achieved nearly all As and Bs. I liked mathematics and performed well in math classes, including algebra, which was the bane of many of my classmates. When we got into trigonometry in my senior year, I confess that my math skills were severely challenged. I did not like trig and I struggled the whole time I took that class. In the end, I received a C, a passing grade, and it was the only C that I received during all the courses I took during four years at Roxbury Memorial High.

Interscholastic athletics became an important part of my high school experience, as well. I made the varsity basketball and football teams. It felt good to be part of a team, to join in the camaraderie of being part of an athletic community, and to don our green and gold uniforms and board a bus to go play other schools in and around Boston while classmates, cheerleaders, and teachers and staff cheered us on.

My football career was short-lived. I was a running back my sophomore year and occasionally was put into games and did pretty well rushing since I was big and fairly fast. During my junior year, we got a new coach and he decided to move me to quarterback. During the first game of the season, in a game against our rival, East Boston High School, I went back to throw a pass. I didn't see a large defensive lineman rushing from outside my peripheral vision and he came flying in for a tackle, slamming with full force into my planted leg. I felt a lightning bolt of pain and crumpled to the ground. I could not stand and groaned in discomfort. The game was stopped and medical personnel rushed out onto the field to assist me. It turned out that I had a bad break, a compound fracture. I was carried off the field on a stretcher. The pain was intense—I was flickering in and out of consciousness and I could see people lined up around me. They looked worried and asked me in grave voices how I felt. I remember distinctly picking out my mother's face in the crowd of onlookers. She had been against me playing varsity football from the outset, because of the possibility of getting injured. The last thing I remember as they carried me off the field was my mother, disgusted and shaking her head, saying this: "I told you so . . . I told you so."

The ambulance took me to Boston City Hospital, where I was born. I nearly passed out due to the pain, but I remember seeing a tip of the broken bone sticking out of my skin on my calf and the doctor pushing it back under the broken skin. The compound fracture was on my right leg between my knee and ankle and the surgeon told me that he was going to repair the break and put it in a cast. He chose not to use a metal plate or screws in case I wanted to play sports again. He was a former football player himself and said he recommended that I avoid the hardware and allow the break to heal "naturally."

My career-ending injury came in one of the first football games of the season, in early September, and I spent an entire month at Boston City Hospital in traction, so that my leg would be immobilized, the break could begin to repair itself, and I could heal. I was in a rigid plaster cast from my knee to my foot, with my ankle encased and immobile. My aunt Eunice invited me to stay at her quiet, spacious apartment during my convalescence, which took two more months after I was discharged. Since my aunt did not work—my uncle had a job with the US Postal Service—she was able to help take care of me during the day when my mother was at work. I was largely immobile and could only move slowly and carefully around the apartment with the use of crutches. I was more or less unable to do basic tasks for myself and my sweet aunt Eunice cooked and washed, ironed, and folded my clothes for me.

Finally, after the most difficult and frustrating four months of my life, the fractured bone had healed sufficiently so that I was cleared by my doctor to return to school and my normal classes. Luckily, I did not lose too much ground in the recovery and rehab period away from school because administrators arranged to have a tutor come to my aunt's apartment three days a week to help with my instruction and homework so that I could stay on track in the demanding College Prep courses. Since I had little else to do, I applied myself to my studies with uncommon focus and singlemindedness. There were no distractions and I actually not only did not lose ground, I gained ground, and when I returned to school, I was actually ahead on the syllabus in all my classes compared to my classmates. I heard my mother's voice ringing in my ears, loud and insistent, that my primary focus now had to be higher education and achieving a high school academic record that would get me accepted to a good college where opportunities for advancement would open up to me.

One concern about suffering the broken bone was that I would be knocked out of competing in varsity athletics, particularly basketball, which was my favorite sport. I continued to work very hard at my physical rehab and made a full recovery and was cleared to resume competing in interscholastic sports.

Around the time that I was temporarily sidelined from my promising athletic career, I made an acquaintance with the Reverend Dr. Michael E. Haynes, a native of Roxbury who became the pastor of the historic Twelfth Baptist Church on Warren Street in Roxbury in 1964. He also represented Roxbury in the Massachusetts House of Representatives from 1965 to 1968. He is perhaps best known for his work on the front lines of the civil rights movement. Reverend Haynes became close to the Reverend Dr. Martin Luther King Jr. after he helped organize Dr. King's 1965 march from Roxbury to the Boston Common to support school desegregation. I was a high school student when I met Reverend Haynes. He was a young, charismatic community activist who helped low-income Roxbury teenagers, particularly Black youths, prepare for admission to college. Reverend Haynes also served as program director of the Breezy Meadows Camp in Holliston, Massachusetts, from 1951 to 1962. Holliston is a small town in a rural area about twenty-six miles west of Boston. The summer camp served underprivileged children from the greater Boston area and Providence, Rhode Island. The camp was managed by the Robert Gould Shaw House, named for a Union Army officer who served during the Civil War. Shaw came from a prominent abolitionist family in Boston and he accepted command of the 54th Massachusetts, the first all-black regiment in the Northeast. He supported equal treatment for all soldiers and he led the effort to get Black troops the same pay as that of white troops.

Haynes had attended Breezy Meadows Camp as a youngster and returned to run it as an adult. He came to our Roxbury neighborhood to recruit summer camp counselors and I was impressed with the erudition and passion of Reverend Haynes when I first encountered him. He was a small, intense man who was extremely smart and well read. He had a bachelor's degree in theology from New England College of Theology and a graduate degree in mission and clinical services from Shelton College in New York. Breezy Meadows Camp served low-income and disadvantaged youths in single-gender sessions between the ages of five and twelve. The boys were in residence at the camp during the month of July and the girls took up residency each August.

I was not only won over by the persuasive recruitment talk by Dr. Haynes, but I badly needed a summer job to help my mother in her financial struggles. Reverend Haynes became a mentor and a significant figure in my life and maturation into manhood, and Breezy Meadows Camp helped me grow in my efforts to become a teacher, a leader, and role model for kids. I went to work for Reverend Haynes and worked as a camp counselor for several summers during high school and throughout my college years. The camp was surrounded by large tracts of wooded acres and a nice pond for swimming. Our campers were almost entirely African American children who came from disadvantaged backgrounds. We spent our days leading kids in races, sports competitions, arts and crafts, and swimming. We all gathered for a church service on Sunday.

All of my sisters attended Breezy Meadows Camp and so did many of our friends from Roxbury and other poor neighborhoods. Not only was it restorative to get out of the congested city to breathe fresh air and walk in the silent woods, it was also an opportunity for children who came from difficult backgrounds to feel cared for and empowered. Reverend Haynes said he recruited me because I was an excellent student, as well as an athlete whom the children could look up to. He made it clear that he wanted me to be a good influence and a role model for the campers. Breezy Meadows was a sleep-away camp and the children came for either a two-week session or for an entire month. I enjoyed my summers work-ing at the camp—it helped develop leadership skills in me, improve my communication skills, and it helped me grow out of an innate shyness.

Being a camp counselor, I quickly learned, was no summer vacation. The children came from a variety of backgrounds, many dysfunctional, and we had to help them cope with a wide range of anxieties as well as traumas they had experienced in their young lives. You learned how to be a counselor in the true sense of the word, an authority figure they could trust, confide in, and come to with problems for which they sought wise counsel. It was a privilege to serve as kind of a surrogate parent for at least a couple weeks, a chance to do good social work by uplifting and enriching the lives of these disadvantaged youths. I was able to save up some money from my summer camp job, as well as help out my mom with household finances. It was mentally and physically exhausting work and I was tired by the time school resumed each September.

When I returned to Roxbury Memorial High for my senior year, my leg cast was off and I could return to my physical education classes and resume playing basketball. I followed my mother's wishes and chose not to return to the football team. One major injury was enough for me. I liked the independence and the power that having some money in the bank gave to me. During the years I worked at Breezy Meadows Camp, one of my favorite back-to-school rituals was taking some of my paycheck and going to Filene's Basement to shop for school clothes—learning from my mother how to stretch my budget by assembling a fall wardrobe from the sharply reduced racks at Filene's discount store.

In my senior year, I also became involved for the first time with student government at my high school. That was another positive influence because my classmates active in student government were also high academic achievers and college-bound. At the same time, I saw some of my friends falling deeper into a dark hole of wasted opportunities and stunted dreams marred by alcoholism. I didn't mind if I was occasionally mocked as a straight arrow. I did not want to waste my chance to attend college and to better myself by hanging around on the street corner, with one hand clutched around a brown paper bag and the other holding a cigarette.

I wasn't completely regimented and focused on my studies, however. I liked to have fun and I made time for romance. In my senior year, I had some friends who were a year or two older and who already attended college. They introduced me at parties to young women who attended Boston University. I did make a nice connection with Sylvia, a beautiful Black woman from New Jersey who was in her freshman year at Boston

University. We dated casually. She didn't seem to mind that I was a year younger than she was and still a senior in high school. I was able to pay for small dates with my summer camp money and I also still had my job at the drugstore, which provided spending money.

I learned to become a multitasker, juggling my various activities. In my senior year, I worked hard to get back into shape and to return to the basketball team. I was made captain of the Roxbury Memorial High squad and I had a breakout senior season, averaging about twenty-two points per game, the second-leading scorer in the Boston City High School Conference. I was chosen for the All-Conference team, a wonderful honor and a testament to my hard work following my serious leg injury. I played center and had good post-up moves. I stood six feet three and although I was still thin, I was strong and wiry and could use my height and strength to get position and score from inside the paint. It was a different era, of course, and I did not dunk the basketball, especially after my leg fracture. In fact, though, dunking had not yet become popular and it was decades from being the integral part of the offensive game that it is today.

When I look back on my senior year of high school, it is a blur of activities. I'm somewhat amazed that I managed to juggle so many things while also maintaining high academic success. I ran for senior class president with my vice president running mate Bob Cohen, a buddy of mine from the basketball team. We came up with a catchy slogan: "Get on the Ball with McCall . . . And Keep Goin' with Cohen." Apparently, it worked. We won the election. My student government involvement amounted to one meeting a month presided over by the principal, who spent most of the time lecturing us instead of getting our buy-in or even asking for our perspective. That's the way it went in that era, a strictly top-down style of leadership. I also served as editor of our high school yearbook.

Luckily, those months of rehab when I had a tutor paid dividends because I was ahead of the pace in most of my classes and did not feel stressed about juggling multiple extracurricular activities. I did not want to give up my job at Laurel Drugstore for reasons beyond the steady income. I liked the sense of authority and purpose it gave me. I worked the Friday and Saturday evening shifts, 6 p.m. to close, and I worked at the soda counter and sold soda and ice cream as well as cigarettes, beer, and liquor. I also liked the owner, Abraham Charney, who treated me well, paid me a fair wage, and taught me valuable lessons about running a business.

One of those lessons was imparted to me every Friday night, when a precinct commander for the Boston Police Department came into the drugstore and filled a grocery bag with a couple of cartons of cigarettes and a bottle or two of whiskey. And then he turned and walked out the front door without paying. I was shocked the first time I saw it, but Mr. Charney quickly instructed me on the reality of graft. The brazen precinct commander performed what amounted to shoplifting in the open and with a nonchalant and even arrogant air. It was a straightforward transaction and a cost of doing business for Mr. Charney. What I learned is that the cops allowed Mr. Charney to break the law by selling whiskey illegally on Sundays—in an era when the so-called blue laws were in effect and strictly enforced—and the Friday evening free shopping spree was the payoff for turning a blind eye to the Sunday alcohol sales infraction. I saw how things operated in the real world and, although I did not know the term at that point, I was witnessing the sort of quid pro quo that was commonplace in the arena of politics—as I later came to learn.

During the winter of my senior year, the time approached to begin preparing college applications. I had no shortage of mentors and prominent African American men from my Roxbury community willing to offer advice and guidance. Reverend Samuel Laviscount urged me to apply to his alma mater, Howard University. Wade McCree advised me to apply to Fisk University, his alma mater. My counselor at Roxbury Memorial High, Mr. Barnes, did something he told me he had never done before: He recommended that I apply to Boston College, from which he graduated. Even more remarkable, he informed me that he was prepared to write a personal check for $100 to cover the cost of my application to Boston College, a predominantly white college that had a reputation as an elite institution. The prestigious Jesuit university, founded in 1863, was the city's oldest and widely respected for its rigorous academics.

As my senior year wound down, it was all something of a whirlwind. I hardly had time to pause to consider my extraordinary opportunities and the remarkable support and guidance I was receiving from exemplary leaders. My mother was extremely supportive, but she also trusted my instincts and my ability to do my due diligence and to find the college that best fit my needs and areas of academic interest. In the years that my father had left us during which I had assumed the role of the ad hoc man of the house, our relationship had changed and become less of a mother-son hierarchy and more of a pair of colleagues committed to doing the best thing for our family, my sisters, and our entire household. My own personal checklist in the college application process was to find a small school that was outside Boston because I had come to accept the fact that our apartment was small and crowded and it was difficult to find quiet time to study there.

I also was becoming concerned that I was consuming valuable time during these months of important decisions about my future by focusing so much energy on student government, scholastic sports, my part-time jobs, and community involvement. I always understood that, despite our household's ever-precarious financial state, I was very fortunate to be in such a position of privilege. Not only had I watched kids my age who chose the wrong path and ended up on the street corners, but even classmates who were moderately committed to their studies were not focused as intently as I was on going to college. Their hesitation seemed more about a lack of confidence or not getting strong support from home and mentors as I had. It certainly was not due to the fact that I was smarter than they were. There were plenty of kids in my class who got better grades or tested higher than I did. But I would say I rose above and excelled when it came to discipline, hard work, focus, and sacrificing in the short term for long-term gain.

A turning point came when the Reverend Michael Haynes took the time to organize a tour of New England colleges for myself and three of my friends from our church who were also neighbors. We got on the road and it was a glorious trip over a long weekend. We visited in rapid succession University of Massachusetts at Amherst, Amherst College, Williams College, and Bowdoin College. They all seemed impressive and important, in their own right. But as we drove into Hanover, New Hampshire, for our fourth stop, I spied the copper roof, clock tower, and white steeple of the landmark Baker-Berry Library at the heart of Dartmouth College. It was love at first sight. What did I know, a poor kid from Roxbury? But to my eyes it just looked the way a great college should. It had a New England sensibility, with stately red-brick academic buildings, swaths of manicured lawns ringed by shade trees, and a feeling of grandeur and solidity. Dartmouth College, I learned on our tour, was founded in 1769 and is one of the world's greatest academic institutions, a small liberal arts college that is Ivy League and highly selective. I also happened to see a few Black students on the Dartmouth campus, although far fewer Blacks than I had seen during our stop at University of Massachusetts at Amherst and about the same as I had seen at the other private colleges we visited—which was to say, not very many. For some reason, the fact that I did not see many other students who looked like me on those campuses was not a red flag or deal-breaker for me. I accepted it as a fact of life. Somehow, deep in my heart, I just felt like Dartmouth was the college for me and the place I should be. Admissions counselors say that the college search often comes down to an immediate emotional connection during a campus visit and that's the way Dartmouth was for me.

We stopped at one or two more colleges after Dartmouth, but I knew I had made my choice and I said as much to Reverend Haynes and to my friends who were on the road trip with me. When we returned to Roxbury, I went to work to solidify my choice and to improve my chances of getting accepted to Dartmouth. I reconnected with two Dartmouth alumni I knew from our neighborhood, two prominent Black community leaders and role models: John Shelburne, Class of 1919, an All-American football player at Dartmouth who played professionally and also was director at Breezy Meadows Camp; and Matthew Bullock, Class of 1904, also an All-American Dartmouth football player who earned his law degree at Harvard Law School and who became a revered elder of Saint Mark Congregational Church. Bullock lived at the end of our block on Harold Street in a modest two-family house.

I reached out to Bullock and Shelburne and both readily agreed to write recommendation letters on my behalf to Dartmouth. After that part of the process was completed, I had to meet with application interview committee members, who were Dartmouth alumni living in the Boston area. It was difficult for me to schedule an interview time with the committee because we did not have a telephone in our apartment since we could not afford it. The committee made an accommodation and sent a telegram to our apartment, with an interview time scheduled. Despite my nervousness, the meeting went well and I was pleasantly surprised that the application committee members, whom I did not know, seemed supportive and encouraging. I left feeling that I had a good chance of being accepted to Dartmouth.

And then I waited. It was extremely difficult to remain calm and to tamp down my anxiety during the winter and spring months leading up to graduation when my fate was being considered by Dartmouth admissions officials. My classmates and I waited with great anticipation as spring acceptances and athletic and academic scholarship offers were received and sent ripples of excitement through the senior class at Roxbury Memorial, as well as our teachers, guidance counselors, and administrators. The coach at Boston University offered me a basketball scholarship, but I declined. I met with Mr. Barnes to explain that I needed to get away from Boston. He was a good and kind man, and he understood completely.

One day in May 1954, as my mother retrieved the mail, she discovered two letters from Dartmouth in the mailbox and she came rushing to let me know. Time seemed to stop as I opened the envelopes. My mother and I stood side by side in silence as I carefully drew my index finger along the inside edge of the envelope, tore open the top, and removed the first letter. It was one of the most special moments in my life as I read the letter aloud and recited the words I had been dreaming about for months. "Congratulations. You have been accepted to Dartmouth College." I hugged my mother. Tears rolled down her cheeks.

"This is what I have been praying for every night," she said.

The second letter explained that I would be receiving an academic scholarship that covered tuition and I would be given a job in the dining hall in exchange for room and board. But there were other living expenses and academic fees that I could not afford. That's when Matt Bullock offered to assist me financially. He was the trustee of a charitable foundation and he said he would make sure that the foundation would cover all my other expenses so that I would not have to take out loans and could focus on my academic work without worrying about going into debt. I had so many people to thank who had mentored and assisted me up to this point, and Bullock did not stop there. He also directed money from the foundation he oversaw to help support my graduate school studies.

I could not believe my good fortune. My dream was becoming a reality. Everything had changed, and changed entirely. I was headed to the Ivy League.

Chapter 5

Dartmouth

There was one hitch: I had to figure out how to get myself and my belongings to New Hampshire. My mother had bought me a foot locker to take to Dartmouth and I filled it with everything I owned, which was not much: mostly clothes, toiletries, a few books and photographs, and a couple of personal mementoes. We did not own a car and I did not have a driver's license even if I could afford to rent a car, which I could not. My uncle Ted, my aunt Eunice's husband, owned a car. He offered to drive me to college. He worked for the US Postal Service and took a day off from work delivering the mail in order to drive me to school.

After a three-hour drive, my uncle Ted and I arrived in Hanover in September 1954 for freshman orientation at Dartmouth. I came with great excitement, a slight stir of trepidation, and enormous gratitude for the sacrifice and support of my mother, and the selfless mentorship of the Black men who were pillars of my Roxbury community. I was thankful for the kindness of Uncle Ted, who helped me carry the foot locker to my dormitory room. Since I did not have anything else and my uncle was not one to make small-talk, we said our goodbyes and I waved as he drove off. Instead of feeling afraid, I felt comfortable and calm, like I belonged here. I also had the advantage of other Black pioneers who came before me at Dartmouth, including the two who most likely sealed the deal for me with their recommendation letters—Dartmouth alumni Shelburne and Bullock.

Dartmouth had a long history of desegregation. The college taught its first African American students in 1775 and 1808, putting them ahead of the curve in terms of equal opportunity for Blacks. By the end of the Civil War, twenty Black men had enrolled and been educated at Dartmouth College or its medical school. Dartmouth had a solid reputation among the Black community and among Black intellectuals as a place where opportunity, acceptance, and tolerance awaited.

When it came to gender equality, however, Dartmouth lagged. It was the last Ivy League college to admit women. In 1972, Dartmouth's board of trustees approved enrollment of 1,000 women that fall, or slightly less than one-third of the 3,412 total student population.

It was an all-male institution when I attended and there was a strict set of rules and decorum that I was determined to follow with as few missteps as possible. Luckily, I had read the Dartmouth handbook in advance and came prepared for that evening's reception on my first day on campus. A jacket and tie were mandatory. As I mingled with my fellow freshmen, I felt a sense of pride that I had achieved admission to this prestigious college, that I had overcome the challenges of being from a low-income family headed by a single mother. Even on that first night, I realized that Dartmouth could offer a leveling of the social order for me and it would provide me with opportunities that would not present themselves if I had stayed in Roxbury. I felt this was just what I daydreamed about during those endless hours poring over textbooks in the library during high school. It seemed like a dream come true.

Thankfully, homesickness did not become an issue for me and drag me down emotionally as it had with some of my classmates. It was not that I felt like I had to flee Roxbury or that I was running away from my family, but I was just so glad and thankful to be at Dartmouth and in that beautiful New England setting. It seemed something like a fairy tale compared to where I had come from.

I also never experienced overt racism at Dartmouth. When I entered, in 1954, the number of Black students who were admitted each year doubled from four to eight. They never called it a quota, but I suppose that is what it was. I was fortunate that the number of Black students doubled my year, which might have been the difference in my being admitted. Although

I felt comfortable and accepted there, when I pondered that statistic in later years, I felt a sense of outrage that some arbitrary administrators made the determination that in the entire United States there were only four Black men who had the qualifications to be accepted to Dartmouth before I attended. That is not the way they would have phrased it, but the admissions policy was exclusionary regardless.

Fortunately, I never felt ostracized or shut out by the white students. Their attitude seemed to be that even though we were few in number, the Black students had all the necessary qualifications and academic standing to become Dartmouth students and they understood and respected all we had endured to be admitted. There was never any sense, at least to my mind, that we were second-class citizens or that we were anything other than equal members of the Class of 1958, to which I belonged. As far as I was concerned, I was welcomed with full acceptance as a freshman student who happened to be Black.

When it came to Greek life at Dartmouth, however, there was open racial discrimination. Most of the fraternities at Dartmouth were affiliated with national fraternities and many had clauses in their bylaws that excluded Blacks and also Jews in some cases. In 1954, these exclusionary practices became a national issue and Dartmouth students and administrators had begun to push back against the fraternities that excluded Blacks and to demand racial justice. It turned out that many of the national fraternities had large, strong, and prominent chapters at colleges and universities in the South and they refused to change the policy. Despite the complaints, Dartmouth officials felt like they were stuck with a problem that was not of their own making and at that point, at least, they were not willing to take decisive action and to ban those fraternities from campus who did not admit Blacks.

Jewish students established their own fraternities as a counter to exclusionary practices, including Pi Lambda Phi and Tau Epsilon Phi, which had Dartmouth chapters. Those two Jewish fraternities accepted Black students. There were also a couple of local and independent fraternities at Dartmouth who were not beholden to national bylaws and they accepted Black students, as well. I decided that I wanted the Greek life experience and the camaraderie of a fraternity, since I never had a brother and had grown up in a house with all women. I pledged Gamma Delta Chi, which had admitted its first Black member, Tom Young, the year before I arrived. I was the second Black admitted. They were not nationally affiliated and made their own rules. I liked the fact that they had a fraternity house on North Main Street adjacent to campus, although Dartmouth rules stipulated that students could not live in a fraternity house until their senior year. I also was drawn to the Gamma Delta Chi motto: "Live by the spirit of brotherhood and achieve growth in character." That last part about character appealed to me. Gamma Delts, as they were known, also had a reputation of being academically minded and not focused primarily on partying and socializing as other frats on campus were known to be.

Out of the eight Black students in my freshman class, six joined fraternities: three became members of the Jewish fraternities, another joined a local unaffiliated fraternity, and I settled in with Gamma Delta Chi. In our experience, there were no Black students who could not join a fraternity if they wished to join one. The two Black students who did not join a frat made that choice on their own. We were fully accepted and well integrated into all facets of fraternity life and the same was true of the time I spent in Hanover, where I was generally accepted and not made to feel unwelcome when I went into town to shop or go to a bar or restaurant.

I do recall one instance of racism during my time at Dartmouth, but it occurred off-campus during the Christmas break. I received an invitation from someone I did not know personally, a female college student who lived in Newton, one of Boston's wealthiest suburbs. The invitation said she hoped I would join other Dartmouth students from the Boston area at a Christmas holiday party. I wasn't particularly interested and did not think much about the invitation until a couple of white Dartmouth students approached me on campus and asked if I received a party invitation. They apologized and said it had been a mistake and the hostess realized afterward that I probably would not be comfortable and she picked my name from the college student directory, which did not include pictures. I saw where they were going with this unexpected visit and I thought I would have some fun with them, so I said they should not worry, that I would be comfortable, and that I already made my plans to attend the party and was looking forward to getting together with my fellow Dartmouth students. I could tell the white students left with a sense of consternation that they had failed their assignment, which was to stop me from attending the party to which I had been invited in Newton.

In the end, I did not attend the party in Newton. I never had any intention of going. I planned to meet up with friends coming back home to Roxbury on break from other colleges and we had a couple events scheduled with other Black fraternities. I had no time for the Newton nonsense and realized from the moment I received the invitation that there had been some confusion with my name and that there was no way that they were inviting me, a Black man, to their lily-white suburb for a Christmas party.

I do not want to give the impression that my race was a major issue during my four years at Dartmouth or that being Black hindered me in any significant way. I do not believe that it did, although there were occasional unfortunate incidents when I was reminded that we were nowhere near being race-blind or that we lived in a postracial society. Race mattered and being Black brought various challenges on an Ivy League campus.

One prime example was the recruiting visits by corporations who came to the Dartmouth campus to recruit Dartmouth students in the spring of their senior year. I thought it would be instructive and useful no matter what I decided to do after graduation, so I signed up to be interviewed by several companies that were making recruitment visits. When the time came, I heard from several of my fellow students, who all happened to be white, that they were getting scheduled for interviews by the corporate representatives. I was not getting contacted, so I stopped by the office coordinating the interviews and said I had not heard anything yet and wanted to find out why I was being left out. I finally got a straight answer out of one of the office assistants. He told me that these companies were not interested in hiring Black students. I let that sink in. I took some deep breaths and checked myself before I said anything I might regret or lost my cool. Instead of complaining or pleading to get an interview, I simply turned and walked away. But I never forgot that and I pledged to work even harder to succeed; I silently vowed that nobody would hold me down because of my race.

From the outset, I took my academics very seriously. I majored in government and chose to steer away from science courses, which were my weakest subject. I wasn't interested in the sciences and took a geology course because I thought it would be an easy way to fulfill the science course requirement. It turned out to be much harder than I imagined. We went on field trips early in the morning, which I disliked, and I found it tedious and hard to concentrate when we spent hours studying rock specimens and sediment stratification out in the field. I had a hard time concentrating on geology, but I stumbled along and receive a grade that was barely passing. It was my lowest grade during my four years at Dartmouth, but it was good enough. I had fulfilled the science course requirement by the skin of my teeth.

I went out for the freshman basketball team at Dartmouth, ended up making the team, and soon earned my way onto the starting five. But my leg had not fully recovered after the double-compound fracture I suffered playing high school football. I had already decided not to play football at Dartmouth because I was worried a big hit could reinjure the leg and perhaps cause permanent damage. I figured basketball was less of a risk, but after one season I still had pain and discomfort in the leg after practices and games, so I decided to curtail my basketball career after my freshman year. I did not pursue varsity athletics in either sport at Dartmouth. Instead, I threw myself into my studies and into student government.

I lived in Woodward Hall on campus and liked the camaraderie of dormitory life and I made good friends in my building. Each dormitory elected a chairman of the dormitory to represent the dorm at the collegewide Dormitory Council. I was elected chair of Woodward my first two years. At Woodward, my roommate my freshman year was Wilburn Durousseau, who was of Haitian descent and known as Will. We did not get to choose our roommates; they were assigned. I don't recall if all eight African American students were paired together. It did not matter to me. Will and I got along fairly well. We went through our usual minor squabbles and strains that all roommates do, but nothing lasting or serious. I would not say we became really good friends, but we did alright as roommates.

For my junior and senior years, I switched roommates. Robert Grayson McGuire III was my new dorm mate and we shared a room in Woodward Hall—where I stayed for all four years at Dartmouth. His father, Robert Grayson McGuire Jr., was a 1932 Dartmouth graduate and he ran his family's very successful funeral service in Washington, DC, where generations of McGuires had lived. His father was prominent in civic affairs and fought aggressively for equality and racial justice in segregated Washington. He was a member of the DC Board of Elections and Ethics, former president of the Washington Urban League, and vice president of the DC Chamber of Commerce. He received the Whitney M. Young Jr. Memorial Award from the Washington Urban League for his role as a pioneering Black businessman and citizen-activist. He died in 1982 but, unfortunately, had to bury his son, Robert, my roommate, in 1975. I learned much about Black society from Robert and he was a good friend who also shared with me his deep political and business connections through his father. Despite his prominent family, he was easygoing and low-key about his social status. I miss Robert and his friendship was an important part of my time at Dartmouth.

The matter of politics and race seemed always to be in the air, whether addressed directly or only hinted at. Growing up, most of the people in our church in Roxbury were Republicans and most of the Black political leaders in Boston, including my mentor, Ed Brooke, were active members of the Republican Party. That is the backstory of my brief and temporary affiliation with the Republicans. It turned out even my joining the Young Republican Club at Dartmouth was not a lasting connection. I think I only went to a couple of meetings before I drifted away. Nonetheless, when I ran for governor, the Republican incumbent, Governor George Pataki, exploited this fact and mentioned on the campaign trail more than once that I was actually a Republican rather than a Democrat and he used my membership in the Young Republican Club at Dartmouth as evidence. It wasn't exactly a dirty trick, but it was a distortion of my involvement, which was a brief and shallow connection to the GOP.

Another fact emerged from my time at Dartmouth that some found hard to believe since it is a rite of passage among college students to get drunk and to party to excess by abusing alcohol. I was not a drinker. If that made me a straight arrow, I guess I was. Since we were an all-male school at the time I attended, on weekends I went with my Dartmouth friends to the nearby all-female colleges, including Smith, Mount Holyoke, and Skidmore College in Saratoga Springs. The Skidmore women, referred to as Skiddies, were probably the No. 1 choice for weekend visits among Dartmouth men because the drinking age in New York State at the time was eighteen years old, compared to twenty-one years old in New Hampshire. Also, downtown Saratoga Springs had several popular bars and taverns that catered to college students. Saratoga was often our destination on the weekends.

Since I did not drink, I was usually chosen as the designated driver. I became adept at driving a car borrowed from one of my friends, crammed with our buddies, on the nearly three-hour trip each way between Hanover and Saratoga. I was a popular choice for these weekend forays because I was a reliable designated driver and, I like to think, because I was good company, as well. It wasn't entirely altruistic. I enjoyed meeting young women on these weekend getaways and I met a very interesting young woman on one of our trips to Skidmore. She was from Atlanta and she was one of the relatively few Black women at Skidmore. She came from a well-educated and upper-class Black family in Atlanta. I was impressed with her beauty, smarts, and Southern charm. We were more or less matched up by one of her girlfriends, who described me as a "nice young Black man from Dartmouth." During my junior and senior years, we dated. I had to wait until I was asked to be a designated driver because I did not have a car. And she would have to find a ride to Hanover, which was infrequent. She came to see me on campus for some Dartmouth football games in the fall. I ended up getting to know Saratoga pretty well because I was a frequent visitor to see her at Skidmore and I came to enjoy the city and to appreciate the historic Victorian architecture and the open and welcoming nature of the people who lived there. Alas, my brief courtship of the woman from Atlanta ended after I graduated from Dartmouth. She was a year younger than me and we broke it off in her senior year at Skidmore because I had moved out of Hanover after graduation, my life took a different direction, and I was not in a position to continue making trips to Saratoga Springs.

My connection to the Spa City continued, though. My daughter, Marci, attended Skidmore College and my wife Joyce and I owned a townhouse overlooking Saratoga Lake. I still love the city and especially enjoyed the sporting and cultural riches to be found there in summer, including thoroughbred racing at the Saratoga Race Course and concerts at Saratoga Performing Arts Center—both of which we attended regularly.

There was one drunken incident that represented an indelible memory of my time at Dartmouth and one that swore me off hard liquor for the rest of my life. Dartmouth had a reputation as a hard-drinking school. I knew from experience that the biggest single item in a fraternity's budget was the cost of kegs of beer. I always said I felt like I didn't get a very good deal since I paid my fraternity dues, while all that beer budget was lost on me. My drink of choice was ginger ale. But as you can imagine, there was a lot of peer pressure to get me to drink, which I managed to deflect. At one point in my senior year, the pressure became unbearable and I finally relented and said that when we finally got close to our graduation, I would give in and have an alcoholic drink or two. My fraternity brothers reminded me of this pledge as we approached our comprehensive examinations, the final hurdle before commencement. I was anxious as I started my comprehensive exams, but my confidence grew and by the time I finished I thought I had done quite well. When our grades were released, I did well, I had cleared my final hurdle prior to graduation, and I felt happy and almost giddy at how far I had come and how much I had accomplished. "Let's have that drink," I said to my friends.

A bunch of guys came to my room at the dormitory and they brought a variety of bottles of alcohol. I started with a glass of Scotch. More bottles of liquor were opened and poured and I kept going. I felt elated and was letting off steam after an arduous final semester of my senior year. I started drinking around 6 p.m. and I don't remember much after midnight, but I am told I was still drinking at about 4 a.m.—although it was a blur to me at that point. I passed out at some point, woke up the next afternoon, and thought my head was going to explode. I had a raging headache and was so immobilized with pain in my head and a queasy stomach that I could not even lift my head off the pillow. I was experiencing my first hangover, and it was debilitating. I had consumed a lot of alcohol and, being inexperienced and inept, I had managed to mix several types of liquor—dark and clear—which was a rookie mistake. I had set myself up for a truly crushing hangover. I barely moved the next day and I was still shaky and fragile two days later. It was the kind of epic hangover that taught me a lesson. I had made myself sick and had lost a few days of my life because I could not function until the alcohol cleared my system. I promised myself that I would not let that happen to me again. And I stayed true to my word. I have not consumed hard liquor since then. I have not been drunk since that episode. I finally stopped being a teetotaler when I reached my thirties and started drinking a glass of white wine at special dinners and functions. White wine is still my drink of choice, but I consume only in moderation—nothing remotely like the excessive drinking that contributed to my first and last hangover.

My major in government gave me a solid foundation for my future work in government service and I put into practice much about the lessons I learned in our textbooks and in classroom lectures. The best part of the program was the guest lecturers who came to speak to us, including members of Congress, officials from state, county, and local governments, and legislators from all levels of government.

One memorable guest teacher who left a lasting impact on me was Austin Tobin, executive director of the Port Authority of New York, which was the precursor to the Port Authority of New York and New Jersey. Tobin ran the organization from 1942 until 1972 and he oversaw the planning and authorized the construction of the original World Trade Center—destroyed during the September 11, 2001, terrorist attacks. What made Tobin's presentation so resonant with me was how he talked about the essence of metropolitan areas and how to function properly when those overlapping metro areas cannot be defined by political boundaries. The Port Authority was an outstanding example of working together and intrastate cooperation. The Port Authority operates bridges, tunnels, and airports jointly and both share equally in their operation. I wrote down a lot of notes and, more importantly, took Tobin's message to heart. I remember sticking around after class to meet Tobin and ask him a few additional questions. I adopted for myself that concept of a metropolitan government that transcended boundaries and political divisions. One never knows how each experience can impact one's later life. In my case, my encounter with Austin Tobin was auspicious. When I ended up working in government service in New York City, that lecture from Tobin echoed in my head and in 1985 I was appointed a commissioner of the Port Authority of New York and New Jersey. I remember mentioning that I heard Tobin speak while I was a student at Dartmouth. The longtime Port Authority staffers spoke about Tobin with reverence and said he was one of the key reasons why it had developed into a great institution. It was my honor to be appointed to the position by Governor Mario M. Cuomo and I had the distinction of being the first African American from New York to serve as a commissioner.

Although I was living in the moment and enjoying my time at Dartmouth, I did not focus on it in any obsessive way. The issue of race was never far from my mind. It often lurked just below the surface of daily life. By any objective measure, I had not been discriminated against at Dartmouth. I was elected chairman of the Dormitory Council, which put me on par with the leader of the Inter-Fraternity Council—the highest level of student government leaders on campus. It was heady stuff. I was also selected to Palaeopitus, a Dartmouth senior society founded in 1899. Membership was limited to high-achieving, active students and ex officio members such as the senior class president, the president of the Student Assembly, and the editor of the campus newspaper. It was a high honor from one's peers. When we had a ceremony or official function for Palaeopitus, we wore all-white outfits: white slacks, white sweaters, white shirt, and white shoes.

I also felt a sense of pride that all eight of us Black students in my class graduated in four years. I felt that was an important fact and it demonstrated that if we were given the opportunity to attend an Ivy League college like Dartmouth, we could compete equally with the white students. We were not exactly pioneers, but our solid academic showing across the board with all eight of us succeeding academically helped pave the way for successive generations of Black students being admitted to Ivy League colleges. We were proud that we had dispelled myths and showed that we belonged. I would not say it came easy. It was not like we had to work twice as hard as our white classmates, but we did have a sense that we were being observed and judged more than most. That is one of the reasons why I accepted a leadership role in student government: to show that a Black student had what it took to reach the highest echelon of student affairs at Dartmouth, and to succeed.

Fortunately, the mid-1950s was not a period marked by racial unrest on college campuses. Dartmouth was no exception. There were some Black students at our college, however, who complained of feeling marginalized. Garvey Clark, who graduated a year ahead of me, in 1957, was a Black activist during his years at Dartmouth and later, in 1972, he helped lead the effort to create the Black Alumni of Dartmouth Association, known as BADA. He was among the founding alumni who partnered with members of the Afro-American Society of Dartmouth. I was supportive of BADA and helped finance their initial annual conference, which I attended. The gatherings highlighted the work of BADA members who went on to prominent careers in the law, medicine, business, and many other fields. There were Black students at the conference who expressed criticism of the way gay Black students were treated at Dartmouth and they shared their personal experiences, which were quite emotional and painful to hear. I never witnessed or heard of any homophobic behavior during my time at Dartmouth, although that was an era when most gay men remained in the closet due to social stigma.

Despite some minor and major hurdles regarding race relations at Dartmouth, I speak from my own experience and say I felt that I did not face any overt racism. There is a strong network of about three thousand Black alumni of Dartmouth College. I have always been proud to count myself among them.

Another foundational experience at Dartmouth was my joining the Army ROTC program my freshman year. The Reserve Officer Training Corps, or ROTC, is a college program offered at more than 1,700 colleges and universities across the United States. It prepares young men and women to become officers in the US military. Cadets commit to serve in the military after graduation. I chose ROTC as an excellent opportunity to develop leadership skills and to adopt the rigorous discipline of the military. I picked the Army over Navy ROTC. I was required to spend an hour each week in a class with lectures about military history and combat tactics. In addition, we spent three weeks each summer at a military base near Boston. As ROTC cadets, we received a small monthly stipend that helped cover personal expenses at Dartmouth. The catch was that I was obligated to spend two years in military service after graduation. That was a deal-breaker for some of my friends at Dartmouth, who expressed initial interest but dropped out after reading the fine print.

My years in Hanover, from 1954 to 1958, were a relatively placid period socially and politically in the United States that bore none of the volatility, violence, and widespread unrest during the anti–Vietnam War protests and civil rights eras.

When commencement approached in the spring of 1958, it did not seem possible that I was about to graduate with my bachelor's degree from Dartmouth College. The four years had flown by and I had been right during the tour of college campuses with Reverend Haynes. I felt like Dartmouth was the right fit for me. And it was. I had made the most of my time in Hanover and I had grown and matured in every way possible: personally, socially, academically, and psychologically. I had learned how to live on my own, how to manage my own time and make my own choices—and to live with the consequences. In a way, when my father left our family, it forced me to grow up early and to behave in a way that was older than my biological years. Some of my friends suggested that I was an old soul. Perhaps I was.

Graduation day was even more momentous than when I opened the acceptance letter four years earlier, that day that made my mother so happy. Seeing her only son walk across the stage of Dartmouth was even more special, a proud and happy occasion for her. She came with my aunt Inez and they beamed as I processed as a class marshal, a high honor. Our commencement speaker was the Reverend Theodore Hesburgh, president of Notre Dame University. I cannot remember precisely what he said during his commencement address, but I remember he was impressive and inspirational. Mostly, I remember seeing my mother beam the entire day. I had made her proud. I felt good about that, but somewhat apprehensive about my future. I had been so focused on doing well academically and having a well-rounded experience as I completed my degree that I had not given a lot of thought to what my career trajectory might look like.

Of course, part of the decision of what came next was made for me. I had enjoyed the benefits of being a member of the Army ROTC, after all, including the monthly stipend. Now, it was time to repay the debt I owed: two years of obligatory military service. I knew what I was getting into and had entered into this bargain with my eyes wide open.

My timing was fortuitous. Since the Korean War had ended five years earlier, in 1953, the world was enjoying a period of relative peace. The postwar geopolitical situation was fairly calm and the need for the US Army had lessened, which meant the troop strength was allowed to draw down. Happily, as a result, our ROTC obligation was reduced from two years to six months of active duty. I graduated in June and would not have to report for duty until February. I could postpone worrying about my career goals for a bit. The summer of 1958 beckoned.

Chapter 6

Military

That summer, after graduation, I needed to earn money and I went back to work at Breezy Meadows Camp. The Reverend Haynes had moved on and I was promoted to program director. It was a nice step up in responsibility and in pay, but I needed to think about a career path beyond seasonal summer camp work and the six-month army obligation. My major in government at Dartmouth had been worthwhile, but it did not necessarily lead directly into a career track. It was a means to an end. I gave serious consideration to becoming a teacher, since I was influenced by wonderful teachers in the Boston public school system and because I felt I had a talent for molding young lives from my experience as a camp counselor and I needed a job to pay the bills.

I took the next step and went to the Boston School Committee, headquarters of the public school district. It was located at 15 Beacon Street in a landmark Beaux Arts building from the early 1900s, which is now an upscale hotel. I didn't have an appointment, walked into the large office, and told a receptionist I was interested in a teaching position. She handed me an application form. It took me a few minutes to fill it out. Almost as soon as I finished, they quickly sent me upstairs for an interview. I never expected things to move so quickly, but I guess they were in need of new teachers.

I was ushered into an office and introduced to Miss Fitzgerald, who was in charge of recruitment and placement for the school system. She saw me enter and nearly jumped out of her seat. She could hardly hide her excitement and said: "You're just the man I need for Jamaica Plains High School. You're big and can keep order," she said. At that time, the school was enrolling more Black students. She did not need to say anything more overtly, but it was clear that she meant that Black students were unruly and needed order, rather than a quality education. I let what went unsaid sink in. I thought about it a lot the rest of that day and in the weeks, months, and years after the encounter. It was subtle, but it was a defining moment in what would become a lifelong commitment to providing a high-quality, affordable public education for Black students and students of color.

I was hired almost immediately, without the usual delay for interviews or background and reference checks. I was a permanent substitute, to begin with, and I would be paid $80 a week to teach English, geography, and history at Jamaica Plain High School. I signed on the bottom line. Of course, I had no direct experience as a high school teacher and I needed some assistance in the form of professional guidance from a seasoned teacher.

Assistance came in the form of a former classmate of mine at Roxbury Memorial High. Her name was Cecilia and we had socialized during our high school years, although she attended the all-girls side and I was on the all-boys side. The library, the middle ground, was my refuge and she also was a serious student and a studious one who spent long hours in the library as I did. She also got involved in student government and we intersected in that area, as well. Cecilia was very bright and she was one of the top students academically in her class. That drew my attention, as well, and I was aware of her and was impressed with her many positive qualities, but I was not romantically interested in her and she expressed no interest in me, either. We did not date or have any serious attraction to each other in high school, although she also lived in my neighborhood in Roxbury and I saw her both inside and outside school. She never wavered from her early career choice of becoming a teacher. When I want off to Dartmouth, she stayed close to home and enrolled at State Teachers College of Boston—which later became known as State College at Boston and Boston State College.

I lost touch with Cecilia, but she stayed true to her goal. She studied with a single-minded sense of purpose, graduated with a bachelor's degree in education, earned her teaching certificate, and began teaching in the public school district in the Boston suburb of Newton, Massachusetts. She won accolades for her teaching skills and her name was suggested to me as somebody who could help me in preparation for my position as a substitute teacher at Jamaica Plain High School.

That is how I reconnected with Cecilia. She was helpful in assisting me in developing lesson plans. As she helped coach and prepare me for my high school teaching debut, we developed a personal relationship that grew into a budding romance. My teaching position and the courtship with Cecilia was short-lived. The army summoned. I was ordered to report to Fort Benning, Georgia, in February 1959. It was the first time I had traveled below the Mason-Dixon line. My exposure to the South was a new experience and would have plenty to teach me as a Northerner and an African American. I had a learning curve when it came to pronunciation. I packed my gear and flew into the airport at Albany, Georgia, located about seventy-five miles from Fort Benning. I learned Southerners pronounced it *AL-benny* as opposed to the *ALL-buh-KNEE* that I knew in New York.

It was my first plane ride and I sat next to a guy my age who had just graduated from Yale. He happened to be white, he had joined the ROTC to help pay for his tuition, and he was going to Officer's Training School at Fort Benning as I was. We were both slated to spend two months in an officer's training assignment, which included field experience and classroom instruction. He was a very nice fellow and we hit it off and had a nice conversation during the plane ride. It turned out the flight had been delayed and by the time we arrived in Albany and were transported from the airport to the bus station, it was very late and we had missed the last bus out of Albany bound for Fort Benning. That bus left at midnight, over thirty minutes earlier. The next bus to Fort Benning was scheduled to depart at 6 a.m.

I was in my dress uniform as an army lieutenant and I was happy that the bus station, which was empty at that hour, was at least nice and clean. The guy from Yale I had befriended on the flight looked around and assessed our options. I was hungry and thirsty and noticed a lunch counter at a far end, which happened to be open at that hour. I stepped up to the counter and was about to give the cook my order, when he stopped me with a wave of his hands. "You know, you can't do this," he said, motioning to the counter where I was about to sit at one of the leather-topped chrome stools. "You can't eat here. You have to go outside to the colored section."

My Yale pal, who was white, just looked at me incredulously. He looked like he was about to say something to the cook, but I shook my head and muttered that I was going to let it go. I made my way out the door, around the side of the station, and I spotted a dark and dirty little alcove at the end of the building. A small sign said: "Colored." I looked into the poorly lighted space and saw eight or nine Black men. Most of them were crowded onto a rickety wooden bench and those who could not fit sat on the floor against a grimy wall.

I took it all in without saying a word, but I felt my blood pressure rise. Here it was. I had come face to face with overt racism. I had never witnessed it before in Boston or Roxbury, or even in Hanover. The white people got to eat in a nice, modern lunch counter inside a clean, modern station while Black folks were relegated to a dingy little shack. The white guy from Yale had a look of anger and consternation on his face. He had never experienced such racism on display. We just exchanged glances.

I was hungry for a sandwich and thirsty for a hot cup of tea, so I went inside the shack, past the cluster of Black men. The same cook who had refused to serve me inside opened a screened window and asked me what I'd like to order. As if this was the most ordinary thing in the world, this blatant racial discrimination. I had been given an introduction to the South that would stick with me the rest of my life. I refused to eat in the dirty shack, to where the color of my skin relegated me. I would rather go hungry and thirsty than to implicitly condone that terrible treatment. My white friend, also an army officer, and I sat alongside each other on an outside bench. We waited for the 6 a.m. bus in silence.

We finally arrived at Fort Benning, were joined by about two hundred other officers, and were told to line up for roommate assignments for the double rooms. The Yale guy and I decided we'd ask to be placed together in a double room. Without any review of the paperwork, we were told that would not be possible since we each had been assigned to different rooms and separate roommates. I was given a room number and when I got there, I met my roommate, a Black man and Howard University graduate. I accepted this not-so-subtle form of segregation without comment. My roommate was a nice guy. He didn't want to make a fuss and stir the pot either, since the army was a rigid chain-of-command hierarchy and we were lowly short-timers anyway. I later learned that the six Black officers were all paired up in three rooms. Here was the unspoken color line in practice.

A week or so later, our commanding officer, a general, gave a speech at a formal reception for us two hundred officers-in-training from ROTC programs around the country. He spoke about how the army listened to its soldiers and if any of us had any questions or concerns, we should not hesitate to contact him. After he finished and we mingled in a reception room, I walked up to the general and said I had a concern. I said it was my understanding that President Harry Truman had integrated the US Armed Forces in 1948, in advance of the Korean War. I said I noticed six Black officers in our group of two hundred and we were all paired together as roommates. I felt emboldened and asked that if the army had been integrated a decade earlier, why were the Black officers given no choice of roommates and all placed together in a segregated fashion.

The general looked me right in the eye and without a hint of irony said this: "Well, this is the South and that's the way it is here. Of course, personally, I'm all for integration. I have a Black driver." I told him what I had experienced in the bus station and said I thought the army was above that sort of discrimination, but I said the room assignments were a disappointing reminder that the army was not truly integrated. I could see that his jaw was starting to clench and he looked around the room to get away from this uncomfortable discussion. He ended the conversation by saying I could make an appointment to see him at his office to discuss my concerns further.

I made an appointment for the following day. When I was ushered into his office, he clearly was not happy to see me. He told me that I could take my complaints to my congressman in Boston. I told him my congressman was Adam Clayton Powell Jr. and that I knew him person-ally from Harlem. I said I would call Congressman Powell. The general did not say a word. He was lost in thought.

Powell was the first African American elected to Congress from New York. He served in the US House of Representatives from 1945 until 1971 and was a powerful national voice in the Democratic Party leading the fight for civil rights and issues of social justice. In 1961, he became chairman of the Education and Labor Committee, one of the most powerful posts in Congress. Of course, I did not have to give the general this background. He knew how powerful Powell was and that a complaint from a Black officer and Dartmouth graduate would get some unwelcome media atten-tion. I could see the general's mind working quickly upon this scenario. He paused and said he had heard my concern, that it had registered, and he would consider a change in policy that would allow both Black and white officers in the ROTC program a choice of roommates.

I was summoned to his office a couple of days later. This time, he welcomed me warmly and a smile creased his lips. He said he had insti-tuted a new policy for officers' training school, to take effect immediately. From now on, when officers arrived, they could pick their own room-mates, regardless of race. I just nodded my head. I thanked him and said I appreciated the change in policy.

I did everything I could to not let out a whoop of joy in the hallway. I did allow myself a fist pump as I walked outside. It was an important education about how political power worked and the importance of lever-age and how the perception of something counted almost as much as the thing itself. I am glad he did not call my bluff on Powell. Many years later, when I had an opportunity to meet Powell, I told him the story about the general and changing his policy. He just laughed and said he would have taken my call and he would have been more than happy to travel down to Fort Benning to set the general straight on the army's policy of integration of its troops.

The two months of army training school in Georgia passed very quickly. In fact, as we counted down to the conclusion of our service, I started to grow slightly wistful. I had learned valuable lessons beyond my standing up to the general. I found that the discipline and the training had appealed to my leadership qualities and I enjoyed the camaraderie of the other two hundred officers. Soon, the day to leave arrived and I was assigned to Fort Devens, located about thirty miles outside Boston, to finish the rest of my required service. They assigned me to the transportation company and put me in charge. I oversaw thirty young soldiers who drove army trucks. The routine was that every morning at seven o'clock, my soldiers all lined up in front of their trucks and it was my job to go out to inspect each one. I was lucky that I had a good sergeant I could rely upon because the thirty guys in our unit came with a lot of baggage. They were a diverse group of Black, white, and Hispanic young men. Some were troublemakers, others tried to shirk their duty, and others clearly needed a person in authority or perhaps a father figure to straighten them out. Again, I tried to look on the bright side and realized that I was gaining valuable leadership experience as a teacher and a molder of men. It was an extension of the role model I had become with my students as a substitute teacher at Jamaica Plain High School.

The months fulfilling my ROTC commitment passed in a flash and all of a sudden Cecilia was there to pick me up at Fort Devens. I still lived at home with my mother and sisters, but she had her own apartment and a car, and our relationship flourished after I completed my army stint. I was at loose ends again and was grateful that she wanted to be with me because I did not have a job and no concrete employment prospects. I spent a lot of time thinking about what I might do next in terms of a career and I talked things over with Cecilia. She enjoyed her job as a teacher and encouraged me to make teaching my career, but I did not feel that was the right fit for me. I gravitated toward two career paths: lawyer or minister. I felt like I could be successful, build a good life, help others, and support a family by practicing the law or leading a congregation. I had role models who were notable lawyers and ministers among the Black men who mentored me in Roxbury.

As I thought more about a possible career path, I knew I wanted to make a difference, to be able to do something about the racism I encountered in the bus station in Georgia, or about racial quotas at Dartmouth and about the lack of opportunity for my poor, Black students at Jamaica Plain High School. I wanted to have a job that put me in a position to change that entire system of racial inequality. I was an idealistic young man and I thought about my mother's dream of making sure I received a good college education, in my case an Ivy League degree.

I also thought a lot about how I fit into the African Diaspora and the continuum of African American struggle. I always considered myself a moderate or even leaning more toward the conservative side of the spectrum—although I would call myself a liberal on social issues. I had friends growing up and throughout my college years who were much more militant in their philosophy and how they expressed their blackness. For instance, I knew a fellow from Roxbury named Louis Eugene Walcott. I called him Gene. He was born in the Bronx, but his family moved to Roxbury after his stepfather died when Gene was three years old. We were a few years apart in age. He was a member of Saint Cyprian Augustine Episcopal, a very conservative church. We hung around a little bit, but he did not play basketball and football with me and the other guys in the neighborhood. He played the violin. In fact, he was a violin prodigy and he became a legend in the neighborhood because he was such a talented musician. He won national competitions and it was a big deal when he was chosen to go on tour with the Boston College Orchestra when he was just twelve years old. We had a lot of neighborhood pride when Gene was selected to appear on the popular television program, the *Ted Mack Amateur Hour*, the first Black person to be chosen—and he won a prize for his violin playing.

We lost touch after high school. He traded the violin for a guitar and reinvented himself as a Calypso singer known as "the Charmer" and "Calypso Gene." Gene didn't come back to Roxbury much after that because he toured the country, learning about the teachings of the Nation of Islam. He met the leader of the Nation of Islam, Elijah Muhammad, and became friendly with one of his most charismatic followers, Malcolm Little, who was arrested for a series of burglaries in Boston and had served several years in Charlestown State Prison in Massachusetts. While in prison during the late 1940s and early 1950s, Little joined the Nation of Islam and adopted the name Malcolm X—to symbolize his unknown African ancestral surname, he explained. Malcolm X became a powerful and extremely influential Muslim minister who served as Islam's most well-known spokesman and public face for many years. He advocated for Black Nationalism and Black empowerment and became a vocal critic of the mainstream civil rights movement because of its emphasis on nonviolence and racial integration. In the 1960s, after growing disillusioned with the Nation of Islam and its leader Elijah Muhammad, he broke with the organization, founded the Muslim Mosque, Inc. and began referring to himself as el-Hajj Malik el-Shabazz. His conflict with Nation of Islam followers intensified and his critics alleged he espoused violence and racism. He was assassinated on February 21, 1965, in New York City and, despite murder convictions of three Nation of Islam members, conspiracy theories about who was involved in the killing of Malcolm X continue to swirl.

Meanwhile, my old neighborhood acquaintance, Gene, also converted to Islam, changed his name to Louis X, and led a Boston mosque that was part of Malcolm X's Nation of Islam organization. He later became the influential and controversial Muslim minister Louis Farrakhan. The Southern Poverty Law Center describes Farrakhan as a Black nationalist, Black supremacist, and leader of a hate group.

Some of my friends from Roxbury later became followers of Farrakhan, but I always kept him at arm's length. On a political spectrum, I considered him far too radical for my belief system. Although I was never drawn to the militant and radical side represented by Farrakhan, I tried to find a middle path more along the lines of Martin Luther King Jr., whose philosophy of nonviolence I espoused. I was willing to listen to the other side and stayed open to various interpretations of how to bring about social change and racial justice.

I admitted to myself early on that I certainly did not have all the answers, but I was willing to ask the right questions. I was still trying to figure out who I was and who I wanted to become, a universal rite of passage for all young people.

I knew from my own experience that to achieve racial equality and social justice it was better to work within the system and vigorously hold public and private institutions accountable by challenging them to do more to bring about a just and equitable society. I decided that I could be more effective by working in traditional ways to build consensus for change—slowly, steadily, consistently—rather than espousing overthrow of institutions by militancy and even violence. My philosophy of rational, respectful leadership would soon be challenged in ways I could not yet contemplate.

Chapter 7

Ministry

With my army service completed, I now had to make a major decision about my career path. I felt like my degree from Dartmouth was a great accomplishment and I was well prepared academically, but a bachelor's degree was more of a first step than a final stop. I felt more and more that graduate school was going to be crucial for whatever career I pursued, whether that was the law or education or something else. I also thought of the role models I had growing up in Roxbury and the Black ministers in our congregation, St. Mark Congregational Church. In particular, the Reverend Michael Haynes was the single biggest influence in my life outside my family and I valued his wise counsel. I met with him and other prominent Black men in our church, including lawyers and physicians, to sound them out about my career direction. I was privileged that they thought enough of me and my potential to take the time to help me sort through the possibilities.

Several confirmed my interest in a legal career and I applied to the University of Chicago Law School. I was interested in Chicago and thought it would be an interesting city to live in. In doing some research on the law school, I found out that I could pay for a portion of my tuition by serving as a counselor in an undergraduate dormitory at the University of Chicago. I would need a job like that to make law school a viable option. But I did not follow up on the law school application because I felt pulled strongly in a different direction. I felt a calling to the ministry.

73

The Black church has been the single most important institution in my life and it had made it possible for me to overcome economic barriers and other obstacles I faced in order to graduate from Dartmouth College. I never forgot and never forgave a sociology professor of mine at Dartmouth. I wrote a paper on the role of the Black church in the Black community and I called it the single most important institution. The professor strongly disagreed with my thesis and as a result he said he could not give me an A and I would have to settle for a lower grade. I was angry at this man, who happened to be white. I vowed to prove him wrong.

That disagreement with the professor lurked in the back of my mind as I applied to Andover Newton Theological School, a graduate school and seminary outside Boston. A number of the ministers of the United Church of Christ whom I knew had graduated from there. They had all spoken highly of Andover Newton, the oldest graduate school in the nation, which formally affiliated with Yale Divinity School in 2017. The location in Newton was close enough to my mother and to Cecilia and I also learned that it had a generous scholarship program, which I would need to be able to afford the tuition.

I was accepted to Andover Newton and I had the same sense of excitement and anticipation I felt when I started at Dartmouth. It was a three-year program and I lived in a dormitory there. I received academic scholarships and financial support from St. Mark Congregational Church and Matt Bullock's foundation. I also worked as the part-time leader of the church's youth group and worked on weekends to help pay for my education.

I also married Cecilia during my first year at Andover Newton. She was teaching at an elementary school in Newton, within walking distance of the apartments reserved for married couples where we lived. We were both twenty-two years old, both graduates of Roxbury Memorial High School. She was raised Catholic, but was no longer active in her church, so we got married in Roxbury at my church, St. Mark Congregational. We had a small wedding for family members and a few friends. Living in the apartment complex was not ideal, but we were both just getting started in our chosen careers and we focused on that—she on her teaching and me on my coursework.

I didn't feel challenged by the coursework, compared to the academic rigor of Dartmouth. I did not have to work very hard to earn high grades in courses such as History of Christianity, the Old Testament, and New Testament. I was still called to the ministry but felt that training for a parish appointment did not really suit my interests and ambitions. I came to realize I wanted to work in a ministry that was larger than working in a single parish. I was drawn to community organizing work and realized I needed a different educational background to prepare for that.

I took advantage of a study abroad program and enrolled at the University of Edinburgh in Scotland, which was recruiting seminary students from the United States. I was drawn to one of the world's oldest and greatest universities and a desire for international travel since I had never been out of the country before. Unfortunately, Cecilia could not get a work permit and she could not get an extended visa, so she remained behind in Roxbury and continued to teach school. I was very grateful that she made the sacrifice to stay behind and support me because she knew how important an opportunity like this was for me in my graduate studies. I was also fortunate to be receiving financial assistance from Matt Bullock's foundation.

I faced culture shock in Scotland. It was cold and damp and the people of Edinburgh were even colder. I never felt terribly welcome. Luckily, the university had a diverse student body, with students from Asia, Africa, the United States, and Europe. Graduate student housing was very limited and the university housing office referred me to a rooming house run by Mrs. Lyntton. I spoke with her on the phone and told her I was a graduate student from the US. When I went to meet her in person, I could see a bit of surprise register on her face when she saw I was a Black man. She gave me a big hug and said she took in students of color from Africa and Asia and elsewhere—students who often had a hard time finding housing in Edinburgh. I felt comfortable and welcome and made friends with the other students living there. We ate breakfast and dinner together and enjoyed the ritual of high tea in the late afternoon. It was a lovely way to connect with each other and that is why, to this day, I am a tea drinker and not a coffee drinker.

I had a fifteen-minute bus ride to the sprawling urban campus. The theology school was located in a historic building and the campus looked like a movie set. The university was founded in 1538 and several of the structures dated from the seventeenth century.

My two closest friends at Edinburgh were Fred and Diane Foster, a couple of free spirits who seemed to spend as much time planning their next adventure as they spent studying or attending class. They purchased a Volkswagen Bug in Germany on their way to campus and drove it to Edinburgh. It was a luxury for students to own a car. I met Fred and Diane occasionally for lunch at a casual Indian restaurant in town. They always had big plans and fun ideas. I was happy when they invited me to join them on their spring break trip throughout Europe. The three of us could squeeze into the VW Bug and I could share the driving because the idea was to explore several countries and cover many miles.

We booked separate rooms in pensions or inexpensive hotels and were an inseparable trio during the European road trip. One night, Fred's stomach was acting up and he told Diane and me to go to dinner without him. When we returned, I picked up my room key from the desk clerk. Diane did not request her key because Fred was in their room. I got a call as soon as I entered my room. The desk clerk spoke in German or French, which I did not understand, so I hung up the phone. The clerk came up to my room. I now understood that he was looking for the woman in my room. I tried to explain Diane was not in my room and she was in her husband's room, but the desk clerk did not understand English. He proceeded to scour my room, looking under the bed, in the closet, and behind the shower curtain. He left no space unchecked. I eventually ushered him into the hallway and locked my door. He left puzzled. I couldn't help but wonder whether it was a puritanical streak or, perhaps, a reaction to the fact that I was a Black man and Diane was a white woman. At any rate, it was a story I told Fred and Diane and we had a good laugh about it.

That road trip by VW Bug with two good friends was probably the highlight of my study abroad program at Edinburgh. Nothing else topped it in terms of exploring new countries, experiencing different cultures and having an awful lot of fun and camaraderie along the way. We traveled from England to Belgium, Germany, Austria, Switzerland, Italy, and France.

The year at Edinburgh ended in spring and it was a good experience on balance. I was glad I took advantage of the opportunity, I achieved good grades without feeling too stressed, and all the courses transferred with full credit to my transcript at Andover Newton. Summer passed quickly and uneventfully. I reunited with Cecilia in Roxbury.

Since Cecilia was on summer break from her teaching job, she and I both spent the summer of 1961 as administrators at Breezy Meadows Camp—me as director of the boy's camp and Cecilia as head counselor for the girls.

I settled into my third and final year at Andover Newton in September and, fortunately, Bullock's foundation provided the financial support once again that made it possible for me to attend without taking out large loans or sending me into deep debt.

A terrible loss occurred in October of that year. My mother died at age fifty from complications of rheumatic heart disease. Her heart valves had been permanently damaged by rheumatic fever and we understood her vulnerability and high risk for dying at a young age. Still, nothing prepared me for the shocking reality and the crushing blow of losing my rock, my inspiration, my biggest supporter, and my best friend. Also, Caroleasa was the glue that held our family together and with her gone, I feared the center might not hold. Her death required a period not only of deep mourning but also of reorganizing and restructuring the family dynamic.

Shortly before my mother died, unbeknownst to me at the time, two of my sisters had located our father and visited him in New York City. They had not told me beforehand because they knew it would make me upset, which it did. I had done my best to put that hurt and anger behind me and to move on with my life without him. My sisters also did not tell me that they invited our father to our mother's funeral, which was at St. Mark Congregational Church. His appearance unsettled me on a day when I wanted to give my full attention and devotion to my mother. It had been more than ten years since he abandoned our family when I was just eleven years old.

I did not want to see him, but he appeared and he put on what I felt was a phony performance of grief. He cried and apologized for leaving us. I felt angry and embarrassed by his presence. What was worse, he spent two days with us at our apartment in Roxbury. My sisters doted on him. I did my best to ignore him and had as little interaction with him as possible. He and I did not spend much time talking. I felt he had nothing to say that I cared to hear. His actions spoke loud and clear. I resented his reemergence on a couple of levels, particularly because I was trying to grieve the loss of my mother, for whom I was deeply and genuinely bereaved. He drew my energy and attention away from that in our embittered and fraught relationship. I preferred the path of least resistance. I did not want to get into a fight or angry shouting match with him. Instead, I stayed silent and swallowed my anger. I was happy to see him leave the apartment two days after the funeral and return to New York City. It was the last time I saw him for a long while. So much remained unsaid and unresolved.

My mother was also the caretaker of my four younger sisters and they could not live independently. Two of them went to live with our aunt and the other two moved in with Cecilia and me at an apartment we rented in Roxbury. The apartment was crowded and less than ideal.

Meanwhile, I had to focus on completing the last year of study to receive my theology degree and I had to think of what came after Andover Newton. I didn't have a plan and there were few job prospects. I had to create an opportunity since none presented itself. Andover Newton students were required to complete an internship at Boston City Hospital. They were trained to provide counseling to patients and their families. This was important instruction for future ministers. The hospital setting did not appeal to me. I pivoted and created a proposal for an alternative internship program and presented it to Andover Newton.

I based this proposal on the East Harlem Protestant Parish model, which started in the late 1950s with graduates from Union Theological Seminary in New York. It was influenced by the ecumenical movement and collaboration among various faith traditions. East Harlem was becoming mostly Hispanic and there was no mainline Protestant church presence there. The seminary graduates filled a void and served the community almost like a domestic Peace Corps. The emphasis was on helping underserved, low-income, inner-city communities. It was seen as a successful experiment: it produced graduates who became prominent church leaders, and it became a model inner-city ministry that others studied and emulated.

I noticed firsthand the shifting demographics of Roxbury along the western corridor of the city along Blue Hill Avenue. With increasing velocity, Jewish families were moving out and being replaced by poorer Black families recently arrived from the Deep South. This influx of poor Blacks without the requisite corresponding community services made for a changing socioeconomic dynamic in the community.

I perceived a need in the Blue Hill Avenue area of Roxbury and I developed it into a proposal: to offer a series of internships for service-oriented Andover students who would serve as a new community support network, to link the newly arrived poor Black families with essential social services. I enlisted support from one of my favorite professors at Andover Newton, Dr. Harvey Cox, author of *The Secular City*, published in 1965. The book became an international bestseller and is one of the most influential books of Protestant theology in the twentieth century. As his reputation soared with the publication of *The Secular City*, he was recruited by Harvard Divinity School and started teaching there in 1965. I was influenced by his courses and his scholarship, particularly by his vital research on the interaction of religion, culture, and politics. His specialty areas, which he covered in his coursework, included urbanization and Jewish-Christian relations—which were apropos for my Roxbury proposal.

Professor Cox was always encouraging and supportive and he agreed to be an adviser on my project, along with the late Reverend Dr. Meredith Brook Handspicker, who preferred to be called Jerry. He passed away in 2016 and he had served as Professor of Practical Theology at Andover Newton for thirty-six years. Both professors were tremendously helpful as I formulated the criteria for the internship and the project itself.

Now, of course, I had to recruit students to consider the internship. One of the requirements of third-year theology students was to preside over and preach at one of Andover's weekly chapel services for the entire population of seminary students and faculty members. I took the opportunity to use my service as a recruiting tool. In my sermon I expounded on the theme in a book by Gibson Winter, published in 1962 and titled *The Suburban Captivity of the Churches: An Analysis of Protestant Responsibility in the Expanding Metropolis*. Protestant ministers and churches were abandoning the cities, moving to affluent suburbs and leaving behind poor, disadvantaged young people. I preached that some of us must return to neighborhoods in urban areas.

My sermon had the desired effect. The first two students to sign up for my project were two female Andover students, Nancy Warren, a first-year student from western Massachusetts, and Yvonne Delk from Norfolk, Virginia. Yvonne went on to serve for four decades as a minister in the United Church of Christ and she was the first African American woman ordained in 1974. She became a highly respected national leader in the UCC.

My next challenge was to find a space for the project and I scoured the neighborhoods of Roxbury. I was excited to find some available space at a key corner on Blue Hill Avenue in the heart of my community focus. There was a pharmacy on the ground floor of this corner building, but the second level was empty and I negotiated an affordable monthly fee for the entire second floor, which consisted of several rooms of various sizes. The location was central and highly visible and the right price for us.

Next was to come up with a name and we kept it simple and straightforward. The Blue Hill Protestant Center was born. I was grateful that we received strong financial support in the form of a grant from the Boston City Mission Society. Renamed City Mission Boston, this ecumenical group founded in 1816 is the oldest multiservice agency in New England. It was created by members and clergy of Old South Church United Church of Christ and the Park Street Church in response to the hardships facing Boston residents in the early 1800s. It espouses "spiritually sound and socially responsible" programs and it works to act together to advance economic and racial equality for underserved families. It was a nice fit for the project I was developing, and we were grateful to them for providing critical seed money to help get us up and running.

Our recruitment efforts yielded about a dozen Andover students, most of them first-year students, and I was able to get administrators to agree to provide course credit for their internships. In addition, we got community volunteers to assist Bill Strickland, a friend of mine from high school and a graduate student at Harvard, who helped recruit more student interns from Harvard and Boston University. Further, an appeal to suburban churches produced their unused furniture, chairs, tables, and desks that we used to furnish our spaces.

As we prepared to launch our community center, we benefited from a legal provision related to the separation of church and state that provides release time for religious education from the public school curriculum. We made use of the legal right of parents to release their public school students for two hours each week during the normal school day in order to attend religious education. This was utilized by Catholic, Jewish, Muslim, and, in our case, Protestant faith communities. This made a big difference and we drew a sizable number of elementary and middle school students, a program element that we borrowed from the successful strategy in East Harlem.

This required a lot of outreach and laying the groundwork, particularly with school superintendents, principals, and administrators. We put in the effort and managed to get buy-in from the Roxbury school district, as well as leaders of elementary and middle schools. We began with about sixty children released from their local schools one day a week for two hours. We were able to develop a lively curriculum for religious education. We borrowed some elements of East Harlem's program and we developed important relationships with families, who also sent their children to us for after-school tutoring, for Saturday programs with arts and crafts, and other group activities. We also developed a recreational basketball team that was very popular with teenagers and helped channel their energy in a positive direction instead of succumbing to the allure of the streets.

We had many wonderful success stories, including one family I recall in particular, the Wallace family from Georgia. They were having difficulty both economically and socially in a racist white community that did not want to provide social services or support for Black families like theirs. Instead, they purchased those families a one-way bus ticket to Boston or New York City as a cynical way of dealing with their problem. The Wallace family consisted of the parents and five children and they arrived in Roxbury with essentially the clothes on their backs. We managed to help the husband find a job and we got the five Wallace children involved at our center's after-school programs as well as Saturday activities and our Sunday school class. We helped them get an apartment and also put out the word that they needed furniture and household goods and donations poured in. The Wallace family was an example of the wonderful outcomes that could occur when the community collaborated to provide needed assistance—and when secular and religious organizations worked together.

For the first year of our existence, I served as director and manager of the Blue Hill Protestant Center. It was a part-time position because we could not afford to pay a full-time salary. In reality, I worked more than full-time in my role and I transitioned into the full-time director's job in 1962 after I graduated from Andover. In addition to overseeing the center and staff of interns and volunteers, I was in constant fundraising mode in order to keep the operation afloat. I made countless visits to the predominantly white pastors of affluent suburban churches as I described our program and made the case for the need for their congregations to support this urban ministry that empowered poor Black families. I was not very comfortable asking for money initially, but I got better at it as I went along and my secret weapon was that I believed with my heart and soul in the need for our center and that we had already lifted up many struggling poor families in Roxbury. I knew that we could do even more if we could increase our funding and our capacity. In addition to securing considerable financial support, I managed to make invaluable contacts with the leaders of suburban churches around Boston that would serve me well in future endeavors.

Meanwhile, my home life had settled into a predictable rhythm. Two of my sisters were sharing the apartment with Cecilia and me. My sister Audrey was very active at the center and worked in the crafts program on Saturdays and she was helpful to our efforts. Cecilia continued her teaching and I was spending a lot of time at the center.

I also faced some challenges from within my own community. Specifically, the members of St. Mark Congregational wanted to know what was I doing focusing all my time and energy and resources on Blue Hill and improving conditions for poverty-stricken newcomers, instead of taking a leadership role in the church that nurtured and helped raise me? I tried to explain to them that I felt like I was engaged in a vital ministry that was as much social work as spiritual guidance. I said that I was doing the important work of helping families find jobs, or keeping their children engaged and committed to being part of the Christian tradition. About six months after we opened, I organized our first Sunday service and we drew about fifty people, including families with young children, who filled our meeting space. I preached and invited other student ministers to preach and we also added Bible study classes and prayer services on other days throughout the week. I felt like we were becoming a full-service program that addressed all the needs of our families in a holistic way that did not separate the spiritual from the practical, but instead saw all of it as part of an integrated whole.

We managed to patch together enough money from my fundraising efforts among suburban churches and our grant from the City Mission Society of Boston to sustain us throughout the first year, and it was enough to pay me a modest salary. I was the only one on the staff who was paid. The rest were interns and volunteers. We truly became a year-round program by renting a school bus in the summers. We took the children who had attended our programs during the school year and added summertime trips to parks and swimming pools and other places the kids never would have been able to go to on their own.

I also had to step up our fundraising efforts and I was fortunate to have a strong message that we were making a difference in the lives of at-risk children in an underserved community. Progressive pastors in wealthier suburban congregations began to add our programs as a budget item and we also received support from many individual donors who recognized the value of our work. I felt like I had made a valuable contribution and that I had brought together not only my theological training and my desire to serve in ministry, but also a variety of skills including team building, community organizing, and development. The Blue Hill Protestant Center had a strong foundation that we had created and it was built to stand on its own for many additional years, until the early 1970s.

I also examined my own philosophy and I recalled Gene Walcott from the neighborhood, who was now Louis Farrakhan. The mosque he started was just a few blocks from our center, but a world away in terms of teachings and temperament. I parted ways with his message of hatred for the white community and belief that they needed to develop an exclusionary Black nation. I did not deny that racism had deprived the Black community of dignity and worth, but I believed we could create lasting change by challenging the white community rather than trying to overthrow it or ignore it.

I had an inherent distrust of the police already, based on an incident shortly after I graduated from high school. I had joined the Breezy Meadows counselors for a celebration at Revere Beach Amusement Park near Boston. We stayed late and the only transportation leaving the beach late at night was a train from Revere Beach to Dudley Street, where I planned to transfer to a bus to travel the rest of the way into Roxbury. But I missed the last bus at 11:30 p.m. and was planning to jog home the rest of the way, a distance of about two miles. As I was leaving the Dudley Street station and had settled into a comfortable lope, someone shouted at me as I passed the doorway to a bar. "Where are you going?" a man yelled to me.

I stopped jogging and could see it was a policeman and as he weaved toward me, it appeared that he had been drinking. He was in a uniform and he said his name was Duke. He told me I was pretty big and he wanted to see who was tougher: him or me. He challenged me to step back into a darkened alley to fight him. He said since I was much larger, I would probably win. I told him I had no interest in fighting and started to walk away. He rushed over and got into my face and started taunting me. He kept egging me on when another police officer approached. He appeared to be sober and he told Duke to stop bothering me. Duke told the other cop I was a wise guy and he wanted to teach me a lesson. I said that I never spoke back or said a word to him. The other cop finally got Duke to relent and he walked away, unsteady on his feet, as the other cop guided him. That incident stuck with me as much as being denied service at the food counter in the bus station when I served in the army. There was an undercurrent of menace and ugliness.

During my time at the Blue Hill Center, there was a horrific crime in our neighborhood that incited anger and fomented rage. A seventeen-year-old African American girl was returning from a babysitting job in Roxbury and was the victim of a sexual assault—the assailant ended up murdering her. The homicide happened in the early evening and Black folks took to the street in angry protests demanding more police protection and more frequent patrols in Black neighborhoods—which they contended always received less robust security compared to the white neighborhoods.

The NAACP called a community meeting in the wake of the slain Black girl. I attended. It drew a large crowd and people were outraged and fearful. They demanded immediate action from the police. I was selected to lead a committee and develop a regular series of meetings and discussions with police officials about the lack of officers and resources in poor Black neighborhoods like ours.

We got their attention. Two nights after the community meeting, three police cars with the top brass from the Roxbury Police Precinct showed up at our apartment. It was late, after 10 p.m., and they said they wanted to talk to me about the meeting. They told me that if I had an issue with the police, I should take it up with the precinct commander. I just listened and said I would do so. After they left, my sisters and Cecilia told me they felt intimidated and worried about my safety.

When I finally got an appointment with the precinct commander, I went to the station with several committee members and we were not offered a seat the entire time we were in his office. They made us stand while the commander sat behind his large desk. It was clearly a power play and meant to intimidate. We made our statement and the commander dismissed any complaint and said everything was fine. He never once thanked us for coming and he eventually dismissed us.

I was angered and disappointed by the lack of respect, which was overtly racist and demeaning because we dared to make demands and question their authority—which had previously been absolute and unquestioned.

Eventually, our passion and energy flagged and the movement to demand more and better community policing slowly faded away. Our efforts at the center came to the attention of the national offices of the United Church of Christ and the head of the Office of Urban Affairs, Dr. Archie Hargraves, who took an interest. He was able to help us obtain some funding from the UCC national office. A couple of months after a visit by Reverend Hargraves, out of the blue I received a call from Dr. David Barry from the New York City Mission City Society. He heard about what we were doing and he told me he thought I had the skill set, temperament, and leadership qualities they were looking for to fill a community organizer position in Brooklyn. They wanted me to consider applying for the position. This unexpected opportunity was one I had to consider seriously and I also asked my family members to offer their opinion whether I should pursue the job in Brooklyn, or stay put in Roxbury.

I was beginning to get the sense that I had done as much as I could in Boston and Roxbury. By staying in my hometown, I was limiting my potential to grow in new and different ways. I felt that I was ready for a change and that a fresh start with a new opportunity in New York City seemed like an exciting chance that I did not want to pass up. After a meeting with Dr. Barry and a few ministers in New York, I was convinced this was an excellent opportunity I should not miss. I worried about how leaving Boston and moving to New York City for a new job would be welcomed at home. To my surprise, Cecilia was excited by the prospect of going to New York City in order to attend graduate school and earn her PhD in education. Secondly, my sisters were supportive because I planned to let them continue to live in the apartment while we moved to Brooklyn.

I wanted to make sure I left Roxbury on good terms and that the Blue Hill Protestant Center, into which I had poured all the talent and skills that I had, would continue to survive and thrive. I discussed my position with my leadership team. I was leaving the center in a solid position, with strong support in the community, a dedicated staff, outstanding programs, and financial security.

I was confident that I would be leaving Blue Hill Center in a solid condition, well established and valued in the Roxbury community. I had helped it gain recognition as an innovative example and national model of a successful urban ministry. The Reverend Virgil Wood was recruited to succeed me. He was a graduate of Andover Newton Theological School, five years before me, and he was active in the civil rights movement and had been a minister at a church in Virginia. Virgil focused on economic development during his tenure and Blue Hill Center continued to operate seven years after I left under Virgil's leadership.

I prepared to leave for the new job in Brooklyn in early June 1964. I was twenty-seven years old and it was a very big step that took me way out of my comfort zone. I had only been in New York City once, and that was during a brief road trip.

Cecilia seemed ready, as well, to start fresh with a new adventure in the great metropolis.

Chapter 8

Brooklyn

I had been attracted to New York City for a long time, probably since I was a teenager and listened to a radio station that carried a live broadcast from the famous jazz club Birdland in Manhattan. I listened late at night to a jazz disc jockey who called himself Symphony Sid and broadcast live from the nightclub to radio listeners up and down the Eastern Seaboard. Birdland hosted an amazing lineup of great Black jazz artists who created one of the most important contributions to American culture. Listening to jazz from Birdland hour after hour in my darkened bedroom is how I developed a deep love of jazz. Symphony Sid's real name was Sid Torin and he happened to be white, but he is credited with introducing bebop and jazz superstars to the mainstream. He grew up in Brooklyn and got his start in radio in the Bronx in 1937. After World War II, he was one of the best-known jazz disc jockeys in the country, he was heard in dozens of states on WABC on the ABC Radio Network, and he brought the jazz of Miles Davis, Charlie Parker, and other jazz greats to a mass audience. I loved listening to Symphony Sid in the wee hours on WEVD AM and I became fascinated by his descriptions of Birdland and the famous jazz musicians who played there. It is where Charlie Parker was a headliner and where the John Coltrane Quartet appeared regularly in the early 1960s and recorded *Live at Birdland*.

Now, I had the opportunity to move to New York City as a result of this intriguing job offer. Although it was difficult to leave my family and friends behind in Roxbury and Boston, my hometown was starting to feel confining to me after four years at Dartmouth, my stint in the military, and studying for the ministry in Scotland. All those experiences expanded my horizons and gave me a taste of a bigger, wider world and a sense of boundless opportunity far beyond the narrow confines of Roxbury's Harold Street. I had the sense that I had achieved all I could in the place where I grew up and that, even in Boston, I would face certain limitations on my professional career there, as a Black man. On the other hand, New York City seemed like a place full of opportunity and possibilities and it was both the most populous and most diverse city in the United States. It was America's melting pot. I felt like I wanted to experience what it had to offer and to challenge myself against what many considered the greatest city in the world. "If you can make it there, you can make it anywhere," I recalled Frank Sinatra singing in "New York, New York" and I wanted to see if it was true, and if I had what it took to succeed there.

The job offer that brought me to New York City was for a new position, director of the Church Community Services of Brooklyn, which was sponsored by the New York City Mission Society. Cecilia did not finish up her teaching responsibilities at her elementary school in Boston until the end of June, but I had to start at the beginning of that month. I loaded up the station wagon we had bought—I used it to shuttle kids to programs and to transport furniture donations for our programs—and drove to Brooklyn. It was June 1, 1963, and it was a meaningful date that marked the beginning of my career in New York. I was looking forward to working in Brooklyn, which had 2.6 million people, making it equivalent to a major American city. It was the most populous borough in New York City and its most diverse borough as well, with about 35 percent Black and 20 percent Hispanic residents, and a minority white populace of about 30 percent. Brooklyn was also known as a "borough of churches"; Black ministers wielded an enormous amount of social and political clout there and the borough also became home to emerging Black political leaders.

My job was created by ministers of Black churches in Brooklyn who felt they needed to respond to the civil rights movement and the activism of the Reverend Dr. Martin Luther King Jr. and other civil rights leaders in the South. Black congregants in Brooklyn were beginning to ask, with increasing urgency, what the Black ministers in their borough were doing to push for racial justice and advocate for improvements in the lives of Black people. The ministers pooled their resources and received a grant with the support of the New York City Mission Society to hire someone to begin this important work. My job was to organize and build programming to support the Black community. The ministers had to focus on managing their large congregations and, while they recognized the need for this outreach, they had neither the time nor expertise to do it themselves.

The members of the Black church congregations were beginning to demand more community-based programs such as day care and after-school programs for teenagers and academic tutoring to help Black youngsters excel in school. I was hired because of my experience as a community organizer and program developer in Boston and also because I was an ordained minister who would be able to seamlessly meld the secular and the religious when it came to programming.

But before I settled into my new position or even unpacked the boxes in the station wagon, I had something more pressing to take care of: a pilgrimage to Birdland. On the night of June 1, just hours after arriving in Brooklyn, I quickly checked into the Bedford-Stuyvesant YMCA where my office would be located. Since I did not yet have an apartment, I drove into Manhattan and made my way to the corner of Broadway and 52nd Street, paid a few dollars admission, and fulfilled a teenager's dream by walking into the Birdland Jazz Club. Here was my long-anticipated pilgrimage to this jazz mecca come true. I don't remember who played that night, but it was a magical evening that lived up to the great expectations I had created in my mind after listening to Symphony Sid night after night. There was something epic at Birdland because of the Who's Who of jazz artists who had performed there, and all the signed photographs of my jazz heroes hung on the walls. It was even more thrilling than the night I bluffed my way into the Storyville jazz club in Boston. I was still in high school and not yet of legal drinking age. I also did not have a fake ID, as some of my friends did, but I was big for my age and acted like I belonged—even though a bouncer would have kicked me out if anyone bothered to card me. George Wein was the owner of Storyville, he grew up in Boston, was a jazz pianist, and had attended Boston University. In addition to opening the Storyville club in 1950, Wein also established the Storyville record label for jazz and taught a course on the history of jazz at BU. Incidentally, I met George Wein some years later and I developed a good relationship with him and his wife, Joyce, who was from Roxbury. George always gave me special treatment when I attended the Newport Jazz Festival that he established, as well as jazz festivals in Nice, France, and Saratoga Springs, New York. My friendship with George solidified a lifelong love of jazz.

Although Birdland was legendary for marathon jazz sets that stretched into the predawn hours, I did not stay late, even though I was mesmerized by being inside that amazing club. I had a lot of unpacking and preparation to do before I started my new job on Monday morning.

My new job came with a salary of $10,000, a sizable increase from what I was making in Boston, and I also had a secretary and a budget for programming. I found a modest two-bedroom apartment in the Fort Greene neighborhood for $300 a month, not far from my office in the Bedford-Stuyvesant YMCA. Bed-Stuy, as it was known, was on the northern edge of Brooklyn; it was predominantly Black and included large public housing projects. The neighborhood struggled with the effects of discrimination and a lack of opportunity: high unemployment, widespread poverty, and a problem with teenage truancy. The ministers expected me to create programs and organize grassroots groups to begin to confront those by-products of systemic racism.

I reported initially to the Reverend Dr. David Barry, a highly regarded Presbyterian minister who was executive director of the New York City Mission Society, an interdenominational Christian organization focused on alleviating the city's urban problems and fulfilling its social service needs. It was founded in 1812 and focused on the needs of the poorest residents of New York City, including the neighborhoods of Harlem, the South Bronx, and Brooklyn. I was familiar with the organization through my work with the City Mission Society of Boston and felt it had an important mission and executed valuable projects. It was one of the oldest charities in New York, and Barry previously served as director of urban research for the Presbyterian Board of National Missions and also for the National Council of Churches. Dr. Barry introduced me to one of his important supporters, the daughter of Marjorie Merriweather Post and E. F. Hutton, the actress Dina Merrill, who carried on the family tradition of philanthropy and was an active board member and major donor to the New York City Mission Society. Merrill was a Republican and officer of the New York City Republican Committee who also was a contributor years later to my Democratic campaign for the state senate. She was an important positive force for the New York City Mission Society and I valued her support and friendship.

Those who oversaw my newly created position were four of the leading Black ministers in Brooklyn, who led some of the largest and most dynamic congregations in the borough. The ministers were: Reverend Gardner C. Taylor of Concord Baptist Church of Christ, a renowned pastor called the "dean of the nation's Black preachers" and leader of Brooklyn's largest Black congregation that numbered thousands of members; Reverend Sandy F. Ray, pastor of Cornerstone Baptist Church and an acclaimed orator who was a close ally of Reverend Dr. Martin Luther King Jr. during the civil rights movement in the South; the Reverend William Jones, pastor of Bethany Baptist Church, a young and active congregation; and the Reverend Milton Galamison, a Presbyterian minister and activist pastor, a leader in championing education reform in New York City public schools and organizer of two school boycotts that caused some to label him a Communist.

I learned many valuable lessons about leadership from these four revered and powerful Brooklyn ministers who wielded enormous influence in their congregations and the larger community. I also was thrust into a fierce rivalry between Taylor and Ray that required finesse and treading a fine line between the two over their ideological differences. Ray was a high-ranking official in the National Baptist Convention, the largest and oldest Black church organization in the nation. It was founded in 1880 in Montgomery, Alabama, with 151 people from 11 states. The longest-serving president was the Reverend J. H. Jackson of Chicago, who led the national group from 1953 until 1982. The National Baptist Convention was a conservative group and Jackson opposed the work of King because he didn't think a church leader should be leading demonstrations or getting arrested and hauled off to jail. This led to a split in the organization and Taylor broke away from the National Baptist Convention to form the Progressive Baptist Convention, which, as its name implied, had much more of an activist approach and was aligned with King and the civil rights movement. Although Taylor and Ray had an ongoing national rivalry, they cooperated in Brooklyn, never made me feel uncomfortable, and never did anything to undercut each other when it came to my work.

I unpacked and settled into our apartment in the University Towers apartment complex in Fort Greene, near the Long Island University's Brooklyn campus and in the heart of the borough's busy commercial district. My first week included attendance at an annual staff retreat for the New York City Mission Society, a great opportunity to network and make new acquaintances. I developed a friendship with another attendee, Reverend Calvin O. Pressley, who would become one of my closest and most longstanding friends. Calvin was born in Harlem, one of six children of a teacher and a railroad worker, and raised partly in South Carolina. He earned his bachelor's degree at Drake University in Iowa, where he met his future wife, Iona. When I met him, Calvin was a young minister recently graduated with a divinity degree from Drew University in New Jersey. Shortly after we became acquainted, Calvin was assigned to serve as pastor of a small church in Fort Greene called the Church of the Open Door. Calvin helped introduce me to other ministers and Black leaders and he also was my reference for our Fort Greene apartment. I was happy to welcome Cecilia to Brooklyn at the end of June and she helped organize and decorate our apartment. I introduced her to Calvin, who ultimately became as close as a brother to me during more than forty years of friendship and collaboration until his death from cancer at age sixty-nine in 2007—a deep personal loss to me.

Calvin also helped Cecilia find a job as a teacher at an elementary school near his church and, with Calvin's selfless support and guidance, we made a seamless transition to living and working in Brooklyn.

The first couple of weeks of my work involved developing a job description. What does a community organizer do, after all, especially one connected to ministers of Brooklyn's leading Black churches? After discussions with the four ministers, we settled on the following focus areas: improvements to education, housing, and increased voter registration. These were similar to the areas that were among my priorities in Boston.

In my fourth week in Brooklyn, as I began to build a foundation for my community organizing, an unexpected opportunity involving politics arose. Racial tensions were building in New York City during the tenure of Mayor Robert F. Wagner Jr., a liberal Democrat who broke with Tammany Hall and served three terms, from 1954 to 1965. Despite his efforts at quelling racial unrest, Wagner became the target of numerous protests. In 1963, a coalition of civil rights groups including the Brooklyn chapter of Racial Equality, the NAACP, and the Urban League of Greater New York organized a sit-in at Wagner's office and demanded that all city-funded construction projects stop until discriminatory hiring practices that blocked Blacks were banned. At the same time, a group called Congress of Racial Equality, or CORE, stepped up the pressure on Wagner by demonstrating at construction sites throughout the city demanding that state and city government agencies and the Building and Construction Trades Council begin hiring Blacks, Puerto Ricans, and other minority workers.

At the same time, Governor Nelson A. Rockefeller had embarked on an ambitious campaign to build and upgrade the facilities of the State University of New York, including new campuses and new buildings throughout the statewide SUNY system. Rockefeller had championed a $25 million construction project in Brooklyn to build a new facility for Downstate Medical Center, which included a hospital and medical school that was part of SUNY. It was located in the largely Black neighborhood of Flatbush, which suffered from high unemployment and poverty.

Members of CORE began organizing pickets and launched a demonstration at the construction site of the medical center. What stood out to me about the CORE members was that they had an unusual amount of diversity, including large numbers of whites as well as a majority of Blacks. CORE was a national organization with a commitment to nonviolent direct action and was active between the 1940s and the late 1960s. CORE membership grew out of the civil rights movement in the South and they demanded an end to segregation and discrimination against Blacks and minorities. They were far more radical than traditional Black organizations like the NAACP. CORE pushed the Black ministers to get more involved in protests like the one at the Downstate Medical Center construction site through active CORE chapters in Brooklyn, the Bronx, Harlem, Queens, the Lower East Side of Manhattan.

The four Brooklyn ministers who supervised my work sent me to meet with the CORE leaders to determine how the pastors and their congregations might get involved. CORE urged us to join them and the ministers readily agreed. I took a lead in organizing the church effort. Our plan came from the playbook of Dr. Martin Luther King Jr. and his nonviolent protests. We kicked off our demonstration with a rally of hundreds at Cornerstone Baptist Church on a July morning. We carried picket signs, chanted in unison, and marched to the construction site, where we were joined by hundreds of protesters. We followed the plan we had developed and sat down on the ground in front of the entrance to the site, thus blocking construction vehicles and workers from entering. Our tactic shut down the site and drew a large media presence. Police officers were prepared, as well, and came in force to clear the site and arrest protesters, including myself and the prominent ministers who had hired me.

We were arrested, loaded into buses, and driven to the nearest police precinct headquarters on Empire Boulevard, where employees hastily converted a vast basement space into a temporary holding cell. We were led down into the basement in a peaceful and orderly fashion. There was no resistance and no abuse or show of force by the police. It was a powerful feeling to stand shoulder-to-shoulder with more than two hundred people—Black and brown and white, young and old. Collectively, we made a statement against discrimination and we were willing to get arrested in the struggle for racial equality. There was an incredible energy among the group of detainees and over the course of several hours of confinement, we turned it into a celebration that included impromptu speeches, impassioned preaching, and singing protest songs. I felt uplifted by the entire experience and it was something I will never forget. I spent the entire time with the Reverend Calvin Pressley, who became a lifelong friend. I also met two other young ministers who were arrested with us, the Reverend Leon Watts, who was Black, and the Reverend Jim McGraw, who was white. We bonded in that basement jail and never forgot the transformative power of that group protest. The four of us connected in a special way through that experience and we became friends and collaborators for the rest of our lives.

We were released late that afternoon and held a press conference and rally back at Bethany Baptist Church. The church members were energized by the demonstration. I felt proud that I was at the heart of this community organizing for a vital purpose and I could feel that a new dynamism was at work and could bring about change. The ministers made me the spokesman for the group and I did a lot of media interviews and was pleased to have Calvin by my side serving as an adviser. I had been in Brooklyn only a few weeks and it felt like a once-in-a-lifetime peak experience. I felt good about the decision I had made to leave Boston.

We kept the pressure on and led several smaller demonstrations each day at the construction site. We continued to receive media attention as our cause gained widespread support from other churches and grassroots community groups across Brooklyn and New York City. It was a growing movement and it got the attention of Governor Rockefeller. He did not like being the target of criticism or being labeled a racist for allowing discriminatory hiring practices at a state construction project. The Reverend Sandy Ray was a prominent Republican who had a long-standing relationship with Rockefeller. On the other hand, both Ray and his church members helped organize the protests. The governor called Ray and implored him to help stop the protests and demonstrations. Ray explained that he supported the demands to hire Black and Puerto Rican workers at the state construction site. Rockefeller said he would set up a meeting to try to negotiate a solution.

Ray, James, Taylor, and Galamison asked me to attend the meeting and serve as the group's spokesman. They also asked me to draw up a list of demands to bring to the meeting with Rockefeller in the governor's Manhattan office. Here I was, the new hire, having lived in Brooklyn for only two months and I was being tapped to take charge of perhaps the biggest and most important demonstration against racial discrimination in the borough in recent years. I took a deep breath, gathered myself, and went to work. I immediately reached out to McGraw, Pressley, and Watts. We had become brothers in arms during our arrest and confinement; I was impressed with the three young ministers and valued their insights.

We drew up a draft of our list of demands, which included immediate hiring of Blacks, Puerto Ricans, and minorities from the neighborhood around the construction site. We also wanted the state to set up state-funded programs for job training and access to jobs in the most impoverished neighborhoods of New York City, where the residents faced extremely high unemployment. I remember the meeting got off to a good start because the governor was open and listened empathically to our issues. He spoke frankly about his experience helping to oversee the construction of Rockefeller Center and the contentious relationship he had with labor union management who were unwilling to hire minorities, inflexible with their rules, and unwilling to negotiate. They had all the leverage too, Rockefeller explained, because if he did not give in to the union leaders' demands that all hiring of workers was done by union control, they would shut down all work at the site. The governor said he clashed repeatedly with the union leaders, but he was unable to break their iron grip on hiring and the entire construction process. He voiced solidarity with our struggle and pledged to work toward ending the process of racial discrimination in hiring workers at state-run construction sites. Within days, he used his power to get a construction company at the site to hire twelve Black and Puerto Rican laborers who were nonunion to work at the site.

In addition, we agreed at that meeting that we would form a job training program, with state funding from Rockefeller. We settled on the name Job Opportunities for Brooklyn, or JOB. The governor made it happen in short order and he sent state representatives to get JOB up and running. Bethany Baptist Church was selected as a central location where people would receive job referrals for state government and private-sector jobs in New York City through the New York Employment Service. It quickly ramped up and became a very successful job referral and training program run by the Reverend Walter Offutt, associate minister at Bethany Baptist Church. This state-supported effort had the intended effect for Rockefeller. It was embraced by Brooklynites and the demonstrations at the construction site ceased. People saw Black and Puerto Rican workers getting hired—they felt like their voices had been heard and positive change was taking place. For myself and our four supervising ministers, we considered it a decisive victory. It showed the value and purpose of my work. They had achieved a solid return on investment after creating my position and funding the programs and staff to organize the community-engaged church members in taking a stand against systemic racism in hiring practices. It was an early validation of the program and my organizing skills and helped me in my future interactions with Black ministers throughout Brooklyn and New York City.

I was riding pretty high, but then came the six days of rioting that began in Harlem and spread to Bedford-Stuyvesant, Brownsville in Brooklyn, and to South Jamaica in Queens. I was right in the middle of it and it was terrible, one of the most terrifying events I have witnessed. The rioting spread to major American cities, including Jersey City, Paterson, and Elizabeth in New Jersey, as well as Rochester and Philadelphia. The racial unrest became known as a national race riot. It started on July 18, 1964, after an off-duty white police officer, Lieutenant Thomas Gilligan, shot and killed a fifteen-year-old Black youth named James Powell in Harlem. The killing took place in front of Powell's friends and a dozen others following a confrontation with an apartment manager who complained the Black teens were loitering on a stoop in a white neighborhood.

I could not believe the scenes I witnessed in and around our office in Bed-Stuy. We tried to calm the situation and deescalate the violence, but the outrage was a force that burned like a furnace. The Black folks in those neighborhoods had been oppressed and harassed by the cops for so long and their anger exploded. There were also opportunists, including the looters I saw—men who carried a couch out of a department store with a television on top. For the most part, I and my minister colleagues felt helpless to stop the rioting. Eventually, after six long days, the fury subsided. But the anger was stirred up again after a grand jury cleared Officer Gilligan of any wrongdoing in the killing of Powell. All charges were dropped and Gilligan continued to say he was justified in killing the teenager. The Black communities of Bed-Stuy, Brownsville, and Harlem lost more faith in what they considered a racist criminal justice system.

Seeing the riots firsthand was traumatic and I spent time trying to process what I had observed, both as a community organizer and as an ordained minister. I came to see that the demonstrators were young Black men, many of them teenagers likely raised by single mothers in the kind of poverty I knew in Roxbury. Unfortunately, I had to assume that those who turned to looting, burning, and destroying property had not had the kind of positive role models I had—my mother, Black ministers,

Black lawyers, and Black businessmen who served as surrogate fathers. I could understand and empathize with their anger and frustration over their unemployment and lack of opportunity. They lost hope after being passed over at construction sites and other manual labor positions in favor of white men who were no more qualified. However, I drew the line at illegal and destructive behavior.

While I understood their grievances, I never condoned criminal behavior regardless of the cause. It was my goal as a community organizer to channel all the potential and ability of these young Black men into something more productive than smashing windows and looting businesses. Instead, I wanted to get them into job training programs and provide access to college or technical schools. I wanted to show them alternatives to the rage that terrified all of us for those troubling six days in the summer of 1964. My message was that burning down your own community does not work and does not make sense, and that we must work for meaningful change through grassroots organizing and by engaging in the political process. One thing I could do was to use our limited amount of funds to buy pizza and soft drinks and invite the angry, wayward Black teens of Bed-Stuy to come off the streets and into our office at the YMCA or into church community halls to talk about their anger and rage. We could brainstorm about how to channel that force into more constructive activities.

The race riots were a wake-up call and given the groundwork that organizations like ours had been doing, we were able to tap into the momentum and sweeping new policy initiatives, legislation and programs initiated by President Lyndon B. Johnson's administration. Johnson laid out his agenda for a "Great Society" in May 1964 during a speech at the University of Michigan, and by the time the ambitious social program was put into place it was widely considered the largest social reform plan in modern US history. With his unparalleled ability to work the levers of the federal government as "master of the senate," Johnson quickly got Congress in 1964 to pass a suite of meaningful bills intended to help the poor and underprivileged, including the Black and Puerto Rican residents of Brooklyn. The goal was to break the cycle of poverty by developing job skills, furthering their education and providing avenues to employment.

In essence, what we were doing on a small scale writ large, with the full force and funding of the federal government behind it. In quick succession in the spring and summer of 1964, Johnson created the Office of Economic Opportunity and pushed through the Economic Opportunity Act. He created a Job Corps that would provide employment for one hundred thousand lower socioeconomic individuals and he ordered state and local governments to create work training programs for an additional two hundred thousand unemployed citizens. The Great Society initiative also became known as LBJ's "War on Poverty." Another key element was a community action plan for residents to begin to tackle poverty within their own communities.

It was exactly this grassroots, community-level organizing and program creation that I had been spearheading in Brooklyn through the support of Black ministers. For the next two years, I rolled up my sleeves, put my head down, and rode the wave of the Great Society initiatives, using federal funding to expand the programs I had already begun. In my experience, a fundamental problem in Brooklyn and other underserved communities I had worked in was that, since there were so many Black folks who had not registered to vote, there was a political disconnect and a sense of powerlessness and disenfranchisement. Thus, voter registration became one of my key focus areas. I hammered home the message that they needed to use their numbers and political power to demand the services and attention they deserved from government officials. But as long as they did not get involved in the political system, focus on changing policy, or lobbying for racial equality, the wounds that created the 1964 riots would continue to fester and would periodically break out in violent ways.

I had the advantage of being an ordained minister and working directly with Brooklyn's most powerful Black ministers, who had the clout and community respect to make things happen in their communities. Since we were already organized, we were able to access federal funds and community block grants from the federal government as part of Johnson's Great Society efforts. We benefited in Bed-Stuy with grants that allowed me to help form a Youth in Action chapter with enough funding to hire staff and social workers to develop federally funded job training, with programs, opportunities, and access to higher education. Two of the wonderful people I hired were Carlos Russell and his wife Jackie Woods, with whom I worked in Brooklyn and beyond for many years. The fact that we now had federal money was a game-changer, and the frustration and sadness I felt after the summer of '64 riots were being replaced with a sense of hope and optimism.

By the summer of 1965, we were making rapid progress and many groups wanted to join us and to make use of federal funding. I was part of an ecumenical effort that formed the City Coordinating Community. We brought together a new coalition of Protestant, Catholic, Jewish, and Muslim congregations and civic organizations to create and expand youth programs in a direct response to the previous summer's rioting. I was invited to a meeting at City Hall and asked to collaborate with the new Neighborhood Youth Corps, which created 2,500 jobs for us to distribute. All of the funding was distributed through de facto community centers— the churches, synagogues, and mosques of New York City. We could hire teenagers at $1.25 per hour, which was roughly the minimum wage at that time, and it was wonderful and transformative to see the same teens who had been smashing windows and looting stores the summer before now cleaning up blighted neighborhoods, restoring abandoned parks, repairing broken playgrounds, reclaiming vacant lots, and fixing up youth playing fields and gym facilities. I witnessed firsthand the success of the program and how a small bit of assistance like a minimum-wage job made a world of difference in turning around wayward youths and helping them become productive members of their communities.

I was buoyed by these positive developments, but I was feeling the itch of politics calling me. I got involved with the mayoral campaign of John Lindsay, a promising young congressman who bucked his own Republican Party and established a liberal voting record in the US House of Representatives. In spite of my mentorship by Black Republican ministers and professionals in Roxbury, and a brief involvement with Republicans who ran the student government at Dartmouth, I switched my party enrollment from the GOP to the Democratic Party when I moved to Brooklyn—for ideological as well as pragmatic reasons. I was in a Democratic stronghold and a deep blue state, and I did not want my temporary political past to be held against me. I looked beyond party affiliation when it came to Lindsay. I found him to be a dynamic and refreshing young political figure and I supported Lindsay in his bid to unseat Democratic challenger Abraham "Abe" Beame, who was then the city comptroller. It was noteworthy that Lindsay was a rare Republican who garnered the support of the Liberal Party of New York. I was not a fan of Beame's because he represented the Tammany era and the worst kind of cronyism that maintained the status quo. The Lindsay campaign was happy to accept my volunteer services because Lindsay was in a tough three-way race with Beame and well-known conservative commentator William F. Buckley, who ran on the Conservative line. The 1965 mayoralty race was hotly contested, but Lindsay prevailed. I thought he was effective and made progress on addressing racial inequality. He served two terms and later switched his party affiliation, as I had, and registered as a Democrat when he ran unsuccessfully for the presidency in 1972.

After getting a taste of politics once again, I was beginning to grow restless in Brooklyn. I was offered a new job opportunity I felt I could not refuse in the fall of 1965. I was offered the job in the national headquarters of the United Church of Christ in New York City after my friend, the Reverend J. Archie Hargraves, left the position to become president of Shaw University in Raleigh, North Carolina. Archie suggested this was a wonderful opportunity, urged me to take it, and gave me a glowing recommendation.

The new position gave me a chance to continue to work in New York City, but it felt less confining and more challenging than my limited portfolio of programs in Brooklyn. What seemed like a tremendous opportunity in reality was difficult and challenging. One of the biggest drawbacks was that there was far more travel required than I understood when I took the job. I felt like I was hopscotching around the country between UCC offices and programs, dropping a few ideas and trying to seed new programs here and there. But I didn't get to stick around enough to see if any of them took root and flourished. I was exhausted from the travel, frustrated by the rootlessness, and felt it was further straining my marriage.

I found refuge in going to hear jazz at Birdland, the Village Vanguard, and smaller jazz clubs around the Village. I was purely a fan, though, and never a musician in my own right. I am the first to admit

I possess no musical ability whatsoever. Even all the times I presided over Sunday services or preached at Black churches, I never developed an ability to sing well, or on key. I managed for all my career to mouth the words and to fake it as a vocal accompaniment to the church choir. I still remembered, with some shame, that I was so off-key during chorus singing at my elementary school in Roxbury that my teacher sent me on an errand so that I would not muddy the sound of the students. I took that as a lesson and, from that point on, I became a great music lover—and a lip sync expert who appeared to be singing without making any out-of-tune sounds.

What I also took away from my love of jazz was that life was also a kind of improvisation, of being attuned to subtle shifts and being willing to pivot and go in a new direction at any moment. I took that to heart when I got a phone call out of the blue from an executive at the Taconic Foundation. Like a soaring saxophone solo, it caught me by surprise, altered my improvisation, and changed the tempo and tenor of my professional career.

While I got ready for a new chapter, I would carry with me a connection to my family and friends in Boston. When we moved to Brooklyn, Cecilia and I bought a summer house on Martha's Vineyard, an island off Cape Cod in Massachusetts, so we maintained that link to our families. It was a popular summer destination for Black folks from Boston, New York, and cities along the East Coast and beyond. People of African descent first arrived as enslaved people in the 1600s to work on the farms of early settlers on Cape Cod and the islands. After their emancipation, freed Blacks worked in the fishing industry and as domestic servants to wealthy white families on Martha's Vineyard. By the late nineteenth century, Black middle-class families began to rent homes and purchase property. A Black community was established in Oak Bluffs because it was the only town where Blacks were welcome and allowed to purchase homes in an era of widespread racial discrimination and redlining.

We joined a large migration of Black professionals, including celebrities and people prominent in politics and the arts, who spent summers on Martha's Vineyard and especially in Oak Bluffs. Eventually, Blacks spread

out to all areas of the island when redlining ceased and multiple generations of Black families from across the country gravitated there and formed
lasting social, political, and business relationships on Martha's Vineyard.
It was the summer place to be for Black families of means.

I started going to Martha's Vineyard when I was a student at Dartmouth.
My aunt Inez and uncle Richard bought a cottage in Oak Bluffs around
1956 and they invited me to visit them during the summers. I thoroughly
enjoyed my time there and Richard was on the lookout for properties Cecilia
and I would be able to afford. He found a small, two-bedroom cottage for
us in Vineyard Haven in 1965. We could afford it because it was a fixer-
upper and Richard helped me do repairs on the cottage. We also built a
deck on the back of the house. After making improvements, we sold that
starter home in 1970 and rolled the profit we made on the sale into a nicer,
larger three-bedroom house in Oak Bluffs. The location was terrific, with a
view of the ocean, next to a public park, and a ten-minute walk to Circuit
Avenue, the town's main street. I also enjoyed the fact that it was a short
walk to the town tennis courts, and I came to love the sport and spent a
lot of time playing matches there each summer.

Beginning in 1965, each summer when the school year ended in June
for Marci and Cecilia, by now a member of a college faculty, we drove
to the Vineyard. They spent wonderful summers there and I commuted
each weekend to join them. It was not always easy to get to the island
using a plane, ferry, car, or bus, but I thoroughly enjoyed the Vineyard
and did whatever it took to get there in that summer wonderland. I took
two weeks' vacation each August and joined Marci and Cecilia and all our
family and friends in Oak Bluffs. It was an idyllic time and place. We also
spent fall weekends there and a few Christmas vacations, as well, because
our house was built for year-round use.

What I loved about Martha's Vineyard, along with feeling a deep
pride in my Black heritage, was the fact that it was a connection to my
family and Boston friends along with business, political, and social colleagues, both Black and white, from New York City. It was a truly wonderful experience on the Vineyard and I have nothing but fond memories
of my time there.

Chapter 9

Taconic Foundation

I t did not take long for me to realize that the job with the United Church of Christ was not a good fit for the long term, and not what I had hoped it would be. The unexpected call from the Taconic Foundation was followed by a job offer. The Taconic Foundation was a philanthropic organization whose leaders had funded and followed my work in Brooklyn through the Mission Society of New York City. It was established in 1958 by philanthropists Stephen and Audrey Currier. Audrey was the granddaughter of industrialist Andrew Mellon, an heiress to a considerable fortune. Her mother, Alisa Mellon Bruce, was the only daughter of Mellon. Andrew Mellon, who died in 1937, built his wealth as a banker and financier. He later got involved in politics and became the US Secretary of the Treasury. He was also a noted philanthropist and art collector. Audrey Currier's father, David K. E. Bruce, was a prominent diplomat who served as ambassador to France, Germany, and the United Kingdom under President John F. Kennedy—the only American to serve all three countries. Her father received the Presidential Medal of Freedom with Distinction in 1976, a year before he died.

Stephen Currier came from a notable family that included the renowned lithographer Nathaniel Currier of Currier & Ives fame. Stephen was raised mostly in Italy and later attended Harvard University. It was there that he met Audrey Bruce, a student at Radcliffe College, the all-women's sister institution to Harvard. Her family was comprised of conservative Republicans and he came from liberal Democrats. Their elopement in 1954 caused some turmoil and stirred tensions in both their families. She inherited a fortune estimated at more than $100 million, worth nearly $1 billion today. Her husband brought his own solid portfolio of assets to the marriage.

The couple could have easily enjoyed lives of idle richness, but both had been inspired to undertake philanthropy and to use their wealth for societal good. Stephen Currier was influenced by a close family friend, Marshall Field, founder of the Chicago-based department stores that bore his name. Currier credited Field as a mentor who encouraged him to aid progressive causes and to embark on a vocation of service.

Stephen and Audrey Currier established the Taconic Foundation four years after their marriage. The name related to the location of a farmhouse and vast acreage they owned in the woods of Danby, Vermont, that they named Smoky House Farm, in Vermont's Taconic Mountain range.

Another one of Stephen Currier's mentors was New York attorney Lloyd K. Garrison, who became one of the chief counsels and architects of the Taconic Foundation. His great-grandfather was William Lloyd Garrison, the famous American abolitionist, and his grandfather, Wendell Phillips Garrison, was literary editor of the left-wing magazine the *Nation*. Garrison was a successful Wall Street attorney but also served as dean of the University of Wisconsin Law School, chairman of the National Labor Relations Board, and chair of the New York City Board of Education. He was a fierce defender of civil rights and civil liberties, a political reformer who challenged and beat the entrenched Tammany Hall machine in New York City. Presidents Franklin Delano Roosevelt and Harry S. Truman tapped Garrison for several key federal posts. His primary mission was to expand economic opportunity and increase citizen participation in political life. He died at his home in Manhattan in 1991 at age ninety-two. Coincidentally, an elementary school near where I grew up in Roxbury was named for his great-grandfather, the abolitionist.

It was 1965 when the call from the Taconic Foundation came without warning and I was very receptive to the offer. I knew about the Taconic Foundation and they knew me because they had funded my work in Brooklyn. The interview process went well. I was impressed with what I heard about their organization. I felt comfortable, at ease and energized by meeting Stephen and Audrey Currier, as well as Lloyd K. Garrison. This was clearly a high-quality operation with big ideas and even bigger hearts. Stephen was reserved and soft-spoken, with a brilliant mind and an ability to take in and absorb a lot of information very quickly. He listened intently and when he spoke it was with carefully chosen words that carried the weight of authority.

Stephen Currier's deep commitment to civil rights began in earnest in 1963, following the assassination of Medgar Evers, the field director for the National Association for the Advancement of Colored People, or NAACP. Evers was gunned down on the night of June 12, 1963, outside his home in Jackson, Mississippi, and the killing deeply upset Stephen. He immediately organized a fundraiser for the NAACP at the luxurious Carlyle Hotel in Manhattan, attended by nearly one hundred corporate executives and philanthropists.

Currier also began meeting privately with leaders of the so-called Big Six civil rights organizations and he directed the Taconic Foundation to award hundreds of thousands of dollars in grants to efforts aimed at improving race relations. That same year Currier arranged a meeting with the Reverend Dr. Martin Luther King Jr. to discuss opportunities for collaboration between civil rights groups and funding from the Taconic Foundation. Currier's meeting with King helped pave the way for the establishment of the Council for United Civil Rights Leadership, or CUCRL, which brought together and forged strong cooperative relationships between the NAACP and the Student Nonviolent Coordinating Committee, or SNCC, and wealthy white donors who wanted to help their causes. Currier was also instrumental in CUCRL's work at creating a centralized civil rights movement, and he helped organize the 1963 March on Washington. Currier donated $1.5 million to CUCRL and was named cochair of the council.

I was the first Black executive hired at the Taconic Foundation and I joined the Curriers' small group of employees. Running the Taconic Foundation was Stephen's full-time job and his passion. His wife Audrey was mostly occupied raising their three children and she also was a horse breeder and accomplished equestrian. She spent considerable time at their magnificent two-thousand-acre estate in The Plains, Fauquier County, Virginia, which they named Kinloch Farm. I was later invited for an overnight visit there. It was a spectacular property.

Stephen gave me an office in their elegant corporate spaces at 666 Fifth Avenue in Midtown Manhattan at West 53rd Street, a couple of blocks from Rockefeller Center. The Currier's butler, Henry, often spent the day at the office when Stephen was there. He trundled down the hallway with a cart that carried tea and coffee, water and soda, and cookies and sweets. It was such a wonderful afternoon ritual to see Henry coming with the cart and we'd all take a break for tea and cookies. That epitomized the mood of the office and its small staff: very civilized, caring, and supportive.

My assignment reviewing grant proposals, identifying potential new grantees, and engaging with grassroots community groups, particularly in minority neighborhoods, allowed me to remain immersed in the daily life of New York City.

My first major undertaking was to evaluate the Taconic Foundation's Voter Education Project, based in Atlanta with various chapters and activities across the South. I met a young Black lawyer there named Vernon Jordan, head of the Voter Education Project. I spent the day with Jordan and his staff at their office in Atlanta. I reviewed their records, spoke individually with staff members, and put the operation under a thorough review. They were doing a very good job increasing voter registration among Blacks in segregated Atlanta, where Jordan grew up, and throughout the Jim Crow South. This was just after the landmark federal legislation, the Voting Rights Act of 1965, was signed into law by President Lyndon B. Johnson in August of that year. In theory this prohibited racial discrimination in voting, but in practice it was a long uphill battle yet to be waged.

Vernon was very personable and offered me warm and wonderful Southern hospitality. After a full day of reviewing his operation, he invited me to his house for dinner with himself, his wife, and daughter. We had a lovely meal and wonderful conversation and that was the beginning of a very long friendship with Vernon that continued to his death in March 2021.

Vernon came of age in Atlanta's segregated society of the 1950s and struggled against racism as the only Black student in his class of four hundred at DePauw University in Indiana. Later, he earned a degree at

Howard University School of Law. He went to work for a law firm in Atlanta that specialized in civil rights cases and eventually moved into activism as his full-time profession. He held positions in the NAACP, Southern Regional Council, and the Voter Education Project before leading the United Negro College Fund and the National Urban League. His long friendship with Bill Clinton led to him serving as a close and trusted adviser to the president during the Clinton administration.

My first meeting with Vernon was at the beginning of his distinguished career and I learned a lot by observing him and his successful leadership style. When I met him, he was one of his generation's most promising young civil rights leaders in the South. He played a central role in the civil rights movement and he had a personal connection to Dr. King. My job was to assess his operation and I was impressed by what Vernon and his staff were doing. In the end, I completed my report, gave the Voter Education Project a positive review, and recommended that the Taconic Foundation continue to fund it. We were one of the largest funders.

One benefit to my position was being asked to sit in when Stephen invited a wide range of civil rights leaders for meetings at our Fifth Avenue office. In addition to Vernon Jordan, I met Dr. Martin Luther King Jr., National Urban League head Whitney Young, and NAACP executive director Roy Wilkins.

I got to see each of these extraordinary civil rights leaders at close range, learned from them, and was left with lasting impressions. Wilkins was very diplomatic and more moderate, even conservative, compared to his colleagues. Wilkins was a pioneer in civil rights and dedicated his life to racial equality. He led the NAACP for two decades, from 1955 to 1977, during a crucial period of its development and growth.

Young struck me as more of a social worker and his focus was on increasing employment opportunities for Blacks through the National Urban League. He was responsible for taking a relatively passive organization and reshaping it into a more aggressive force for providing socioeconomic access and upward mobility for Black people. He injected a new energy and dynamism into the organization.

Although all three were major civil rights leaders of that era and each had a slightly different approach and style of leadership, it seemed clear to me that Dr. King was the one to whom they all looked for leadership. In my brief time in his presence, I was impressed with Dr. King and found him very charismatic. It was clear that he was passionate and committed to the civil rights movement with every fiber of his being. He was extremely eloquent and also blunt about how much work remained to be done and his expectations for everyone involved. As a young person, I remember feeling very fortunate to be in their presence, and also in awe of these giants of the civil rights movement.

I remember that Dr. King came with private security, which was understandable given the threats being made against his life. I remember how focused Stephen was, and how he listened with deep concentration to the updates and summaries of the work that each of their organizations was doing. This firsthand knowledge helped Stephen make his own decisions about the Taconic Foundation's philanthropy, and also to leverage funding from other heads of private foundations and wealthy donors whom he knew.

I could immediately see that the Curriers were genuine and committed and they were highly regarded by Black civil rights leaders. Their Taconic Foundation was one of the largest donors to the civil rights movement. Through his wife's Mellon fortune, Stephen had substantial financial resources and the couple chose to deploy their wealth in the service of racial justice.

While I was still new in my job at the Taconic Foundation, the election of John V. Lindsay, a liberal Republican, as mayor of New York City created a wave of change in local politics. It caused a great deal of consternation and considerable interest from political observers. Lindsay had built a reputation as a young progressive and he defeated New York City comptroller Abraham Beame by a narrow margin. He immediately brought a fresh face and a new approach to urban issues and the extremely difficult job of running the largest city in America.

I followed this shift in New York City politics very closely. Lindsay promised to attack social problems that had been ignored or neglected during the three terms of Democratic mayor Robert F. Wagner Jr. Lindsay was the first Republican mayor since Fiorella La Guardia, who was in office from 1934 to 1945. Lindsay brought into his administration well-qualified experts, and he promised to wage a war on poverty, to address racial inequality, and to enhance community development through funding social programs. He was forty-five years old, handsome, and dynamic. His campaign theme was: "He is fresh and everyone else is tired." He also brought in fresh talent to his administration, including proven leaders Ed Logue as his head of housing and Mitchell "Mike" Svirodoff to lead social revitalization efforts. Svirodoff had developed antipoverty programs that helped revitalize his hometown of New Haven, Connecticut, which had become a model for urban renewal and social welfare programs. Meanwhile, conservatives attacked Lindsay as a "limousine liberal" and criticized his efforts to improve life for minorities in New York.

Svirodoff's main responsibility was to establish a new agency in New York City, called the Human Resources Administration. The purpose was to consolidate a disorganized slew of social service programs and bring them under one umbrella that would provide a convenient one-stop approach for the citizenry. Lindsay and Svirodoff approached Stephen and the Taconic Foundation to help fund a task force to develop the Human Resources Administration as part of a new type of public-private partnership. Stephen assigned me to serve as the foundation's liaison and it was my job to be the point person with the task force. I relished the opportunity to inter- act with brilliant young professionals and civic leaders, including Stanley Brezenoff, who later served as president of New York City Health and Hospitals Corporation, the world's largest nonfederal health care system, under Mayor Ed Koch. Brezenoff also served as executive director of the Port Authority. Other members of our task force included Bill Grinker, Henry Cohen, Jack Krauskopf, Dr. Kenneth Clark, and other administra- tors who had distinguished careers in both the public and private sectors. I learned so much from these outstanding public servants and it was my introduction to working with the Lindsay administration.

Under the Human Resources Administration, we established the Council Against Poverty to administer the federal, state, and city funds that were earmarked by President Johnson in his War on Poverty. The funds would be distributed to twenty-six districts throughout New York City, which we identified through data collection and research on the poverty indices in each district. My involvement in the development of this program led Mayor Lindsay to appoint me as chairman of the Council Against Poverty in 1966 early in his first term. The council consisted of one representative elected from each of the twenty-six districts. It was a nonpaying appointment and I was happy to volunteer since I was being paid for my work with the Taconic Foundation. Stephen encouraged me to take the position and he gave me the time I needed away from the foundation to fulfill what he considered a civic responsibility. The other key staff person I worked with was George Nicolau, a lawyer who served as deputy director of the US Peace Corps. George was appointed commissioner of the Community Development Agency, the administrative arm of the Council Against Poverty.

George and I faced a difficult task of establishing the twenty-six districts as separate community corporations. Since we were bringing in substantial funding, there was a lot of effort from the outside to curry favor with us, to lobby and to advocate for how the funding should be spent. It was the job of the council to be impartial reviewers and fair arbiters to sort out the competing requests, and to recruit competent and trustworthy people to oversee each of the twenty-six districts.

I felt the pressure immediately because I was stuck in the middle of a political tug-of-war between Dr. Clark and the powerful congressman Adam Clayton Powell Jr., a Harlem political power broker who had been a Baptist minister. He possessed a dynamic personality and expertise on how to work the levers of power, which had earned him a formidable base among constituents. He served in the US House of Representatives for three decades, from 1945 until 1971. Powell became a national leader on issues of civil rights and racial justice and he was the most powerful Black congressman by virtue of his chairmanship of the important Education and Labor Committee. Since I was in charge of overseeing the distribution of millions of dollars in federal aid, Powell and his chief of staff made it clear they wanted control over who would run the Harlem district among the twenty-six New York City districts. The Powell forces wanted to say who would get funding and who would not, as a way to reward political supporters and punish political foes.

Meanwhile, Dr. Kenneth Clark, a psychologist, educator, and social reformer who committed his career to the case of racial justice, was highly regarded as the first Black tenured professor at City College of New York.

Clark served for three decades at City College, where he built a national reputation as the author of seminal books such as *Prejudice and Your Child* (1955), *Dark Ghetto: Dilemmas of Social Power* (1965), *The Negro American* (1966), and *Crisis in Urban Education* (1971). Clark and his wife, Mamie, became a notable scholarly couple who conducted numerous studies on the effects of racism on child development and they published conclusive evidence that segregation was psychologically damaging to both Black and white children. Their study, which found that Black children as young as three years old preferred white dolls to Black dolls, was cited by the US Supreme Court in the landmark 1954 decision *Brown v. Board of Education* that declared segregated education unconstitutional.

Clark did not have the political clout of Powell, but he was a prominent educator with a strong platform because of his acclaimed research and publications. Clark insisted that Powell and his transactional politics be kept out of the funding distribution process. Clark did not appreciate the political dynamics. I tried to play peacemaker and explained to Dr. Clark, a decent and conscientious man whose allegiance was to the underserved Black community, that it was Powell who, because of his connections and political juice in Washington, made the money flow in such a substantial way to New York City. Trying to block Powell's political control was not possible and eventually Dr. Clark moved on and took his colleagues with him, including Dr. James Jones, Cyril Tyson, and Dr. Ken Marshall. They then established the Metropolitan Area Research Council, or MARC.

Powell easily won that round of the political power play and it was clear that he stood astride the New York congressional members who all wanted a piece of the pie for their districts. I felt unrelenting pressure and lobbying from all sides and if I resisted or denied certain outrageous requests for funding, I was labeled an elitist and an outsider. They criticized me for working for a wealthy foundation run by a rich white man, and they also attacked me because I came from Boston and lacked roots in Harlem. Also, as a Republican and a white politician, Mayor Lindsay aroused the deep suspicions of a lot of the Black leaders, both pastors and politicians who, by extension, were wary of me.

These competing forces converged at a community meeting in Harlem. I was invited to explain the twenty-six districts, distribution of funding, and who would lead the program in Harlem. I was grilled over the course of a couple of hours at that meeting in a Harlem school auditorium packed with a few hundred people. I tried to take the high road and explained in a calm, rational manner that my message was simple and direct: We could spend our time engaged in conflict or we could cooperate and make sure the funds were distributed equitably. I said what they considered obstacles I considered assets and I relied on my training as a preacher to try to sell my message. The audience was primarily community organizers, social workers, municipal employees, and neighborhood activists. A few of the more vocal attendees tried to talk over me and I got tough, raised my voice, and said that I was not going anywhere, I was not going to be pushed around—I had a job to do and I planned to do it. I invited them to cooperate instead of fighting me and each other. I used the cadence of the pulpit and made my point: We should be fighting together to get more money rather than fighting over the little amount that has been proposed. We deserve more than a poverty program. We deserve substantial resources to rebuild our community.

There was also a big change after Dr. Clark left the program and his spot was taken by Livingston Wingate, who was a close ally of Powell's. The congressman had put his own guy in place and the roadblocks and opposition quickly went away because people crossed Powell at their own peril. After months of wrangling, we were effective in setting up one of the twenty-six districts in Harlem and the program began operating smoothly.

I had to accept the fact that I was an unknown in Harlem, someone they dubbed an outsider, a carpetbagger. But I was not daunted by the challenge. I took a lot of abuse, but I never backed down. I made connections, expanded my network of colleagues, and eventually developed a reputation as somebody who could get things done. In a way, managing the clash between Clark and Powell became my first trial by fire, which laid the groundwork for my eventual move into electoral politics. Nobody in that crowded, contentious community meeting in the Harlem school auditorium could predict, myself included, that in eight years many of the people in that meeting would be the leaders of my successful campaign to be their state senator. But that's how things work in politics and positive developments occur when you least expect it.

I was fortunate to have the full backing of Stephen Currier and my colleagues at the Taconic Foundation even while I worked nearly full-time as a volunteer Lindsay administration appointee as we established twenty-six community groups, one for each district.

I learned the subtle art of compromise. I went to countless community meetings at night, where people argued and yelled and engaged in long, heated arguments. I did my best to maintain order and to rise above the fray. The most important thing I did was to meet them individually afterward to listen to their perspective and to hear their ideas free of such a contentious environment. I discovered that it all came down to forging strong personal relationships and that's what I did in order to gain a foothold in Harlem and beyond. Even though I was still an outsider, they knew that they could trust me and that I had their interests at heart. I often followed up with an invitation for further discussion at our Taconic Foundation office, where Henry would serve us coffee and tea in an elegant silver service. I wanted to show them the utmost respect and these small gestures helped establish my credibility. Those became key, long-lasting relationships among community leaders and activists throughout New York City and they would be invaluable many years later when I ran for elected office. People remembered me from those days and they were willing to work for my campaigns.

It was easy to understand why so many struggled so mightily to lobby and influence me. The total federal funding for the twenty-six community councils was $60 million in 1965, which would be worth about $500 million in today's dollars. The federal government passed a provision that said all grants would require "maximum feasible participation" of those being served by the program. That became a significant phrase and a bulwark against fraud and abuse. My colleagues and I tried very hard to forward only requests for funding that provided maximum feasible participation by those who qualified for services. We were glad to have the federal government's wording to fall back upon to support our decisions.

I was getting a real-life education in local politics that would serve me throughout my career. I learned to read people and I came across all sorts of folks who wanted to break off a piece of that big allotment for themselves. The challenge was that there were a lot of hands in the process, since the funding originated from Congress and politicians like Powell held considerable sway. And then the money was distributed from one of several regional offices around the United States, and then it was funneled again through the Lindsay administration in New York City and ultimately to the twenty-six community groups I helped to oversee.

One person who took things too far and employed tactics I did not like was Leroy Knight, a community organizer and something of a hustler. One thing I insisted upon from the heads of the twenty-six community groups was transparency and accountability. It was easier said than done. Since they were accepting federal money, it came with strings attached and they had to follow procedures and protocols in order to receive the payments. The system was set up to send every two weeks a check, which arrived on Fridays. It was not uncommon for employees to forget to fill out their time sheets or make clerical errors that held up payment. Then, when they found that their check had not arrived and payment would be delayed, they were outraged and organized demonstrations and complained bitterly about us to anyone who would listen or provide media coverage.

One Friday, I happened to be in the office when one of these disputes broke out. Somebody started pounding and kicking on my door, yelling obscenities and demanding that I come out and pay them the money they were owed since their paychecks had not arrived. I opened the door and saw a short, little Black man rudely pointing a finger in my face and calling me names in a curse-filled tirade. It was Leroy Knight, who was a former addict now running a drug treatment and rehabilitation program and making a name for himself as a rabble-rouser and rent strike organizer. Knight and his followers were very unruly and obnoxious. I finally calmed them down and worked out a way to have their paychecks issued. I decided that would not be the last word between Knight and me.

A couple of weeks later, I had to go to Brooklyn for a meeting and I made a point of stopping by Knight's office at the end of the day. It was after five o'clock and quiet. I started kicking and pounding on the door and yelling his name. He came to the door, and I grabbed him by the collar of his shirt and said through clenched teeth: "I came here to kick your ass." I gave him a strong push back into his office and started to move toward him—I towered a full head and shoulders above him—and he started stammering and apologizing. He said he was just trying to help poor people and get the money they were owed. I did not resort to any more physical persuasion, but he got the point. I told him I knew where he lived—it was a bluff—and that if he ever came to my office or pulled anything like that again I would give him a serious ass-whupping next time. He apologized profusely and promised it would never happen again.

As soon as I left, colleagues of mine heard Leroy Knight calling his network of activists and putting out the word: "Don't Mess with McCall." My confrontation had the desired effect. I had no more trouble from Knight and his crew. And it enhanced my reputation with other activists.

Unfortunately, Leroy relapsed, started using again, and died of a drug overdose a few months later. His girlfriend, who knew I was a minister, asked me if I would officiate at Leroy's funeral. I had nothing against him personally and I sort of admired his audacity, so I agreed to lead the funeral service. The funeral took place at Calvin Pressley's church in the Fort Greene section of Brooklyn and the church was pretty well filled with family and friends, clients from his drug program, and Leroy's colleagues from community activism. I led the service and offered a eulogy and was preparing to leave after the service when his girlfriend asked if I would please accompany the mourners to the veterans' cemetery on Long Island for the interment. That was something I almost never did and I was about to beg off, but I reluctantly agreed to lead the committal prayer before Leroy was lowered into the ground. He was an army veteran and I had a soft spot for that part of his life.

It had rained heavily the night before and the ground was soft and muddy in spots. I wanted to finish this graveside portion of the service as quickly as possible, so I stood solemnly at one end of the gravesite and began the committal prayer. The casket rested on planks of wood that spanned the freshly dug grave, which was still muddy from the rain. As I got one or two sentences into the prayer, I felt the edge of the grave where I was standing start to tilt and give way. And then, with a sudden whoosh, the bank collapsed and I fell feet first into the grave, beneath the coffin and the wooden planks suspending it. I slipped to a fully prone position on my back and my nice black suit, my preacher's suit, was caked with mud. Luckily, the muddy ground broke my fall and I did not appear to be hurt. Of course, my vanity was severely wounded and I was in a state of shock and embarrassment.

Onlookers said it seemed to be some sort of miracle. One moment I was saying the prayer and the next I had simply disappeared. Gone. Without a trace. All six feet, three inches of me.

I needed more than divine intervention. I was trapped under Leroy Knight's coffin. It was another long and embarrassing delay as I lay in the mud and waited for cemetery workers to lift the coffin off the boards, remove the slats, and give me a hand back up to the grass. I don't know how the group of a few dozen mourners held their laughter. I bit my lip and said that concluded the graveside service.

As I slogged in my ruined, muddy suit back to my car, a woman stopped me and said: "Reverend, Leroy wanted to take you with him. He didn't want to go alone."

For years afterward, I ran into people I knew from Fort Greene and they all laughed at the recollection. They shook their head in disbelief. "Leroy almost took you with him," they said. I heard it over and over and after a time I stopped being upset by the memory and laughed along with them.

Stephen Currier was also the kind of boss who not only gave me a lot of autonomy, but encouraged me to bring new ideas and thought leaders to the Taconic Foundation. I was entrusted with vetting opportunities and bringing the best ones to Stephen. This is how I came to know the Reverend Leon Sullivan, a Baptist minister who was also a civil rights leader and social activist whose ministry focused on creating job training opportunities for African Americans. Sullivan was a native of West Virginia and it was Adam Clayton Powell who became a mentor to the young minister and convinced him to move to New York City. It was during the 1940s when Sullivan served as an assistant to Powell at Abyssinian Baptist Church while he also studied at Union Theological Seminary and later Columbia University.

In 1950, Sullivan and his wife Grace relocated to Philadelphia and he became pastor of Zion Baptist Church, where he was known as the "lion of Zion," built a mega-church, and developed a national reputation. As an activist, Sullivan also created the Opportunities Industrialization Center, or OIC, in an abandoned jail in North Philadelphia. It grew into a robust Philly-based organization that provided job training opportunities for

Blacks in fields that were in demand by companies around Philadelphia. Sullivan won a lot of converts to his practical vision of "self-help," which focused on providing clients the tools with which they could help themselves overcome barriers of poverty and oppression to attain well-paying jobs and meaningful employment. It was extending a hand of assistance, not a handout, and it created a path for opportunity rather than delivering services in an entitlement program. Its success was due to the fact that its clients were being trained for existing jobs that needed workers rather than job training for positions that did not exist. That pragmatic focus made an impact on my thinking and it stuck with me.

Sullivan's OIC program was so successful that Black leaders in New York City wanted to use OIC as a model to create similar programs in Harlem and other boroughs of New York. I set up a meeting in New York with several prominent Black ministers, including my friend the Reverend Calvin Pressley, Reverend Sullivan, and the Reverend Milton Galamison, a minister and civil rights activist. Galamison was a powerful force in the NAACP as chair of the education committee of NAACP's Brooklyn chapter.

We had a cordial and productive meeting, although the others were wary of Galamison, who was considered more radical in his beliefs, which leaned toward a variation of Communism. Sullivan was willing to help plant the OIC concept in New York, but he was warned by emissaries of the powerful Powell to stay out of Harlem. He was welcome to establish an OIC program in Brooklyn or some other borough, but Powell controlled everything in Harlem and he should stay off Powell's turf.

After that not-so-veiled threat, Sullivan and his team agreed to take OIC to Brooklyn. I brought Sullivan to meet with Stephen and he agreed that Taconic would put up the money to establish the program in Brooklyn. We hired Pressley to serve as executive director. They leased an empty school building in Brooklyn and received partnership commitments from several companies. They quickly signed up two hundred students for focused job training that would lead to job offers from the partnering companies. It was a resounding and rapid success and OIC branched out to Queens and Manhattan in the next couple of years, with additional money from our foundation and a federal grant. I took great satisfaction decades later when I traveled to Africa and saw OIC programs established on that continent—and felt that, at least in some small way, I played a role in this program that empowered Black people in a pragmatic form of self-help and equal opportunity employment.

It was an eventful three years at the Taconic Foundation between 1965 and 1968 and there were developments in both my professional and personal lives. We moved from Brooklyn to Washington Square Village in Manhattan, a massive apartment complex in Greenwich Village for New York University graduate students. The rent was reasonable and it was a more convenient location for the commute to my office and also for Cecilia, who gave up her job teaching at a Brooklyn elementary school to pursue a graduate degree in education at NYU. While she was completing her master's degree at NYU, she landed a part-time job at Baruch College, which turned into a full-time position as an academic counselor.

During that time, I also received an unexpected phone call from a man I had not seen in many years, someone I had tried to put in my rear-view mirror as I struggled to process my tangled emotions about him: my father. One day, out of the blue, a secretary at our office said my father called. He had read about the work I was doing running the Council Against Poverty and asked for the address of our office. He said he planned to come later that day to see me. I was beyond surprised. I had not seen or heard from him since my mother's funeral, which was seven years earlier. A couple of hours later, he arrived. I did not try to cover up my bitterness. I was silent. He did most of the talking. He said he was proud of me and the work I was doing and he asked if he could come to our apartment to meet my wife and daughter. I tried to take the high road, as a minister should. I agreed that he could come for a visit in a couple of Sundays to meet Cecilia and Marci.

The day arrived and I was a little nervous. I remember he brought his lady friend with him and we made friendly chatter and talked about inconsequential things. I did not have the guts to make a scene and demand to know why he abandoned his wife and children. I forced a smile through gritted teeth and we tried to act like we had a relationship and there was no animosity between us. We put on an act for my wife and daughter. He said he was living in Queens, but did not offer a lot of detail or personal information. There were a few awkward pauses and we said our goodbyes. I never saw him after that. He made a few telephone calls in the ensuing months, but I had no interest in trying to pick up the pieces of our shattered father-son bond. I felt like I had done my part in being civil to the man while we were with my family. I guess he was trying to introduce his girlfriend to me, but I was not about to let him off the hook. He had left our family a long time ago and was never a part of our lives after he departed. I was not ready to welcome him back into the fold with a familial embrace. Let him feel what being abandoned feels like.

Meanwhile, I could not have asked for a more caring and considerate boss than Stephen Currier. He was not only an extremely generous philanthropist; he was personally kind to me. At one of our meetings, he raised the topic of my living situation. He worried we were too crowded in our apartment with the new baby and he suggested we look for a larger apartment to accommodate our growing family. Cecilia found a spacious three-bedroom co-op for sale on Riverside Drive, a very desirable and expensive neighborhood overlooking the Hudson River on the Upper West Side of Manhattan. Even though we figured it was outside of our price range, Stephen encouraged us to take a look at it. I started to say I did not think I could afford such an address, but he waved me off and said not to worry about financial matters at that point, just take my wife and daughter to see if we liked the place. We certainly did. It was an amazing apartment. The catch was that the asking price was $40,000. In today's terms, it was well over $1 million and the sum was out of our league. I told Stephen it was a terrific apartment, but beyond our means. He said he was glad we liked the place and he would help us with the financing. I made arrangements with the broker to take another look at the apartment.

On the day that I was to meet the broker, Stephen and his wife were due to leave for a ten-day Caribbean cruise aboard their new sailing yacht *Sandoval*, which was anchored in the Virgin Islands. The plan was for them to fly from New York to San Juan, Puerto Rico, and then on to St. Thomas to rendezvous with *Sandoval* and its crew. Stephen insisted I drive along with him in his chauffeur-driven limousine to John F. Kennedy Airport so we could catch up on my projects. Stephen gave me a $10,000 check for the down payment on the apartment. He said he would propose a financing plan for the $30,000 balance when they returned from the sailing cruise.

We talked on the way to the airport and Stephen reiterated his support for the work I was doing. We dropped Stephen off at the airport. I watched him walk away carrying a suitcase as he went to meet his wife at the baggage check-in. The chauffeur brought me to the Riverside Drive apartment. My entry was blocked at the lobby by a Black doorman named Ruben. He eyed me suspiciously. He wanted to know what I wanted at this luxury apartment building. I said I was buying a unit that was for sale. I am not sure if we would be the first Black tenants, but Ruben looked at me with a frown and said the apartments were very expensive and he openly questioned if I could afford it. I didn't answer him, but he told me I could not wait in the lobby. I did not argue and went back to the limousine and waited for the real estate agent. I handed her the down payment check.

It was a cold winter day, January 17, 1967, but I was aglow with an inner warmth. All felt right in my world. I liked my job. I was respected and supported by my boss, who also made a point of saying that he hoped Cecilia and I could join them on a cruise aboard *Sandoval* sometime soon, perhaps as a winter break. And I had the keys to the most amazing apartment I could imagine, something that would not have been possible without the generosity of Stephen.

I slept peacefully that night, but I was awakened by a call from our office's secretary the next morning at 5 a.m. She told me to turn on the television news. I caught the end of a report that said that Stephen and Audrey Currier were missing and that the plane they were flying in disappeared from radar about thirty minutes after they took off from the airport in a small private plane in San Juan, Puerto Rico, for the final leg to Saint Thomas. The pilot radioed for permission to fly over the island of Culebra, which was a high-security navy installation at the time, but the request was denied and they were told to fly around it. That was the final radio communication and the last time anyone heard from the plane and its occupants.

Their children—Andrea, Lavinia, and Michael—and other family members were waiting for the couple to arrive. They never did. The Taconic

Foundation hired private pilots and undertook an extensive search with multiple planes and search and rescue teams. Audrey's father, David Bruce, United States Ambassador to the United Kingdom, called in additional resources and the search was extremely thorough. No bodies or wreckage were ever recovered. The rumor mills went to work and there was wild speculation that the couple was kidnapped, that the pilot was involved and they were being held for ransom. None of these conspiracy theories had any grain of truth. They simply vanished and were never found.

On a personal level, I was devastated. I considered Stephen a mentor and a friend and I learned so much from him and had so much more to learn. Professionally, it was a catastrophic loss to the Taconic Foundation and the numerous projects their philanthropies supported, including my own. On a private matter, Stephen had urged me to purchase an above-my-means co-op on Riverside Drive and had given me the $10,000 down payment, but now I felt like I needed to contact the real estate agent, explain the situation, and ask to be let out of the deal. There was no way I could afford the remaining $30,000, even with an extended mortgage loan. It was a very unsettling time for all of Taconic's employees.

A week later, after the exhaustive search had been called off and plans for a memorial service were being made, the executor of their estate, Lloyd Garrison, contacted me and set up a meeting at the office. Lloyd explained that Stephen was always organized and planned ahead, and he had called Lloyd from the airport to go over loose ends before the cruise. In that call, he mentioned our co-op apartment purchase and that he intended to provide me with a zero-interest loan for the remaining $30,000 of the purchase price. Lloyd said that as the estate executor, he would honor that commitment. I was overwhelmed with gratitude. It had been a roller coaster of emotions but I finally had a sense of security and closure on the transaction.

Cecilia, Marci, and I moved into the Riverside Drive apartment and it made us all very happy. I also cherished a lovely gift Stephen had given me, a Patek Philippe watch. It was an extraordinarily kind Christmas present and one I treasure. It is a very expensive Swiss timepiece and I treat it with great care. It is still keeping perfect time after fifty-five years and I have sent it to Geneva, Switzerland, for maintenance a couple of times. I wear it on special occasions. It is engraved on the back: H.C.M. 12/25/65 from S.R.C.

None of us, including the staff or the Taconic Foundation itself, ever fully recovered from the shocking deaths of Stephen and Audrey Currier, the lack of closure with the mystery of their disappearance, or the heart-breaking fact that they left three young children behind.

We were left numb and rudderless at the office. There was still plenty of the couple's fortune left to keep running the Taconic Foundation and its projects, but a pall hung over the place. Remarkably, there was no talk of layoffs or disbanding the philanthropy, but I could not see myself staying there. I could not bear to work at Taconic for somebody other than Stephen. He was one of the most remarkable people I ever worked for during my career. He never made a show of his wealth. He went about his work with humility and grace. He managed to present himself as a regular guy, although that was not really possible. Still, he shared his resources and himself and he became a true friend. I was most impressed by his idealism and his focus on trying to address social and racial inequality. He was deeply concerned about suffering and urban problems that he observed and he committed his life and his wealth to fighting against those things, whether it was the brutality of segregation in the South or lack of job opportunities for Blacks in the Northeastern cities. His wife was his partner in philanthropy and she was an active board member of the Taconic Foundation. She came to board meetings and had valuable input. Shortly before she died, she made a presentation on a special project she was working on, to assist special needs children in Harlem, and she convinced the rest of the board to fund it. She was quiet and unassuming, but a force for good like her husband, deeply committed to helping underserved children.

I took some time to solidify the funding and organization of my projects and made sure I readied them for a smooth transition. I had nothing but good memories of my nearly four years at the Taconic Foundation and felt I had done some important work on behalf of racial justice, civil rights, job training, and equal opportunities for minorities. I said goodbye to the fine people at Taconic and got ready to face my next career challenge.

Chapter 10

Percy Sutton, Media, and Harlem

The shock of the deaths of Stephen and Audrey Currier lingered for me after I left the Taconic Foundation, which faced a crisis of leadership without its founders and Stephen's guiding spirit. I still had a job as chairman of the Council Against Poverty in New York's Human Resources Administration, but it was a nonpaying position. With a wife and daughter to support, I needed to find a new job opportunity with a salary. Mitchell Ginsberg, a former Columbia University professor of social welfare, whom I knew, offered me the position of deputy administrator of the Human Resources Administration. I took the job, but quickly realized it was not a good fit because it meant functioning as a bureaucrat with very little involvement or direct interaction with members of the community. Although I developed useful administrative expertise overseeing six agencies and nearly three thousand employees who reported to me, the work consisted mainly of managing the large staff and developing budget plans. The glacial movement of the bureaucracy was a sharp contrast to how quickly I could make things happen at the Taconic Foundation and I felt hamstrung by the plodding nature of the work. I stayed in the position for less than a year and decided to strike out on my own because I had a strong reputation as a community organizer with skills that were marketable and in demand.

I started my own consulting business and called it HCM & Associates. My first hire was Jackie Woods, an effective and energetic administrator whom I had worked with when I established Brooklyn Youth in Action. My first client was IBM, the computer manufacturer. They asked me to help run training sessions for their top executives in order to increase their awareness and insight about the needs and concerns of people living in urban and minority communities of New York. New groups of executives arrived every two weeks and HCM & Associates signed a contract in which I would lead three-hour sessions based on my experiences, with lessons and takeaways about what they needed to understand in order to work effectively in minority communities. I billed IBM six hours a month, which was my first income as a self-employed business entrepreneur. I was proud to see my name on the shingle and IBM was so pleased with my work that they agreed to serve as a reference so I could book more clients.

In 1969, I set up my office in a nice Manhattan building on Madison Avenue in the 30s. I may have become a self-employed business owner somewhat naively, without a clear strategy for recruiting and retaining clients. I was extremely fortunate that people started finding me and that lack of a business plan did not doom my enterprise. In fact, I did not accept every client that approached me, and I was fortunate that I could be selective and choose to work with the types of companies that appealed to me. I soon realized that I could not be effective trying to run the company alone and I brought in Bryant Rollins as a partner. I had known Bryant since our high school years in Roxbury. He was a successful journalist and one of the first African American reporters at the *Boston Globe*. He later founded the *Bay State Banner* for a Black readership. He had relocated from Boston to New York City and was doing consulting work and writing marketing materials for a wide range of companies. I had always been impressed with Bryant's skills and his work ethic and I asked him to join HCM & Associates. He accepted my offer and brought several clients with him. At the same time, I was able to add additional accounts and I felt personally satisfied as the owner of a small business. I was also continuing my volunteer activities and registering voters in disenfranchised minority communities throughout New York City.

As the 1970 gubernatorial campaign heated up, I joined an active group of Democratic reformers who were organizing a broad-base group to try to defeat incumbent Republican Governor Nelson A. Rockefeller, who was seeking a historic fourth term. I also became friendly with two of the leaders of the New Democratic Coalition, or NDC, Sarah and Victor Kovner. He was a prominent lawyer and First Amendment expert at a prestigious New York City law firm, and she was a tireless activist and fundraiser for progressive Democratic candidates. They had been instrumental in the Eugene McCarthy presidential campaign of 1968. I was impressed with the passion and commitment of the Kovners and their fellow activists. My main hesitation was that the NDC tended to be largely a white liberal organization with not much minority representation. Still, I got involved because I felt I could bring along more minority members and a perspective that was missing from their ranks. Of course, the NDC had its critics. Detractors and media commentators joked that NDC stood for November Doesn't Count because the organization often supported very liberal primary candidates with narrow appeal who were not electable in general statewide elections.

My involvement in voter registration and assisting the Kovners in their NDC work involved helping organize a series of statewide political forums for candidates seeking statewide office in 1970. At that time I received an unexpected call from Percy Sutton. This was my introduction to a Black political leader and Harlem power broker who would be important to my career in politics. Sutton was a lawyer and prominent activist in the civil rights movement who had been a Freedom Rider and a lawyer who represented Malcolm X. After one term in the state assembly, he was elected Manhattan borough president. He held that powerful post from 1966 to 1977, making him both the longest-tenured and highest-ranking African American elected official in New York City.

Although he was Texan by birth, he made his way at age twelve to New York City because an older sister and brother lived there. He ended up settling in Harlem and during World War II he served as an intelligence officer with the Tuskegee Airmen. He earned a law degree from Brooklyn Law School and was recruited into Harlem politics. He became an organizer of the so-called Harlem Clubhouse, which some also referred to as the "Gang of Four." After building a network and developing a reputation as someone who made things happen, Sutton pivoted from politics to the private sector and made shrewd investments as a businessman. In 1971, Sutton helped found the Inner City Broadcasting Corporation, which bought WLIB, the first African American–owned radio station in New York City. Sutton's entrepreneurship also led him to invest in both the Apollo Theater in Harlem and the *Amsterdam News*, a newspaper that covered New York's Black communities.

Sutton was also the most powerful member of the New York City Board of Estimate, a governing body that had broad review and oversight responsibilities in consultation with the mayor to assess land use proposals, development projects, and other major issues in the city. Sutton was a legend. I remember watching a documentary that featured Sutton's courageous efforts at leading Freedom Riders on buses along dangerous runs into the Deep South in a campaign to demand racial integration and an end to discrimination against Blacks. I felt inspired by him and was fortunate to run into him from time to time in New York, but I did not know him well. I never had a sense he was keeping an eye on me or considering me for a position. I was surprised, therefore, when Sutton called me with no apparent agenda. We had a pleasant talk and he finished our discussion with him urging me to participate in the NDC political forums as a potential candidate for the office of lieutenant governor. It was not something I had considered, but since Percy Sutton asked me to do so, that's what I did. It was a good learning experience.

Sutton was concerned because no Black candidates had come forward to participate in the statewide NDC political forums for any office.

Sutton had a way of inflating everybody's title and general worth and making you believe you were capable of great things. When he introduced me, he intoned that I was "a person of consequence" and it made me want to live up to that description. My work at the Council Against Poverty had received some media attention and later when I formed a group with friends called Black Independent Voters, I garnered some political recognition.

However, I had no money to mount a campaign and no experience related to the lieutenant governor's job. I felt I had nothing to lose and that exposure would be good for any future plans. After careful deliberation, I decided to participate in the political forums that became a clearinghouse to evaluate potential candidates. The forums were held in several cities around the state. I was the only Black participant. In some upstate cities they had never seen a Black candidate. I got a good reception at these events and made some good contacts. Soon, Arthur Goldberg emerged as the front-runner to challenge Rockefeller among the Democratic gubernatorial candidates. Goldberg was a prominent labor lawyer who was appointed US Secretary of Labor by President John F. Kennedy, and he later served as US Ambassador to the United Nations and was appointed to the US Supreme Court. In 1970, he accepted the formidable task of trying to unseat the three-term incumbent, Rockefeller.

Goldberg obviously had strong support from Jewish voters and he cemented his position as the candidate of choice among the Democrats, which ended the need for the political forums I had been attending. To balance the ticket, Senator Basil Paterson of Harlem was chosen as Goldberg's lieutenant governor running mate and that also concluded any slim chance that I had, in spite of Sutton's urging to run for that post. Many people upstate were not happy about the Jewish-Black Democratic ticket and were vocal about their discontent. I became active out on the campaign trail on behalf of our ticket. I got to know Paterson's campaign manager, Harold Ickes, whose father served as secretary of the interior under President Franklin D. Roosevelt and helped develop some of the programs in FDR's New Deal. It was one of the pleasures of working on that campaign that I developed a friendship with Ickes and we worked side by side on voter registration in Harlem. I developed great respect for him and we forged a lasting relationship.

Disappointment came quickly. Goldberg was a disaster as a candidate. I was not the only one who thought he was terrible, and that comes from a supporter of his campaign. He had never run for elected office before and his inexperience showed at every turn. He did not have a friendly personality or a good rapport with people, which is a major liability on the campaign trail. The bright spot was Basil Paterson, who was a terrific campaigner and became the star of the ticket, upstaging Goldberg whenever they shared a stage. It got to the point where campaign event organizers said to send Basil and leave Goldberg behind. Rockefeller rolled to an easy victory and the only winner, of sorts, on the Democratic side was Paterson, whose political star rose considerably. He was promoted to vice chairman of the National Democratic Committee on the strength of his campaign skills and his popularity with people.

The gubernatorial campaign was a bust and pulled me away from building my consulting business, but, in 1970, I did manage to land an important new client, the Florence and John Schumann Foundation. The couple married in 1917, settled in Montclair, New Jersey, and were major philanthropists throughout their forty-seven-year marriage. Florence Ford's father was one of the founders of the IBM Corporation and she inherited considerable wealth. Her husband was a successful investor and financier and the couple created their private philanthropic foundation in 1961. They donated to numerous charitable causes focused on health and education primarily in the area around their home in Montclair. The Schumanns made significant investments in minority communities in and around Newark, which experienced devastating riots after a police officer beat a Black man to death in the summer of 1967. They offered me the position of executive director of the Schumann Foundation, based on my experience at the Taconic Foundation, and as a community organizer. I was recommended for the job by David Freeman, who knew me from my work in Brooklyn when he worked for the Rockefeller Brothers Fund, which supported our programs in Bed-Stuy.

I weighed the offer, but decided I did not want to relocate to New Jersey, so I suggested a compromise. I would serve as a consultant, working part-time, which would allow me to maintain my life and work in New York City. They accepted my suggestion and it seemed like a win-win situation. I realized that I needed help to connect with Newark and Montclair, the communities we would serve. I was able to recruit two reliable consultants. Gus Heningburg had been an executive at the United Negro College Fund and president of the NAACP Legal Defense and Educational Fund. He later served as CEO of the Greater Newark Urban Coalition and he helped make connections and provided advice on groups to fund in Newark. In addition, I recruited Wally Choice, a tremendous basketball player who was a standout at Indiana University as one of the first Black players to compete in the Big Ten Conference. He played professionally and toured with the Harlem Globetrotters before returning to his hometown of Montclair to make his mark as a real estate developer and business owner. Together, we set up summer camp and enrichment programs for hundreds of underserved children in Montclair and those programs recently celebrated their fiftieth anniversary.

While Montclair was anchored by a solid white middle-class culture, it had a large working-class Black population while nearby Newark had deep-seated urban problems, including severe poverty and racial conflicts that occasionally boiled over into violence. I made the best of my split position and commuted from our apartment on Manhattan's Upper West Side to New Jersey two or three times a week. Luckily, I was driving mainly against the heavy traffic and could usually make it to my office in Montclair in about thirty-five minutes. During my time with the foundation, we supported youth programs, day care centers, educational and scholarship services, as well as arts and cultural programs.

I continued to build my client base in Manhattan and developed a stronger relationship with Percy Sutton. The more I worked with him, the more impressed I was in his ability to get things done. I also liked his plan to become a media owner of outlets that catered to the Black community. He first set his sights on the *Amsterdam News*, the city's largest Black newspaper, based in Harlem and owned by C. B. Powell. The son of Virginia slaves, Powell became a medical doctor who specialized in X-ray technology and who owned an X-ray laboratory in Harlem. Powell purchased the *Amsterdam News* for $5,000 in 1935. He nurtured Black journalists, who won acclaim for their reporting and he expanded the paper's coverage of national and international news while making solid investments in the news-gathering side of the operation.

Coincidentally, Powell was a lifelong Republican who became friendly with New York's GOP governor, Thomas Dewey, who appointed Powell the state's boxing commissioner. Often, Powell did political battle with Harlem's Democratic congressman, Adam Clayton Powell—with whom there was no family relationship. The *Amsterdam News* gained national renown and respect for its in-depth coverage of the civil rights movement in the South. Powell recruited Malcolm X to write a regular column for his paper, titled "God's Angry Man."

Meanwhile, by 1971, the *Amsterdam News* was struggling with declining readership and significant drops in circulation and advertising revenue. Like other Black-owned media properties that catered to a Black audience in that era, white media conglomerates were expanding their coverage to include Black communities around New York. They also were hiring more minority reporters and editors in an attempt to diversify their staffs—the upshot being that the *Amsterdam News* was facing more and more competition and it was therefore losing market share.

Percy Sutton had his finger on the pulse of these developments, even though he was not supported and was occasionally criticized for his political activities by Powell's editorial writers. Being the forward-thinking entrepreneur that he was, he asked me to join him in meetings with a few key Black business people and political leaders to discuss a purchase of the *Amsterdam News*. Sutton's exploratory group included attorney and real estate developer John L. Edmonds, known as "Big John," whom I knew from his appointment in the Lindsay administration as deputy commissioner of the city's Community Development Agency. The others included John L. Procope, a marketing and advertising executive; Wilbert "Bill" Tatum, also a Lindsay administration appointee who was director of community relations in the New York City Department of Buildings and deputy Manhattan borough president; and attorney Clarence Jones, the former personal counsel, adviser, and friend of Dr. Martin Luther King Jr. It was a powerful group of Black movers and shakers, all of whom shared a deep connection and commitment to Harlem, the larger Black community of New York, and the belief that the *Amsterdam News* provided a vital source of news and information for Black readers that desperately needed to continue.

I felt flattered that Sutton invited me to be part of this influential consortium. The meetings, discussions, and negotiations moved ahead quickly and an offer was agreed upon, it was accepted, and our group became the owners of the *Amsterdam News*. I did not have anything close to the financial means of the business executives Sutton had put together as investors, but I invested $10,000 in the venture, equivalent to about $130,000 in today's dollars adjusted for inflation. That was a substantial financial commitment for me. The five others contributed that amount or slightly more, and Sutton invested several times that sum. We were a coalition of six co-owners. All of us had skin in the game and that meant that we all were committed to working hard to ensure the success of this Harlem media institution under new ownership and with a new direction.

From Powell's perspective, running a paper was a grueling job and he had grown tired of the nonstop stress of the work. He was seventy-seven years old and in declining health when he sold the *Amsterdam News* for $2.3 million to us, a group of Black investors who called ourselves the Amnews Corporation. Six years later, having received a terminal disease diagnosis, Powell committed suicide at age eighty-three. He left half of his estate, or $2.5 million, to Howard University—the largest gift to a college or university from a Black donor at the time. He also left $50,000 to the NAACP Legal and Defense Educational Fund.

For us, the principals of Amnews Corporation, there was a steep learning curve to owning and running a newspaper, even a revered one like the *Amsterdam News*. Sutton was the largest investor of the group, but we still had to take out a substantial bank loan. In addition to our financial contribution, Sutton gave each of us a hands-on job. I was appointed chairman of the editorial board. That meant that I wrote an occasional column about issues to which we wanted to bring focus and attention. I enjoyed doing this and I also used my network of friends and contacts to solicit contributors to our opinion columns. I also met regularly with the editorial page editor and the editorial writers to oversee and discuss op-ed pieces, endorsements of political candidates, and guidelines for publishing letters to the editor. I brought in Bryant Rollins to serve as executive editor, overseeing all the reporters, editors, and photographers. Rollins, who was a partner in my consulting firm, was a prominent Black journalist who had been nominated for a Pulitzer Prize for his in-depth reporting at the *Boston Globe*. He also had worked as an editor at the *New York Times*. We were pleased to land someone of Rollins's caliber to lead the newsroom. It was part of our overall strategy to invest in improving the quality of our staff and our journalism.

In order to herald the new ownership and introduce the Amnews Corporation, we launched a marketing campaign with a new motto for the paper: "The New Black Voice." We created a new energy and brought a little swagger back to our Harlem office and received an overwhelmingly positive response and warm reception from the community. We also immediately launched a drive to sign up new subscribers and to grow our number of advertisers to solidify our financial base.

Sutton became chairman of the board. Jones was appointed publisher, but proved to be a colossal failure, and Procope replaced him as publisher. Tatum held a series of editor's positions and stayed with the newspaper the longest, acquiring control of the *Amsterdam News* in 1983 and becoming its sole owner in 1996. I had previously sold my investment in the corporation. Tatum spent a total of twenty-five years with the paper and was succeeded by his daughter, Elinor Tatum, who serves today as publisher and editor-in-chief. Despite a continuing decline in circulation, it remains the largest Black newspaper in New York City, it is a central force in the community life of Harlem, and is influential in the city's politics.

Meanwhile, Percy Sutton had visions of creating a new Black media enterprise. Since there was no Black-owned radio station in New York City, he set his sights on the No. 2–rated radio station serving a Black audience in the city, WLIB, which broadcast on both the AM and FM dials. It was owned by Harry Novik, a white retailer who, in 1949, recognized the need for a station with programming focused on a Black audience. He and his brother Morris purchased the station from Dorothy Schiff, the owner and publisher of the *New York Post*.

Morris Novik had some experience in radio because, in the 1930s and 1940s, he had served as director of WNYC, the city-owned radio station, during the administration of Mayor Fiorello H. La Guardia. After the Novik brothers took over ownership of WLIB, they replaced the station's stodgy offerings with rhythm-and-blues music and gospel songs, as well as religious shows. They moved the station from the Lower East Side to the Theresa Hotel in Harlem at 125th Street and 7th Avenue. This was the backdrop when Sutton began putting out feelers to the Novik family, who were under increasing pressure to sell to Black owners. The best deal Sutton could get was to purchase WLIB-AM and an option to purchase its sister FM station, renamed WBLS, at a later date.

In that era, with listening habits and technology changing quickly, WLIB could only broadcast during the daytime hours because the radio waves of the more powerful and increasingly popular FM stations filled the New York City airwaves at night, and their stronger signals crowded out the AM stations. Sutton's same group of six principals of Amnews Corporation were also involved with the radio station purchase, which was financed by Chemical Bank. The winds of political change blew in Sutton's favor, too, because commercial lenders and banks were under pressure to approve loans for Black businesses. Additionally, lawmakers had tried to level the playing field so long stacked against Blacks and minorities, by creating legislation that established the Minority Enterprise Small Business Investment Companies, or MESBIC, which was a kind of affirmative action for small firms owned by minorities.

During this time period, there were a considerable number of documented cases across New York City where Black business owners were turned down on loan applications from banks and MESBIC was put in place to address that issue. Sutton and we, his Amnews Corp. co-owners, were forced to go back to the president of Chemical Bank when MESBIC was not cooperating. Even though we were a Black-owned media business, MESBIC claimed they did not have expertise among their loan officers about how to assess financial risk for a radio station. Sutton asked who would evaluate us if we were a white group? Through Sutton's doggedness and refusal to give up, he got the bank president to refer our loan application to the communications lending department. Sutton demanded and we received approval from the bank. Sutton was still serving as Manhattan borough president and he was careful about his public business activities to avoid the appearance of a conflict of interest. In 1971, he formed a new company, the Inner City Broadcasting Corporation. Since I did not hold elected office, I became the president of the new entity. We once again were called upon to be investors and I put in another $10,000, which was the limit of my financial capacity at the time. In addition, I was assigned to find more investors and I worked my network to get friends and associates to invest money. This was hard work and took considerable time and effort on my part. We needed to raise an amount in the high six figures. We ended up with about thirty significant investors, including the jazz pianist Billy Taylor; the singer Roberta Flack; the legendary disc jockey Hal Jackson; the civil rights leader the Reverend Jesse Jackson;

Betty Shabazz, the widow of Malcolm X; and Dr. M. S. Woolfolk, head of Opportunities Workshop, a school that trains Black business leaders.

We closed the deal to acquire WLIB-AM for $1.7 million and transferred ownership from Harry Novik to Inner City Broadcasting, which was approved by the Federal Communications Commission on June 26, 1972, after an extensive review that lasted nearly a full year. The *New York Times* ran a news story under the headline, "Ownership of WLIB Is Passing into Blacks' Hands."

The *Times* story made note of the historic transaction, noting that our radio station was the first in the city owned by Blacks. That station, as the *Times* observed, "has served a mainly black audience for more than 20 years." The article focused on a 1970 Federal Communications Commission ruling that sought to discourage multiple media outlets owned by one company in the same market in order to break up potential monopolies. The article noted that Inner City Broadcasting consisted of mainly the same group of owners as the 1971 Amnews Corporation, which had purchased the *Amsterdam News*. Some of Sutton's political detractors in Harlem seized upon this issue to air criticism over the station's acquisition.

In the *New York Times* story, Livingston L. Wingate, former executive director of the Urban League, called it "a sad day for Harlem." He made the point that he favored Black ownership of the media that serves the people of Harlem but that he was "completely opposed to any situation in which the media merge with the political apparatus." Wingate added that he feared "the politicians will end up using the media to tell the people only what the politicians want them to know."

We pushed back against the criticism of Wingate and others by vowing to open up the radio station's facilities in Harlem to community members and to provide technical assistance to help residents develop community programming. We also were transparent in the second phase of our plan, which involved us exercising our option to purchase the Noviks' FM station, WBLS, which had previously been WLIB-FM. I was quoted in the *Times* article as president of Inner City Broadcasting and I underscored the historic nature of the acquisition.

"This is a significant move because of the importance of a station operating in the nation's No. 1 market and the capital of the communications industry," I told the *Times* reporter. "And it represents a further attempt by a black group to develop a nationwide communications network at a time when the black community is pressing for more control and influence in the communications industry."

As president, I served as the spokesman for our group, but I was not expected to be active in the management of the station, nor was I equipped to be, since I had no experience as a broadcaster or in running a media company.

We faced a serious incident because we decided to remove a popular disc jockey named Joe Bostic. He had built up a large and loyal following for his *Gospel Train* program on WLIB-AM, which ran from 9 a.m. to 1 p.m. daily, a showcase for gospel music. Although his program was very popular and had been a staple at the station for two decades, our market research told us that gospel music was in decline and the audience was steadily being diminished. Advertisers had complained that they didn't want to spend money on gospel programming that attracted fewer and fewer listeners, and many of the remaining listeners were seniors and not desirable for advertisers. We also faced complaints about Bostic from gospel music performers, who said that he exerted too much control of what records got air time. Some of his critics suggested Bostic gave preference to artists and records he had produced, which would be a conflict of interest and highly inappropriate. We weighed all this information and decided to pull Bostic's *Gospel Train* off the air and to terminate his contract.

Bostic pleaded with us that he had such longtime and loyal fans that he wanted to host one final show to thank them for their decades of listening. We were neophytes in the broadcasting business and we made a rookie mistake. We relented and said we would let Bostic back on the air to do one final *Gospel Train* tribute program. It was a nearly fatal mistake.

I was driving back to New York City from New Jersey the next day, tuned my car radio to WLIB-AM, and proceeded to listen to a tirade by Joseph Bostic aimed at the new owners of the station. He was angry and he used his show to complain that he had been unfairly fired and his beloved show cancelled at the hands of the terrible Inner City Broadcasting. He went on to whip up dissent among his listeners and he called on them to demonstrate in front of the radio station offices the following

Saturday. He said he wanted his audience to protest his firing and to pray for Percy Sutton and Reverend McCall so that they will understand the spiritual value of gospel music, repent their mistake, and put *Gospel Train* back on the air at WLIB-AM. Bostic went further. He printed leaflets and posted them around Harlem, urging people to boycott the station. He convinced a prominent Harlem jewelry store owner to pull its advertising. He whipped up a surge of anger.

Since this was 1972 and some recent demonstrations for civil rights and protests against the Vietnam War had gotten out of hand and become violent, we took no chances. We contacted the NYPD and asked cops to erect barriers and to prepare for a very large crowd and potentially aggressive actions by demonstrators. We braced for the onslaught. We were convinced that this could be a deadly blow before we even got started transforming and improving the station.

In the end, about a dozen people showed up, most of them elderly and certainly in no mood for a fight or to incite violence. We were relieved and also felt somewhat vindicated that our market research was correct: that gospel music was in decline, the audience was shrinking and aging out. In the end, we learned that Joseph Bostic did not command the size of audience or depth of loyalty that he imagined.

But we learned a critical lesson: We would never again allow a disc jockey or announcer to go back on the air after we had terminated that person.

I was a quick learner and felt that I managed to avoid potentially harmful situations and mistakes following the Bostic brouhaha. One saving grace was that the majority of investors in Inner City were not expecting to turn a profit or to grow their investment. Rather, they got on board because they felt it was extremely important to champion Black-owned media and to support that effort. I continued to raise money and in 1974 we purchased WBLS and reunited the WLIB stations. We positioned WBLS as the flagship station of the Mutual Black Network, known today as the American Urban Radio Network.

With control of both the AM and FM stations, we held a significant market share of Black listeners in the Northeast and part of my mission was to expand outside the New York City market. We set new marketing plans and launched fresh programming. We added a lot of rhythm-and-blues shows and played modern jazz artists, a nod to the influence of our co-owner Billy Taylor. Mainly, we were responding to the changing taste and demographics of our audience. We kept gospel music only on Sunday mornings, but we also focused on the listening preferences of the audience in each time slot. We targeted housewives during the day and young adults at night and jazz at various times. I was happy to develop a friendship with Billy Taylor, a prominent jazz pianist, educator, author, and ambassador for the distinctly American musical art form. Starting in the 1940s, Taylor had a standing gig as the house pianist at Birdland, the legendary Manhattan jazz club, and over the decades he shared the stage with jazz greats including Charlie Parker, Stan Getz, Miles Davis, and Dizzy Gillespie. Charlie Parker, the alto saxophone genius, was nicknamed Bird and that was the inspiration for the club's name. The original Birdland opened in 1949 on Broadway, a block west of the jazz club row on West 52nd Street. My interest in jazz also forged my ongoing friendship with George Wein.

I also made an important connection in this era with Edward J. Logue, whom everyone called Ed. He was a lawyer, public administrator, academic, and urban planner who was recruited from New Haven, Connecticut, to work with the Lindsay administration and then Rockefeller's administration in New York as head of the New York State Urban Development Corporation. He was an advocate of large-scale urban renewal projects and had a dynamic proposal for apartments and other mixed-use properties on Roosevelt Island in the East River. We connected on a flight to Martha's Vineyard, and we shared our backgrounds with each other and suggested that the two of us could set up a subsidiary of the Urban Development Corporation in Harlem in order to spur revitalization and investment in affordable housing and commercial establishments for local merchants. I was invited to early meetings and Logue ended up spearheading the effort to create the Harlem Urban Development Corporation, which exists to this day. The strength of this and other UDCs is that they use not-for-profit status to apply for federal and state grants and other funding sources. They choose projects that promote urban development and well-being with a particular focus on stimulating growth in minority communities.

Logue hired my firm to do consultant work to assist the Harlem Development Corporation's projects. He also asked me to get involved with a state office project in Harlem that Governor Nelson A. Rockefeller, a Republican with whom Logue had a good working relationship, planned to build in Harlem. Using the state's eminent domain authority, Rockefeller took over an entire block in a prime location that was in the heart of Harlem between 125th and 126th Streets, and between Lenox Avenue and 7th Avenue. The state planned to demolish a row of small stores and shops to construct a new state office building. Predictably, there were protests and demands to cease demolition, since Rockefeller and his team had not bothered to build a coalition or consensus for the plan. They were viewed as rich white outsiders, Republican power brokers who were coming to Harlem to uproot longstanding, Black-owned small businesses and to ruin the neighborhood with a monument to state bureaucracy.

One of the biggest obstacles was a popular community bookstore located in a building on Adam Clayton Powell Jr. Boulevard at 125th Street that was scheduled to be torn down. It was at the heart of Harlem Square, where street speakers for decades stood on stepladders to preach Black Nationalism. The store was owned by Lewis H. Michaux, an activist and proponent of Black Nationalism who died in 1976 at age ninety-two after running the Harlem landmark bookstore for forty-four years. Its official name was the National Memorial African Bookstore, but folks in Harlem called it Michaux's or Professor Michaux's. Michaux slept in the back of the bookstore. W. E. B. DuBois and Malcolm X were customers. Joe Louis, Eartha Kitt, Louis Armstrong, and Langston Hughes held book signings there. Michaux's sold books and pamphlets about African American history—it was a gathering place for the Black community, as well as a source of great community pride. There was an uproar about losing the bookstore and another beloved cultural institution, dubbed UCLA, University on the Corner of Lenox Avenue, which focused on workshops about black culture and African history. Demonstrators were very upset, and rightly so, about losing UCLA, as well, to a state office building.

My job was to try to counter the opposition and disarm their outrage over the state office project, but there was little I could do to change the minds of the Harlem community members. They felt like they didn't need a state office building, and they loved the local businesses that would be lost. I tried to explain that the state was taking great pains to relocate the businesses to other areas of Harlem—at state expense—but this did not assuage their anger. Through eminent domain, the state had the authority to move forward and it did. After the buildings were torn down and the site cleared in preparation for groundbreaking on the new state office building, the demonstrators took their protest to the next level by creating a tent city on the building site and occupying it. The tactic worked and construction was stalled because the police and politicians feared that trying to dismantle the tent city would fuel violence and retribution. It was a volatile situation and it was a long, hot summer in 1969 as the impasse between the protesters and the construction workers carried on week after week.

Logue was expecting me to make something happen, so I scheduled a meeting with state senator Basil Paterson, who represented that area of Harlem, and whom I had known for some time. I wanted to get Paterson's help and to formulate a strategy that could both mollify the protesters and clear the site so construction could begin. Paterson gave me a very practical suggestion. He told me to go across the street from his office and to meet L. Joseph Overton, who was known as Joe. He was a powerful labor leader and head of the United Council of Harlem Organizations, a labor organization including nearly seventy locals across Harlem, including ten Black Nationalist groups. He was the former president of the New York branch of the NAACP and built a base of power as the business agent for Local 338, Retail, Wholesale, Chain Store and Food Employees Union. Overton rose to prominence in 1959, when he organized a large and successful boycott of liquor stores in Harlem that won additional jobs for Black sales people and store workers. His union coalition represented a large number of employees in Harlem. He had a lot of clout because he represented both the poor and the powerful in Harlem. I was glad he agreed to meet with me that same day. I went to his office and we exchanged a few greetings and pleasantries. He led me into one room that was filled with printed signs expressing opposition to the state office building being built, then walked me into an adjoining room and there were an equal number of printed signs in favor of the state office building being built. I asked Overton which of the two signs he intended to use.

Overton informed me he was waiting for a phone call from the Reverend Wyatt Tee Walker, a key strategist in the civil rights movement in the Jim Crow South of the 1960s. He was a grandson of a former slave and grew up in Brockton, Massachusetts. He built a strong reputation as a talented young pastor and activist at Gillfield Baptist Church in Petersburg, Virginia, and was arrested numerous times for leading acts of civil disobedience. He was also an early board member of the Southern Christian Leadership Conference (SCLC) and in 1960 he moved to Atlanta at the invitation of the Reverend Dr. Martin Luther King Jr. to serve as the SCLC's first executive director. He was charismatic and erudite, and he delivered what were described as "dazzling sermons" and later was tapped as King's chief of staff.

When he first came to New York City in 1967, Walker also worked in publishing and he had a plan to create a new encyclopedia that would focus on Black history and culture that he would market and sell to Black churches across the country. But the project never fully materialized and Walker allied himself with Harlem's most powerful Black leader, minister, and congressman, the Reverend Adam Clayton Powell Jr. Walker served as an assistant who preached at Powell's Abyssinian Baptist Church because Powell was facing serious legal problems and was staying away from New York to avoid prosecution. Walker was extremely popular and a dynamic preacher who began to overshadow Powell. Powell was never one to share the limelight and the two had a falling out. Walker went to the smaller Canaan Baptist Church, where he served as pastor for thirty-seven years.

Governor Rockefeller put Walker on his staff as an urban affairs specialist in the 1960s and to serve as the governor's liaison to Black communities around New York. There was a "transaction" between Walker and Overton. All of his union leaders and rank-and-file members would support the construction of the state office building. Overton led all his union workers out onto the street, carrying signs in support of the state office building. This gave the appearance of a large number of Harlem residents in support of the project, which gave Rockefeller's team cover to clear out the demonstrators and to prepare the site for a construction groundbreaking.

It was an eye-opening experience for me and showed me up close how bare-knuckle politics transpired, and how things actually got done in Harlem and New York City. With the demonstrators and opposition cleared away, I was given a place at the table to plan how the state office building would be used. I was happy to play a small role and to raise the issue that it was our responsibility to make sure the building was designed so that it would be as helpful and useful as possible to the Black community of Harlem and not simply a monument to Rockefeller's outsized ego. I was happy that the state's Department of Social Services and Health would have significant staffing, programs, and services in the building, and I think my persistent reminders to make sure the facility served the local community had a positive outcome.

The building was named the Adam Clayton Powell Jr. State Office Building during a grand opening ceremony—it turned out to be an outstanding asset to Harlem and was widely praised. Local, county, and state politicians, including members of the state assembly and state senate had offices there, which ensured that community members could gain easy access to their elected leaders, which had a positive effect on all concerned.

I reflected on what I had witnessed in this case and it was abundantly clear to me that a back-room deal was struck and the impasse was cleared because three powerful men in a room—Rockefeller, Walker, and Overton—worked things out in a mutually beneficial way. It was an outcome that would come to be known as a win-win situation. I was starting to be invited into the inner circle of Harlem leaders and I owed a great deal to the support and mentorship of Percy E. Sutton. I felt good and comfortable about getting deeply connected to Harlem.

And then, although I was not anticipating it, Sutton wanted me to take the next step in my political apprenticeship. He strongly encouraged me to run in 1974 for the New York State Senate district that included parts of Harlem and the Upper West Side of Manhattan. I had remained a resident of the Upper West Side and that made me attractive as a candidate because that area of New York City was very active politically and always had a much higher voter turnout than Harlem. Anyone who could get support from the predominantly white Upper West Side activists would have an advantage in running for the senate seat in the 28th District. That district was home to a diverse group of constituents that included large numbers of Jewish and Black residents.

The 28th District had been a stepping-stone to higher office and greater public service to those who held the senate seat previously, including James Lopez Watson, who was elected to the New York City Civil Court and later was appointed by President Lyndon B. Johnson as chief judge of the United States Customs Court. Watson's seat was left vacant and filled in 1964 by Constance Baker Motley, a civil rights activist and lawyer who became the first African American woman elected to the state senate. She later was the first Black woman appointed to the federal judiciary and she served as a United States District Judge in the Southern District of New York. In 1954, she had gained early fame as a young assistant attorney to Thurgood Marshall as he argued the landmark case regarding racial segregation in public schools in *Brown v. Board of Education*. In the late 1960s, the same senate seat was held by Basil Paterson, who later ran unsuccessfully as the first Black major-party candidate for lieutenant governor, and later was appointed the state's first Black secretary of state under Governor Hugh Carey. I was honored to be considered worthy to join such august company and, after much deliberation, decided to take Percy Sutton's advice and to jump into the senate race. It would be my first time running for elected office and I had much to learn.

H. Carl McCall's mother, Caroleasa, in her graduation photo from high school in Boston in 1928. Author's photo collection.

H. Carl McCall, No. 24, front row, played on the Dartmouth basketball team as a freshman in 1954. An all-conference standout player in high school, a nagging football injury cut short his basketball career at Dartmouth after one year. Author's photo collection.

H. Carl McCall as a lieutenant in the US Army in 1959. Author's photo collection.

H. Carl McCall campaigns with Muhammad Ali for the New York State Senate in this undated photo from the 1970s. Author's photo collection.

H. Carl McCall in 1975 with his Harlem political mentors, from left, Basil Paterson, Percy Sutton, and David Dinkins. Author's photo collection.

H. Carl McCall campaigns for the New York State Senate seat representing Harlem and part of the Upper West Side in 1977 with Manfred Ohrenstein, a Democrat from Manhattan. Author's photo collection.

New York State Senator H. Carl McCall meets President Jimmy Carter in 1978 with US Representative Charles Rangel, a Democrat who represented Harlem. Author's photo collection.

H. Carl McCall shares a private moment with singer Harry Belafonte in an undated photo. Author's photo collection.

H. Carl McCall campaigns with actor Alec Baldwin, right, during the race in 1982 for lieutenant governor as the running mate of gubernatorial candidate Mario M. Cuomo. Author's photo collection.

H. Carl McCall campaigns for lieutenant governor as Mario M. Cuomo's running mate in 1982. Author's photo collection.

H. Carl McCall with Mario M. Cuomo in 1982, when McCall ran for lieutenant governor as the running mate with Cuomo in his bid for governor. Cuomo won and McCall lost. Author's photo collection.

H. Carl McCall, a vice president at Citicorp at the time and a former state senator, speaks with New York City Mayor Ed Koch in 1985. Author's photo collection.

H. Carl McCall speaks at an event in 1986 as a commissioner of the Board of the Port Authority of New York and New Jersey. He was the first Black person to hold that post, appointed by Governor Mario M. Cuomo. Author's photo collection.

H. Carl McCall and his wife, Joyce Brown, center, meet with Nelson Mandela and Mandela's wife, Winnie, in South Africa in 1991, a year after Mandela's release from a long imprisonment. Author's photo collection.

H. Carl McCall and his wife, Joyce Brown, with President Bill Clinton and US Senator Daniel Patrick Moynihan in Washington, DC, in an undated photo. Author's photo collection.

H. Carl McCall campaigns for governor in 2001 with NBA Hall of Fame
basketball legend Magic Johnson, McCall's daughter Marci, and filmmaker
Spike Lee. Author's photo collection.

Prominent Support – Jamie Foxx, Chris Rock, P. Diddy, Chris Tucker

At a Hollywood fundraiser for his gubernatorial campaign, H. Carl McCall is joined by Jamie Foxx, Chris Rock, P. Diddy, and Chris Tucker. Author's photo collection.

H. Carl McCall speaks at a press conference with former president Bill Clinton in 2002 in Harlem during McCall's campaign for governor. Author's photo collection.

H. Carl McCall shares a laugh with President Bill Clinton in 2001 during a gubernatorial campaign event at the New York State Fair in Syracuse after Clinton endorsed McCall over Andrew Cuomo. Author's photo collection.

H. Carl McCall meets with Hasidic Jewish leaders in Brooklyn during his run for governor in 2001. Author's photo collection.

H. Carl McCall and his wife, Joyce Brown, and their dog, Bebe, at their weekend home in Dutchess County. Author's photo collection.

H. Carl McCall, chairman of the State University of New York Board of Trustees, presides over a SUNY commencement ceremony in 2015. Author's photo collection.

H. Carl McCall travels to Haiti with a contingent of SUNY officials and board trustees on a humanitarian mission after Hurricane Maria in 2017. Author's photo collection.

SUNY board chairman H. Carl McCall poses with a group of trustees in this undated photo. Author's photo collection.

SUNY board chairman H. Carl McCall presides over a convocation at the University at Albany with UAlbany president Havidán Rodríguez. Author's photo collection.

H. Carl McCall poses for a photograph with former SUNY chancellor Nancy Zimpher at McCall's retirement party on June 25, 2019, at FIT in New York City. Photo by Paul Grondahl.

H. Carl McCall poses with author Paul Grondahl at McCall's retirement party on June 25, 2019, at FIT. Photo by Paul Grondahl.

H. Carl McCall holds up a largemouth bass he caught in his pond at his Dutchess County weekend home. Author's photo collection.

H. Carl McCall relaxes on the dock after fishing at his weekend home in Dutchess County. Photo by Paul Grondahl.

H. Carl McCall greets a well-wisher at the Executive Mansion on February 14, 2020, after Governor Andrew Cuomo announced the SUNY headquarters building would be renamed for McCall. Photo by Paul Grondahl.

H. Carl McCall poses in front of the tower of the H. Carl McCall SUNY Building after the building's formal dedication in Albany on November 9, 2021. Photo by Paul Grondahl.

H. Carl McCall speaks at the formal McCall Building dedication ceremony in Albany on November 9, 2021. Photo by Paul Grondahl.

H. Carl McCall with his daughter, Marci McCall, left, and his wife, Joyce Brown, at the McCall Building dedication ceremony in Albany on November 9, 2021. Photo by Paul Grondahl.

Chapter 11

Senate Campaign

Even though I was a resident of the Upper West Side based on my home address, I had gained name recognition and credibility in Harlem through my involvement in the Black ownership of the *Amsterdam News* and WLIB-AM and WLBS on the FM dial. All were based in Harlem and had a wide audience among Black readers and listeners. Also, I had been deeply involved in voter registration campaigns in Harlem and residents knew me as someone who had pounded the pavement and went door to door in order to increase Black participation in the democratic process. I had always heeded the advice of Percy Sutton, who told me early on that I would have to wait my turn and be patient if I expected to be elected to public office. He offered me stories from his own experience, which included running unsuccessfully numerous times for a Harlem seat in the state assembly against Lloyd Everett Dickens, a self-made millionaire developer and a veteran Democratic Party district leader who defied the iron grip of Tammany Hall as an ally of Congressman Adam Clayton Powell Jr. Dickens went on to serve in Albany from 1959 to 1964, where he pushed to address racial inequalities and to encourage hiring of minorities. In Sutton's telling, he ran and lost eleven times against Dickens before he finally wrested the assembly seat away, although that number certainly was an exaggeration.

But his lesson was clear. I listened very closely to my mentor and finally replied: "I'm willing to be patient, Percy, but not that patient."

I was entering the state senate campaign in 1974 at a time of transition for Harlem. Harlem had been the arts and cultural capital of Black America, personified by the Black Renaissance in the 1920s. The notable Black writers who lived there included Zora Neale Hurston and Langston Hughes. It was the epicenter for jazz artists including Louis Armstrong, famous jazz clubs like the Cotton Club, and iconic Black performers such as Paul Robeson and Josephine Baker. This underscored Harlem as a Black cultural mecca of the early twentieth century. Its cultural ascendancy ran from the late 1910s through the mid-1930s, an era that is widely considered a golden age of African American culture, with extraordinary contributions in literature, music, and both the visual and the performing arts.

The Harlem Renaissance was fueled by the Great Black Migration in the first two decades of the twentieth century, when Blacks from the segregated rural South numbering an estimated six million began a great northward migration and relocated to the industrial North in search of economic opportunity and with the hope of escaping racism and oppression.

By 1974, when I ran for the senate, the northern area of the borough of Manhattan known as Harlem—from the East River to the Hudson River and from East 96th Street and West 106th Street to West 155th Street—was plagued by demolition in the wake of urban renewal, arson, and abandonment that began in the 1960s. The Black population of central Harlem declined by more than 30 percent in the 1970s. The demographic shift accelerated such that in 2008, Blacks comprised only 40 percent of Harlem's population after a century of being the dominant racial group.

Location and affordability brought a resurgence after 2000, when central Harlem's population had grown from 109,000 to 126,000 according to a January 5, 2010, article by Sam Roberts in the *New York Times* that analyzed new census data. Today, the number of Blacks residing in Harlem is smaller than at any time since the 1920s and the peak of the Harlem Renaissance.

There were two political giants who had the power to move the needle and make change happen in Harlem and first and foremost was Adam Clayton Powell Jr. He was well educated, eloquent, and flamboyant, and he had a bully pulpit as a minister with the force of his important congregation at Abyssinian Baptist Church behind him. His election to the US Congress and his solidifying power in Washington meant that Harlem received a respectable share of federal funding and grants. While I had met him, I did not know Powell well personally, but I had heard him preach and attended a couple of meetings he presided over, and he was a galvanic force. But on the personal side, he drew criticism in Washington and Harlem for a string of ex-wives and glamorous girlfriends, luxury travel and an affluent lifestyle. One speech I heard him deliver contained this passionate defense of his lavish ways that stuck with me. I don't have the quote exactly and cannot find documentation of it, but this is what I remember: "I don't identify with the conditions of my constituents but with their aspirations."

Powell, who died in 1972, would preach at Abyssinian Baptist, Harlem's largest Black church, and after services he would walk across to the Red Rooster, which today is an upscale Harlem restaurant. In decades past, it had been a speakeasy where Powell, Nat King Cole, James Baldwin, and jazz greats liked to mingle. Although Powell had died two years before I ran for the senate seat, his legacy and reputation continued to cast a long shadow over Harlem.

Another giant in the district where I was running was J. Raymond Jones, who emigrated from St. Thomas in the West Indies and started organizing and registering Black voters in Harlem in 1961. Jones was a mentor to many young politicians, myself included. Unlike Powell, he was an insider who worked from within the political establishment. He recruited and promoted talented young Black staffers, several of whom rose to the level of New York Democratic leaders and federal judgeships. He became known as "The Fox" for his sly political acumen and he was the leader of Harlem's Carver Democratic Club, which was nicknamed the Harlem Clubhouse. Jones was credited with advancing the political careers of Sutton, Motley, Charlie Rangel, David Dinkins, and others.

There is an important element of backstory to my 1974 senate campaign, a seismic shift that occurred in Harlem in 1970. It was part of an epic showdown between the newcomer Rangel versus his mentor, the all-powerful Powell. I unwittingly found myself at the center of the titanic power clash of the Old Guard and a new generation of political leader, when Rangel invited me to breakfast at his house in Harlem as the battle royale was about to begin.

Charles B. Rangel was born in Harlem on June 11, 1930, to a Puerto Rican father and African American mother. He always had a side hustle, working in a drugstore at age eight, selling shoes, but he also got into minor trouble, skipped classes, and dropped out of DeWitt Clinton High School at sixteen. He enlisted in the army, served with distinction in an all-Black field artillery battalion, was wounded by combat, and was awarded a Purple Heart, Bronze Star, and other medals for his valor. He was honorably discharged as a staff sergeant in 1952 and the *Amsterdam News* heralded him as a hero.

Rangel made up for lost time, completing his high school degree and earning a bachelor of science degree from New York University in 1957 with assistance from the GI Bill. He completed his juris doctor degree at St. John's University Law School, passed the bar, and began practicing law in 1960. He served as a prosecutor in New York, joined the civil rights movement, and marched with Dr. Martin Luther King Jr. from Selma to Montgomery in Alabama in 1965.

From his base in Harlem, and talented as a dynamic young lawyer, civil rights activist, and a shrewd mind with a bent for politics, Rangel got drawn into the orbit of Albany. He served as an aide to New York State Assembly Speaker Anthony J. Travia in 1965 and, a year later, Rangel was selected by Harlem Democrats to run in the 72nd District. It was a done deal. Rangel was elected to the assembly and slid into the seat that had been occupied by Percy Sutton after Sutton was elected borough president of Manhattan to fill the vacancy left by Constance Baker Motley's appointment to the federal bench. It was a game of Harlem musical chairs and it ran through Albany. Timing is everything in politics, it has been said, and nobody's sense of timing was more finely attuned than Rangel's.

For four years, Rangel played the good soldier in Albany to the powerful Harlem political machine, from which the all-mighty Powell pulled all the levers from Washington. Rangel reached across the aisle and worked well with Republican governor Nelson A. Rockefeller. He carried a lot of water for Powell. Rangel was also astute in reading the political tea leaves. Starting in 1968, Powell got jammed up with congressional ethics investigations, critical media coverage of his lavish and lengthy travels to the Bahamas, and other indiscretions. Rangel was attuned to the declining support for the once-invincible Powell and began to seize his opportunity.

This is how I found myself at a small, private breakfast at Rangel's house in Harlem in the spring of 1970. I was joined by Sutton, state senator Basil Paterson, and a twenty-seven-year-old lawyer and political newbie, H. Patrick Swygert—whom Rangel introduced as Pat. As an aside, much later in his career, Swygert served first as president of the University at Albany and then as president of Howard University—his alma mater.

Rangel announced right at the start of the breakfast that he was going to mount a primary challenge for Powell's congressional seat that September. All of us—including me—sat in stunned silence. Rangel was a decorated Korean War veteran and fearless, but we did not have enough firepower to go into battle against Powell. Rangel turned the floor over to Swygert, who seemed very young and very green. Swygert started laying out the research he had been conducting, which underscored the changing demographics in Harlem and the deepening vulnerability for Powell.

Rangel, Swygert, and his team of advisers sensed that Powell was vulnerable to being beaten by the upstart Rangel. Powell was being characterized as the absentee congressman. He had not been seen in Washington or Harlem in quite some time, he was enmeshed in legal battles, refused to show up for court hearings, and was photographed on Bimini Island in the Bahamas fishing and partying. Despite Swygert's relatively nascent political research and a small team of supporters, including myself, Rangel launched his campaign to knock out the once-invincible Powell from his powerful congressional seat where he had held sway for twenty-six years, beginning in 1945.

I took on voter registration and got very active in Rangel's campaign. He still had the drive and charisma of a platoon leader. We were ready to follow him into battle. My other role was to undertake outreach to prominent Black churches in Harlem, where Powell had been neglectful with his stewardship. Our message was that it was time for a change, and we preached that Powell's time had passed and that Charlie Rangel would bring a fresh voice, fresh ideas, and a youthful energy to Washington. We were a lean and mean campaign force and our message was gaining traction throughout Harlem, assisted by Powell's no-show attitude and being AWOL from his district for so long. I was encouraged day after day by young people across Harlem who took time to listen to me, who said they supported change and would vote for the newcomer Rangel.

In September, the Democratic primary for New York's 18th Congressional District was upon us. We felt a satisfied exhaustion because we knew we campaigned hard and did everything within our power to convince voters it was time for a change. The outcome was in the hands of the residents of Harlem now. There were roughly 25,000 votes cast in the primary and Rangel defeated Powell by roughly 150 votes. It was a historic victory, an unexpected upset. We were elated. Rangel and his small, energetic, and committed campaign team had pulled off the impossible. It turned out that Swygert's research was spot-on and the voters of the Upper West Side, largely Jewish and white progressives, had voted overwhelmingly for Rangel, put him over the top, and were perhaps the most important single factor in Rangel's upset.

We hardly had time to celebrate our improbable victory. Rangel packed up for Washington and brought Swygert with him as one of his key aides. I stayed put in Manhattan and returned to my consulting work and media ownership responsibilities. I needed a break from campaigning and politics. I made sure I never expressed interest in the Harlem senate seat that came open in 1970. I sat it out on the sidelines as three candidates—Sidney von Luther, Rangel's former assistant Virginia Bell, and East Harlem labor organizer Tony Mendez—battled and competed and split the vote. The well-connected von Luther from the Upper West Side won the seat.

Fast-forward to 1974. Four years later, the senate district lines had been redrawn, reconfigured as the 28th Senate District, and I now lived in the district with my Upper West Side address. Percy Sutton and a high-level group of Harlem leaders met with me to express their strong desire to defeat von Luther and take back the senate seat. They talked about the legacy of that seat and the rich legacy of those who had held it, including James Watson, Constance Baker Motley, and Basil Paterson—all of whom had risen to higher office, federal judgeships, and other positions of distinction.

I felt humbled and more than a little intimidated to be considered even in a slight way to be worthy of a discussion among that Harlem political pantheon. The leaders told me in direct terms that they wanted a candidate who would restore prominence and dignity to the seat, which his critics suggested had been lost sight of during von Luther's fraught tenure.

It felt like I was in a strong current in the East River and I went with the flow set forth by these wise, experienced political leaders. I was no kid, but at thirty-nine years old I was a political neophyte who had never held elective office. That did not seem to matter to those supporting my candidacy. My most valuable asset was the fact that I lived on the Upper West Side and had developed a presence, a strong network, deep respect, and a certain name recognition there among the white and Jewish voters, which von Luther did not possess.

I had also developed a certain political astuteness over the years and I made a point to be very public about joining Sutton's Martin Luther King Jr. Democratic Club, which was another point in my favor. One of the most unexpected and strangest twists in my candidacy was a near-reconnection to my long-absent father, who had lived in Harlem and whom I had not seen or communicated with since his visit to my office years earlier. As it turned out, my father's former partner, a kind woman named Mae, was an active member of the MLK Club, and she greeted me there on several occasions and was one of my most energetic boosters. Early on, Mae got involved in my campaign and proudly introduced herself at public events as "my almost-stepson." It was touching and despite my lingering bitterness about my father, I was grateful that she had reached out and made sure this connection was not awkward. Mae filled in a few details and let me know that my father was still alive, but I never crossed paths with him again.

My opponent von Luther did not maintain a district office for his constituents and had very little engagement with the people who elected him. In Albany, other legislators viewed him as a buffoon. He was ridiculed for an episode during a contentious debate on the senate floor in which he challenged a Republican senator to a duel for opposing him. Yet, I was pragmatic about my chances in the race and took nothing for granted. I understood completely that an incumbent had a huge advantage and it would be an uphill battle for a little-known newcomer to defeat a two-term incumbent senator. Still, Team McCall was fully on board and all in. We kicked off an aggressive campaign with a lot of passion, high energy, and not much money. I was greatly encouraged when people came forward to join my campaign. I was helped immeasurably by the political savvy and experience of a campaign manager, Ludwig Gelobter, who was immersed in the Upper West Side community and its politics. Shirley Wasserman also came forward to volunteer her help for my campaign. She was well known and active among educational organizations on the Upper West Side and she was a former staff member to Congressman Bill Ryan (William Fitts Ryan), a lawyer and anti–Vietnam War activist who served in the US House of Representatives from 1961 until 1972.

Percy Sutton was also in my corner and instrumental in my campaign. He introduced me to a group of young people in Harlem who created an influential organization called Blackfrica Promotions, which did its work at the nexus of art and politics. The leader of Blackfrica Promotions, formed in 1968, was a dynamic, passionate young man named Lloyd Williams. Blackfrica and Williams went on to create Harlem Day in 1974 and it soon expanded to Harlem Week. It was eventually sponsored by the Greater Harlem Chamber of Commerce, which Williams leads as president and CEO. Harlem Week has expanded into a month-long celebration featuring arts and cultural entertainment events, educational workshops, special activities for senior citizens, technology programs for all ages, and sessions devoted to entrepreneurialism and economic development.

Lloyd Williams was a creator and catalyst behind Blackfrica Promotions, which celebrated its fiftieth anniversary in August of 2018 with a highly successful Harlem Week. Lloyd had a lot of energy, creative ideas, and passion when, at the urging of Percy Sutton, he approached me at the start of my 1974 senate campaign, Lloyd became the leader of my campaign team in Harlem and he has been a close friend, committed colleague, and strong supporter ever since, throughout all the various stages and positions of my career.

Early on, my campaign team and I zeroed in on the Upper West Side as my focal point and the key to my chances to defeat von Luther because he was Black and had name recognition in Harlem. Our strategy was that even if we split the vote in Harlem I could come out on top by gaining a large edge on the Upper West Side, where I lived and had a presence that he lacked. I was also fortunate to pick up the endorsements of New York State Assemblyman Al Blumenthal from the Upper West Side and City Councilman Ted Weiss. It showed that even as a political newcomer, my message and my campaign was gaining traction, getting noticed, and winning supporters.

I also gained support and signed up volunteers among the young professionals who were very active in an Upper West Side organization of political activists that called itself the Community Free Democrats. One of the most active and energetic leaders of the organization was an activist named Jerry Nadler, who was in his late twenties. Nadler would go on to become a prominent politician, having served fifteen years in the state assembly. Nadler was elected to Congress, where he is a powerful fifteen-term member representing New York's 10th Congressional District and chairman of the powerful House Judiciary Committee, which conducted the House's historic two impeachments of President Donald J. Trump.

Even back in 1974, it was obvious that Nadler had ambition, strong leadership qualities, and a fearlessness that boomed forth from his energetic, nasal Brooklyn tone that could cut through the din of a noisy, crowded room and command everyone's attention. Another young, active member of the Community Free Democrats who joined my campaign was Scott M. Stringer, a friend and colleague of Nadler's who represented the Upper West Side as New York State Assemblyman for thirteen years, beginning in 1992. In 2006, Stringer became Manhattan borough president and was elected New York City comptroller in 2013. Another one of the young, up-and-coming political activists among the Community Free Democrats was Eric Schneiderman, who served for ten years in the New York State Senate and also served as Attorney General of New York from 2011 until his resignation in May 2018 due to allegations by multiple women of sexual misconduct and physical abuse.

I benefited from the youthful energy and creative ideas of this next generation of Democratic leaders and activists. At the time of my 1974 senate campaign, Schneiderman was just twenty years old, Stringer was still a teenager, and Nadler was twenty-seven.

My team and I came up with a couple of campaign slogans that seemed to resonate and connect with voters as we canvassed the Upper

West Side and Harlem: "Time for a Change" and "Time for New Leadership." We were getting strong and steady support, but it was an uphill battle because von Luther had a significant bloc of loyalists on the Upper West Side, and he still had some backers in Harlem, although our campaign locked up the endorsements of nearly all the prominent Democratic leaders in Harlem. I never felt complacent about anything throughout the race against Von Luther.

I also had a disadvantage when it came to fundraising since von Luther had the benefit of an incumbent's strong campaign account. We started with nothing and our goal was to raise about $20,000 to mount a vigorous and competitive primary campaign. It was slow going. But I did have the pleasant experience, somewhat frequently, of strangers pressing checks into my hand as I went door to door campaigning. The first few times I hesitated and felt a little odd, but that discomfort was short-lived. They were making a very public investment in what I stood for and what I promised to change. That was energizing.

At some point, Percy Sutton joined me at campaign events, so I thought I would put the question to Percy. Rather naively, I suppose, I asked him, What do they want me to do for that money they are handing me? I will never forget Percy's response. He told me they were making an investment in their community's future and that my end of the bargain was to provide them with good government and to be attentive to the needs of constituents. I told him I hoped that was true and that I would do my best to live up to my side of the agreement.

My first major fundraiser was an exciting program that had wide appeal. It took place on the Upper West Side and the draw was activist and stand-up comedian Dick Gregory, who performed a very funny and sharply directed set of jokes and social commentary. He was recruited for the party by Jim McGraw, who served as Gregory's editor or coauthor on several book collaborations. Following Gregory's wildly popular comedy set, attendees loosened up their checkbooks and we ended up raising a considerable amount—several thousand dollars as I recall.

I was also careful about maintaining a church and state division when it came to my private business dealings and running for public office. I gave up nearly all my consulting work in order to avoid the appearance of a conflict of interest. The one client I kept working for was the Schumann Fund for New Jersey, with whom I maintained a long professional relationship. Since they were located outside New York State, I determined that there was no conflict in keeping them as a client.

My opponent was certainly nowhere near as active on the campaign trail as I was and he adopted what I can only characterize as a strange strategy. He had his surrogate Stanley Pinsky serve as muckraker and purveyor of dirty politics on his behalf. Pinsky sent out press releases to New York City media alleging I embezzled money in the Brooklyn poverty program I had run, a ridiculous lie that reporters declined to pick up on because he offered no evidence for his preposterous slander. I did my best to take the high road and to ignore his desperate mud-slinging, although occasionally the *New York Post* saw some value in running a sensationalistic political tabloid story. To their credit, they gave me the opportunity to respond; I rebutted the absurd allegations point by point and also suggested I would take legal action against the von Luther campaign if these unfounded lies persisted. Eventually, the candidate's attack dog Pinsky ceased this tactic and moved on to other sketchy moves. I stood my ground, focused on our message of change, and never let their nonsense get to me.

There was one heated incident well into the primary campaign that did get a lot of press attention. In those days, one of the central methods of campaigning was to blanket major thoroughfares and busy pedestrian areas with campaign posters taped to subway station entrances, utility poles, light standards, stop signs, tree trunks, or whatever was in a passing motorist's or passerby's sight line. Our method was to send volunteers out late at night so that commuters and subway riders would see the posters on their morning travels to work.

We had a very committed group of young volunteers who grabbed thick stacks of my campaign posters and fanned out each night to different sections of the senate district along the Upper West Side and Harlem. They taped dozens, maybe hundreds, of my campaign posters in highly trafficked areas night after night. One night, about a week before the September election, I decided to join them on their nightly rounds and met up with about a dozen volunteers, mostly young people. We worked methodically along both sides of Broadway heading uptown on the Upper West Side of Manhattan for a mile or more and, after a couple of hours of work, we cut over one block and started working both sides of Amsterdam Avenue, heading back downtown to where we had begun. When we had nearly finished, we crossed back over to Broadway, and around 96th Street and ran into von Luther, the elusive incumbent senator himself, and several of his campaign supporters. We witnessed them tearing down my campaign posters that we had just put up. This did not sit well with me or our band of young volunteers. His attack dog Pinsky was with him, a man who had been slandering me and making me very angry with his dirty tricks.

Let the record show that Pinsky became the aggressor and tried to attack one of our volunteers, who had done no more than raise his voice and push and jostle with Pinsky's crew. My version, which our volunteers attested to, was that Pinsky, in trying to take a swing at one of my campaign volunteers, slipped and fell and ended up with a bloody nose. This was fifty-six years ago, after all, but my memory of that night's unexpected and unusual confrontation remains vivid to this day.

The standoff and heated argument—there was some pushing and shoving, but never any actual punches thrown based on my recollection—over the von Luther campaign's tearing down our campaign posters and destroying our property reached its denouement when an NYPD squad car pulled up and got out to investigate. This is the scene they encountered: A group of Black men (my young volunteers that night all were Black) were standing over a small white guy, Pinsky, who was bleeding from his nose. Von Luther's crew was mostly white and the police immediately went to them and heard their group's version of the incident while they ignored us. This was only a handful of years after the peak of the civil rights movement. There was widespread police brutality deployed by cops several decades before the current #BlackLivesMatter movement. This was 1974 and Black men were wary and extremely careful in encounters with white police officers. Some things have not changed.

The upshot of the campaign poster dustup was this: Von Luther, Pinsky, and their crew of white aggressors were free to go. I and my young Black campaign volunteers were handcuffed, arrested, and taken to the nearest police precinct. By the time we had been booked and placed in a holding cell, it was about 4 a.m. and I was allowed one call to a lawyer. I called David Dinkins, a friend and an attorney who was in private practice and a fellow investor in Percy Sutton's Inner City Broadcasting Corporation. David came down to the precinct and within an hour or so, he had all of us bailed out and released on our own recognizance.

There was more to the story. The next day, the *New York Times* assigned a reporter to the story and wrote it as a straightforward, brief, and rather routine news story that mentioned that Pinsky complained of a bloody nose and that we had been arrested, booked, and released on our own recognizance. The very same day that the brief news story ran, the *Times* endorsed me on its editorial pages over von Luther in the senate race. It truly was a strange turn of events.

The election itself, after all that had transpired, seemed almost anticlimactic. We were the mavericks and von Luther possessed the power of incumbency, but it was not as close as we all, including myself, had anticipated. We won big in virtually every part of the district, across the Upper West Side and throughout Harlem. It was a sprawling district and it felt like I had walked every block of it during the campaign. I was exhausted. I kept wearing out the soles of my dress shoes. The senate district where I would be serving, the 28th District, stretched from about West 75th Street all the way along the Hudson River and the Upper West Side of Manhattan, north to about 155th Street, and east across Harlem from Central Park West and the West Side Highway, across the Columbia University campus and surrounding neighborhood, as well as Morningside Heights. Throughout the campaign and now as their senator-elect, I had a diverse constituency to represent: Black and Hispanic residents of East Harlem (where I was following in the footsteps of Charlie Rangel) and the white, largely Jewish and very liberal Upper West Side residents, represented in the US House of Representatives by activist and women's movement leader Bella Abzug. "Battling Bella," as she became known, built her political career on the Upper West Side. She beat fourteen-year incumbent congressman Leonard Farbstein in a surprising upset in the Democratic primary of 1970 and she was reelected by a wide margin in 1974.

In assessing my victory, I made note of the fact in my speeches that the Black churches of Harlem were key to my success and I thanked the church members. An important aspect of my campaign was the fact that I was an ordained minister and, on a typical Sunday, I would visit four or five churches across Harlem and shake hands and greet people and explain what I was trying to do in bringing change to Albany. A very active group of Harlem ministers supported me and helped bring out a large voter turnout. Although it took me outside my comfort zone, over time I came to like campaigning and was convinced that I improved as I went along. I had preached to large church congregations and held a variety of jobs, but nothing in my experience compared to campaigning. I took great satisfaction and gained self-confidence standing at a subway stop in Harlem in the morning and greeting thousands of commuters. It forced me to put myself out there, shaking hands and passing out leaflets. The campaign changed me, helped me grow and develop a range of new skills, and helped me see the potential I had as a leader and a public servant.

My electoral success also benefited greatly from working with consummate pros who knew how to get things done in the realm of politics, a prime example being how Jimmy Banks handled our large direct-mail operation. Jimmy had worked in several clubs around Harlem and seemed to know anybody who was anybody. He said he would oversee our mailing operation and through his contacts with the US Postal Service he managed to get our bulk mailings sent out as first-class mail, although we were only charged second-class rates. He saved us hundreds of dollars.

During the campaign, people asked a few times where I grew up because they heard a Boston accent in my voice. I was transparent and straightforward and never hid my roots. I explained that I grew up in Roxbury, one of six raised by a single mother after our father left his family. I told them I had been living and working in New York for a number of years, that we are a city of immigrants, and newcomers and many New Yorkers were like me. They came from somewhere else, but loved the city and stayed and put down roots.

Our victorious election night was a wonderful celebration and we were elated. I shuttled back and forth to the partying volunteers at our

Harlem and Upper West Side campaign offices. Throughout the campaign, I had a couple hundred people volunteering over the course of the race to help me get elected and I think the majority of them showed up for the victory party. I was so glad they did. It was truly a team approach and a collaborative grassroots effort.

After the party wound down in the wee hours, the reality of what had happened sunk in. It truly hit me for the first time that I was now going to become a member of the New York State Senate, the so-called upper house of the New York State Legislature. It was rarified company. I was one of sixty-three senators representing all eighteen million New Yorkers. It was a humbling proposition. By contrast, there were 150 members of the assembly and it was obvious just by the numbers that senators had more power, prestige, and resources compared to assembly members. I say this not to be smug, but as a matter of fact. I was going directly to the senate. Many assembly members toiled in the lower house for many years before they ran for the senate and got promoted, as it were, in the legislature's pecking order.

All along, I had been engaging constituents about the issues that mattered most to voters in the 28th Senate District. First and foremost was the proposed construction of the controversial West Side Highway, which I strongly opposed as a key plank in my platform. Commercial traffic would separate the West Side community from Riverside and Central Park. That was a challenging position for me to take, because the highway had supporters, but my opposition drew strong endorsement from a prominent attorney and leader of the anti-highway movement, Robert Kagan, the father of future US Supreme Court Justice Elena Kagan. Another issue front and center across both Harlem and the Upper West Side was the shrinking pool of affordable housing and the financial burden of skyrocketing rents, stagnant wages, and predatory landlords. I vowed to work toward a solution to this longstanding housing problem. Many constituents who were vocal about raising their most important concerns with me focused on a need to increase spending on schools and to enhance educational opportunities for all, but particularly for minorities in underserved neighborhoods. This was also an entrenched problem, but I said I would do everything in my power to bring about change, increase funding, and make measurable improvement to all facets of the public educational system.

It has often been said in political circles that a candidate campaigns in poetry and governs in prose. Even though I had never held elected office, I knew this to be the case. I realized throughout the campaign that once I got to Albany it was going to take a lot more than a nice turn of phrase and some bold promises in a campaign speech to bring about the changes I had promised to pursue and to be a catalyst for better, more responsive, more inclusive state government.

Fortunately, my timing was fortuitous. I was riding a statewide Democratic wave. At the top of the ticket, in the gubernatorial race, Democratic candidate Hugh Carey defeated Republican governor Malcolm Wilson. Wilson had completed the final year of Governor Nelson A. Rockefeller's final term in office. Rockefeller had resigned on December 18, 1973, to become vice president, after thirteen years as governor. When Gerald Ford assumed the presidency following President Richard Nixon's resignation, Ford nominated Rockefeller to be his vice president, and Rockefeller accepted.

Hugh Carey knocked out Malcolm Wilson practically before the short-term governor finished unpacking at the Executive Mansion. I was grateful to be riding a Democratic sweep.

Winning the senate seat meant that I would be making a lengthy 150-mile commute to the State Capitol in Albany. There would be other significant personal changes and transitions to make, including growing strains in my marriage to Cecilia, who never expressed the slightest interest in politics. She was less than enthusiastic about the fact that my victory would essentially mean that I would be dividing my time between Albany and New York and we would see even less of each other than during the all-consuming campaign I had just finished. This created fresh tensions in our relationship and in many ways hastened our growing divide and contributed to our marital dissolution.

And so, after traveling a long and winding career path that always had seemed to detour around elective politics, I had now committed myself to embarking on a new career and hitching my future to a fresh start in Albany as Senator Carl McCall.

I was ready to write a new chapter in my professional career starting in January 1975 with the kickoff of a new legislative session.

Ready or not, I was Albany bound.

Chapter 12

Albany

I had campaigned and won on two key messages: "Time for a Change" and "Time for New Leadership." Those slogans covered my posters and campaign signs and I used those phrases in all my speeches because they resonated with the district's voters and helped me defeat two-term incumbent Sidney von Luther.

Now, I had to make good on my sweeping promises. It did not keep me up at night, but I was certainly thinking about it, mulling ideas and talking to my team about how we were going to execute reform once I got to Albany and was sworn in as the New York State Senator representing the 28th District. On a practical level, this new position was a major change in my life and career. I had no actual political experience, at least not in an elected position answering to constituents. I focused on immediate priorities: hire a staff, establish a district office in Harlem and the Upper West Side, and begin to build a network and connections in Albany.

There were other considerations I had to address. The base salary for a state legislator at the time was $23,500, which represented a substantial pay cut from my private-sector work. Yet, I still had to maintain our apartment in Manhattan and find some sort of housing accommodations in Albany. Due to ethics rules, I had to forfeit my job with the Schumann Foundation and give up all my clients. Unlike the many legislators who were lawyers and who earned income from private law practice while they served in the state legislature, I had no such supplemental stream of income and I realized my financial situation was going to be tight in order to meet family expenses and new costs in Albany.

I focused on the practical problems I could solve. I applied for and received a grant from the foundation of the pharmaceutical company Eli Lilly, which was making investments in developing new community initiatives in minority neighborhoods by establishing programs and services through Black churches. The grant would support workshops throughout Harlem that would give low-income residents training in job development, furthering one's education and learning marketable employment skills. The Lilly grant would relieve the financial hit I was taking by going into public service. I felt good about taking care of that issue, although there were many more problems to address.

Lilly's grant was meant to develop the Harlem workshops and training programs as models to be put in place in other cities around the nation. I was a part-owner of WLIB and the grant funded a new Sunday radio program to be aired on the station. The program was entitled *Preaching Good News*. The show's title came from the Gospel of Luke: "The Spirit of the Lord is upon me, because he has anointed me to preach good news to the poor." The program included uplifting speakers and ministers reading inspirational chapters from the gospels. The radio show drew upon some of New York's nationally renowned ministers, including the Reverend Calvin Butts from the Abyssinian Baptist Church, the Reverend William Jones at Bethany Baptist, and also the Reverend Herbert Daughtry of the Church of the Lord in Brooklyn. I was included in the rotation of ministers who delivered sermons that fit the desired theme.

At this same time, as I prepared to begin my work as a state senator both in my district in New York City and during the legislative session in Albany, the pastor at Metropolitan Community United Methodist Church in Harlem, the Reverend Dr. William Marcus James, asked me to preach at his church. I agreed to do so because Pastor James, who was born in 1915 in Mississippi, had been serving that church since 1952 and he was highly respected. I thought it would be a one-time invitation, but I connected with his congregation and he asked me back the following Sunday. I have a difficult time saying no to senior pastors I admire, and I was invited to be a regular presence in the pulpit. I hesitated. I never intended to be a full-time minister and saw my ministry in public service. On the other hand, preaching at Metropolitan, which was located on 126th Street in the heart of my senate district, also felt a little like keeping in touch with my constituents. I stuck around after the service to meet and talk with people over coffee and pastries. Preaching on Sundays in Harlem also felt like a way I could stay connected while working during the week in Albany. I was fine with having an arrangement with Pastor James, but he soon gave me the title of Preaching Minister, with no other duties at the church. I liked how that sounded. I said I gladly accepted. I should note that Reverend James died in 2013 at age 97, still living in Harlem and, though long retired, still serving Metropolitan, his church since 1952.

I benefited from the fact that I had gotten to know so many talented volunteers who supported me and the political activists who also gave my campaign a critical boost. They helped me get started in recruiting talented people for my staff. I was very fortunate that I was able to attract very qualified and committed individuals who wanted to help enact the change I had promised. One of my first hires was Jacques DeGraff, a graduate of Hunter College, who had been an extremely capable volunteer on my campaign staff and who was a protégé of Lloyd Williams. Jacque became my first chief of staff, a wonderful leader who commuted, as I did, between Albany during session and our district offices in Harlem and the Upper West Side. I hired as my office administrator Henrietta Lyle, who also had proven her mettle during the campaign and who had been a valued and exceptional employee at WLIB. I brought on Shirley Wasserman, who had been instrumental in building our network on the Upper West Side. The two women made a dynamic duo and they worked seamlessly in handling constituent services and community outreach, and they were both capable, energetic, and highly committed to our mission of working to bring about change in Albany for our senate district. We were a small staff, but we covered a lot of ground. We had office space in the Harlem State Office Building and also an office in the Upper West Side Service Center. I divided my time between the two offices.

I was well aware of the hot-button issues in my district from the campaign and because people were not shy about telling me about their problems, anger, and disappointment over not getting issues taken care of by my predecessor or other public servants. In Harlem, housing was far and away the most urgent concern. In particular they sought a solution to the traumatic and disruptive process of eviction and protection against unscrupulous landlords who mistreated tenants, typically low-income minorities who did not have legal representation or the resources to fight these predatory landlords. Inadequate government services, a lack of investment in public education from kindergarten to college, escalating taxes, underfunded day care, and insufficient preschool programs also drew a loud chorus of complaints by frustrated constituents.

I had been aware of and attuned to these issues as a community organizer and through working with various federal programs in Harlem, but now that I was going to be a New York State Senator I hoped that I would have more ability to fix some of these problems through the legislative process. My naivete was obvious after my first session in Albany, but for now, as a senator-elect, I was still optimistic and trusting in the legislative process.

Percy Sutton, to whom I owed an enormous debt of gratitude, suggested that I should branch out from his Martin Luther King Club, where I was still an active member. He counseled me to start my own club, now that I was a senator, since these clubs functioned as a base of operation for solidifying support and building a foundation for the ongoing need to fundraise and prepare for reelection every two years. With this urging from Percy and others, I took the lead in establishing a new political club in my district. I chose southern Harlem and we called it the New Amsterdam Democratic Club. I took pride in creating a club with a difference. Nearly all the political clubs in Harlem and the Upper West Side and throughout New York City were racially segregated. For instance, the Martin Luther King Club where I belonged was all-Black and the Upper West Side clubs were all-white and primarily Jewish. Since my district straddled both of those neighborhoods and since both white and Black, Jewish and Christian, and a diverse array of people helped me get elected, I wanted the New Amsterdam Democratic Club to reflect that racial mix. From the outside, our club was multiracial and multiethnic and a far more inclusive group than our counterparts. Although we were new, this seemingly radical idea about membership attracted a solid number of new members and especially young, multiracial, politically active people.

We were not one of the deep-pocketed, high-end private political clubs and would never be. We were more in the mode of the low-rent storefront, with a focus on the work rather than the ambiance crowd. But I also got a very early piece of advice as a senator-elect from a political strategist whose advice I valued that could also apply to our new club. "Throw around a little weight at the beginning," he told me. "Let people know you're going to be a player on the political scene. It helps you discourage potential challengers so you can avoid newcomers trying to unseat you after one term." I thanked him for the tip.

Another part of being the winning candidate, the strategist advised me, was essentially to send a message by showing how I would deal with people who did not support me. Uzi Hutchinson was the only Harlem district leader who did not support me and we ran a candidate against her and defeated her. The candidate who ran a strong second in the senate race was Dorothy Gordon. She edged out von Luther and wanted to head the Harlem branch of the NAACP, so our operatives maneuvered and got another person with better credentials to be chosen for the NAACP post, and thus a future opponent was denied an influential platform from which she could have challenged me. I had not even moved into my office in Albany and already I was being schooled in the ways of elective politics.

I entered with a Senate Class of 1974 that was an atypical bunch. Howard Nolan from Albany was considered something of a maverick who had distanced himself from the political hacks of the entrenched Albany Democratic machine. Other newcomers were a cohort of independent, progressive, and outspoken Democrats who had already served notice that we would challenge the typically bland, anonymous, go-along, get-along types who had populated the state senate for decades. The '72 and '74 Democratic arrivals included Karen Burstein, a lawyer, feminist, and antiwar activist from Long Island; Carol Bellamy, an attorney and former Peace Corps volunteer who later became UNICEF's executive director; Major Owens, African American and a native of Tennessee who began his career as a librarian at the Brooklyn Public Library before he became politically active; and Franz Leichter, an Austrian who came to the US as a refugee in 1940 from German-occupied Europe, who served five years in the assembly before being elected to the senate in 1974.

The Republicans controlled the senate in 1974 and that meant the Democratic minority had very little power to pass legislation, but the strident newcomers tried to exert control nonetheless. Traditionally, county leaders decided on the minority leader in the senate, but the independents coming in would not accept the status quo. Instead, there was an air of uncertainty because it was going to be put up for a vote of the Democratic members, including the newcomers. Although their power was waning, the old Brooklyn organization still demanded attention and several of us assumed that their man, Senator Jerry Bloom, who had been a protégé of longtime senator Joe Zaretski (whom Leichter had knocked out), was the odds-on choice to be put into the minority leader's spot. Meanwhile, I supported Manfred "Fred" Ohrenstein, who was one of the dynamic leaders of the New York City Reform Movement in 1960. He helped bring together a coalition that included Eleanor Roosevelt and former governor Herbert Lehman to oust corrupt Tammany Hall Democrats. Ohrenstein had supported my senate campaign and we were both interested in bringing change to the senate so I, in turn, backed his effort to become senate minority leader. The senate Democratic caucus met in a Manhattan hotel and operatives of Jerry Bloom were so confident of Bloom's candidacy that they had a large suite booked with a case of champagne on ice. They never got to pop the corks. Bloom's buoyant optimism was a fantasy. In the end, Ohrenstein prevailed by two votes and I was happy to have backed the winner because it would be good to have our leader in my corner when I arrived in Albany.

Our first day as new state senators resembled orientation for freshman college students. We all had to report early to the State Capitol in January, a few days before Governor Hugh Carey was scheduled to deliver the annual State of the State message to both houses of the legislature. We newcomers met at the appointed hour in the lobby outside the senate chamber and two senior staffers gave us an overview of senate traditions, protocol, and rules on the floor. The master builder and former governor had cemented his political legacy with the just-completed, $2 billion Nelson A. Rockefeller Empire State Plaza, the largest and most expensive state government complex in the country and the world. One of the signature structures in the new plaza was the Legislative Office Building, a vast eleven-story monolithic structure of sparkling white marble where nearly all of the 213 state legislators were given spacious office suites. The LOB, as it was known, all sharp angles and a modernist style in keeping with Rockefeller's tastes, housed the unrivaled collection of modern art he acquired and displayed along the quarter-mile long, underground Concourse of the plaza.

I was coming into the senate with relatively luxurious LOB offices, compared to cramped offices shared by four senators in the Capitol building, at least according to stories that Basil Paterson and others told. The one drawback of the LOB was that it was isolated from the Capitol, roughly a block away, either a short walk outside or underground through the Concourse. That meant that once legislators and their aides went to their LOB office after a session in the senate chamber in the Capitol, they were less inclined to walk back and forth and often missed out on impromptu constituent visits and public demonstrations. There were a few legislators in the prized handful of legislative offices in the Capitol. These handpicked lucky few were in the heart of the action and never missed out on anything interesting and unscheduled that went on.

At our new senator gathering, they called last names of the members and the assigned office number in the LOB. They went through all the senators, but did not call my name. I was standing in the group, looking confused and about to ask why I was skipped over, when one of the senior staffers running things stepped over to me and said quietly: "Percy told me to take care of you." Those proved to be magic words.

He brought me upstairs to the fourth floor of the Capitol, above the senate chamber. It turned out I was the only new legislator, from either the assembly or the senate, who was assigned an office in the Capitol building. It was large and had even more room than the LOB suites. Aside from the central location that would allow me to be in on all the action, it showed that I had political juice and that Percy Sutton, who commanded immense respect, had given me a certain status. That made my fellow legislators take notice of this McCall fellow.

My special office perk made me feel very good and valued, but that feeling lasted just a couple of days, until I experienced the first senate session. It was clear from the bills that were placed on the calendar and available for discussion on the floor that we, the Democratic minority, had essentially no power compared to the Republican majority, who could block or pass any bill at will because they had the votes needed to control the upper house. Also, the Republican members in the majority were assigned to the most prestigious and powerful committees and they were made the leaders of the committees. When our assignments came around, I was placed on the Elections Committee as the ranking minority member. Somebody had done their homework and understood that I had been involved for years in improving the voter registration process and this committee assignment made good use of my experience in that area.

I will never forget the first Elections Committee meeting I attended. John Calandra, a powerful Bronx Republican, was the chairman and he called me in my office about thirty minutes before the meeting was to start in the LOB. Calandra told me in a mocking tone that if I had something else to do or was too busy to attend, it would not matter. Furthermore, he suggested there was no point in my actually showing up because he had the votes to pass all items on the agenda without my input. My attendance would be a waste of time because he would not recognize me and he controlled everything as the chairman. I was not about to be intimidated or pushed around by Calandra and I showed up for the committee meeting, waited behind my chair for a few long seconds so he could see that I stood six feet three and was nobody to try to push around. I slowly took my seat and looked directly at Calandra. He stared back. He did not introduce me or try to make any small talk. It was as if I did not exist. The meeting lasted less than ten minutes because the chairman brought all the Republican bills up for a vote and the Republicans, who had a clear majority, passed them by voice vote. The trouncing of the Democrats was brief and overwhelming. After they passed their final bill, the Republicans stood up in unison, turned, and left the committee room—without any acknowledgment of me. That was my wake-up call and, shoulders slumped, I trudged back to my Capitol office. I now saw how things worked in the legislature, and it was very discouraging. It did not resemble democracy and my campaign promise to make change in the senate all of a sudden seemed like a pipe dream.

A major change in Albany occurred early during the first term of Governor Hugh Carey, a Democrat. There was a major fiscal catastrophe unfolding in New York City on the watch of Democratic mayor Abraham "Abe" Beame. After he defeated Republican senator John Marchi, just months after his election, Beame faced the worst fiscal crisis in the city's history. His mayoralty was defined by desperate measures to stave off insolvency and avoid bankruptcy. When he appealed to Republican president Gerald Ford for federal aid, Beame was rebuffed and Ford vowed he would veto any congressional bailout. This led to an iconic *New York Daily News* front-page headline published on October 30, 1975: "FORD TO CITY: DROP DEAD."

I experienced this stand-off as a state legislator, as a resident of the Upper West Side, and as an elected official who represented thousands of Harlem and Manhattan constituents who gravely needed federal support in order to continue to receive a multitude of necessary city programs and benefits. I was only tangentially involved as the successful Wall Street financier and trusted government adviser Felix G. Rohatyn took the lead in dealing with New York City's fiscal crisis. He was named chairman of the Municipal Assistance Corporation, hastily created by state officials in order to prevent insolvency. With a structural budget deficit amounting to about $11 billion—although city officials suggested the deficit was slightly less than $1 billon—New York City was considered a very bad financial risk, and banks and credit markets would no longer offer a line of credit or loans for the country's largest city. Rohatyn was so highly regarded that he wielded enormous control and influence over the city's spending, and the fact that he was not elected made his position even more unprecedented. He earned the nickname "Felix the Fixer" and he likened his role to the work of a surgeon who is asked to "operate, fix it up, and leave as little blood on the floor as possible."

Another important player during New York City's fiscal crisis was labor leader Victor Gotbaum, whom I knew fairly well, and he worked collaboratively with Rohatyn. The New York State Financial Control Board was created as another layer of review and oversight of the financial management of New York City government and some public authorities. The city first had to request financial support and the authority to create the board. Passing the legislation was contentious and split along party lines. The assembly, controlled by Democrats, quickly passed the bill that set up the control board, while the Republican majority in the senate stalled and blocked it in committee. The feeling among the Republican senators—who were mostly fiscally conservative and represented rural areas—was that they did not feel compelled to bail out New York City because of overspending, incompetency, or both. A common sentiment among Republican lawmakers was that New York City got what it deserved, although they failed to mention or acknowledge that Wall Street and New York City contribute the lion's share of the entire state's tax revenue each year.

One of the stand-up Republican senators I observed at close range was Senate Majority Leader Warren M. Anderson. He represented Binghamton in the Southern Tier and took over his father's seat. Anderson served in the senate from 1953 to 1989 and served as majority leader from 1973 to 1988. I considered him a rare statesman in the senate for the way that he tried to convince his recalcitrant senators to support the legislation because of the cultural, financial, and historic importance of New York City to the state's overall health and well-being. My first year in Albany proved to be the longest legislative session of all time, since it included dealing with the fiscal crisis. Normally, the legislature took up its work in Albany in a legislative session between January and May. However, in 1975, the marathon session continued throughout the summer and into October because the political parties had hit an impasse. Behind the scenes, the state's three most powerful political leaders—Carey, Anderson, and Assembly Speaker Stanley Steingut—met constantly to try to negotiate a solution to the impasse.

Meanwhile, our phones in Albany and our district offices were ringing incessantly with angry, frightened constituents. We received a large volume of letters from municipal employees and retired city workers who feared that they would lose their jobs and perhaps their pensions if New York City was declared insolvent and did not receive some sort of bailout. Following lengthy negotiations between Carey and Anderson, the legislation was finally passed in October 1975. I was pleased to inform my constituents that they could rest assured they would not suffer any long-term damage as a result of the political infighting in Albany.

The dogged work of the rank-and-file legislators, myself included, was instrumental in gaining passage of the bailout provision that saved New York City, the nation's largest, and one of the greatest, cities in the world. The Emergency Financial Control Board helped get the city's fiscal house in order since municipal spending was put under great scrutiny. It was traumatic while it was happening, but all things considered, New York City was stronger fiscally and more careful about its spending going forward.

After the high-stakes drama of saving New York City, the rest of my first session in the senate was anticlimactic. I easily won reelection and the new session began in 1977, and soon enough there was a very important race for New York City mayor. Abe Beame had been badly weakened as a result of the financial crisis, but he nonetheless decided to run for another term. Percy Sutton sensed Beame's weakness and he used his platform as borough president to get into the race. I supported Percy, of course, who was attempting to become the first Black mayor in the city's history. Since Sutton supported Beame in 1973, he expected that Beame would step aside after one term and support Sutton. But that did not happen and a bitter rift opened up between the mayoral opponents.

The 1977 race for mayor of New York grew very crowded when Beame and Sutton were joined in the race by Herman Badillo, Ed Koch, Mario Cuomo, and Bella Abzug. Each of the candidates had a loyal base, but only the top two vote-getters would move beyond the competitive and crowded primary field. It turned out that Cuomo and Koch survived the scrum and came through as the head-to-head opponents for the second round of balloting.

I was a member of an influential statewide group, the Council of Black Elected Democrats. All Black elected Democratic officials were members, and we had the difficult decision of backing either Koch or Cuomo. Cuomo was strongly against the death penalty and that was an important position for Black voters. Koch, meanwhile, in trying to move to the center, began taking more conservative positions and he showed little interest in Black voters. The council formed two groups to vet the two candidates: one led by Sutton met with Koch and the other led by Rangel met with Cuomo. They put each candidate through a series of lengthy discussions and interviews and then made the recommendations to the council for the final decision. The two groups had divergent opinions. Sutton's group presented a glowing endorsement for Koch because he needed the support of Black voters and he therefore made strong commitments to appoint Blacks to high positions in his administration. Koch won more support by making a promise to keep Sydenham Hospital operating in Harlem, which was in financial distress and in danger of being closed. Meanwhile, Cuomo felt that Black voters would support him over Koch and he was not willing to promise anything significant to the council. This was a miscalculation. Rangel's report on Cuomo was negative and did not recommend him to the council. The council supported Koch, who went on to win the race for mayor. He fulfilled his promises and appointed Basil Paterson as a deputy mayor and Herman Badillo as a second deputy mayor—thus ensuring the future support of both Black and Latino voters.

It was difficult for me and my senate Democrats to get any legislation of substance passed, as long as the senate was Republican-controlled. I did manage to bring about one change that I had promised in my campaign. The voter registration process as it had been run for decades was cumbersome, difficult, and inaccessible—which might have been purposeful in order to favor the incumbents. For instance, there was only one office in each borough where new voters could register to vote. I helped organize street protests to raise awareness about this inefficient and politically nefarious limiting of access in order to suppress the people's ability to exercise their constitutional right to vote.

Arthur Eve and I developed legislation, which he introduced in the assembly and I introduced in the senate, to streamline the voter registration process. Our bill would permit registration by mail and allow organizations and individuals to collect registration forms from others and submit them to the Board of Elections. The assembly passed the bill and it was stalled in the senate by the Republicans until Senator John D. Calandra of the Bronx, the chairman of the Elections Committee, surprisingly supported the bill. A few other Republicans joined him and the bill passed and was signed into law by the governor. The state Republican leaders were outraged and they went to court to overturn the legislation.

The attorney general, Louis Lefkowitz, was responsible for defending the legislation in court. We heard from some officials in the court system who had seen a draft of the attorney general's response that it was weak and probably would not prevail. Our informants believed the assistant handling the case was incompetent or personally opposed to the legislation.

Sutton, Dinkins, and I met with Lefkowitz. He was a Republican who grew up on the Lower East Side. He liked to be called "General" and was a close ally of Nelson Rockefeller. When Rockefeller entered politics, Lefkowitz drove him around the state to meet Republican leaders. Lefkowitz's son, Stephen, told me a story about Rocky's first campaign for governor and his concern about the optics of campaigning on a Jewish holiday. Rockefeller called Lefkowitz, who told him that campaigning was not appropriate and he should stay home. He asked Lefkowitz what he planned to do. Lefkowitz, running for reelection at the time, said: "This is an important holiday, so I am going to seven synagogues."

We offered to assist in the court case. Lefkowitz accepted the offer. Dinkins assembled a few lawyers who worked with him to develop a very sound brief. Lefkowitz submitted it to the court. We won. The new law transformed the registration process in New York. I look back on this as my most significant achievement as a legislator.

On a personal level, five years as a senator were also marked by building important connections and making lasting friendships. Howard Nolan entered with me and the group of newcomers in the Senate Class of 1974. We got along very well because he, too, was a reformer who was challenging the suffocating status quo of the entrenched Albany Democratic machine. He also gave me good advice on how to offset the penurious pitfall of being a state lawmaker because he had built outside income through his legal work as a partner in a prominent Albany law firm, and through investing in commercial real estate, including a small shopping center in Delmar, an upscale suburb of Albany. He also was a thoroughbred horse owner, but that was more of a passion and hobby than a source of revenue or investment that paid steady dividends. Howard became my closest friend in the legislature and he invited me to his home for dinner and to socialize with his wife and six kids. He introduced me to the Saratoga Race Track, cultivated my interest in horse racing, and introduced me to other sources of enjoyment in the town. I had developed a liking for the Spa City during my time at Dartmouth, when I made trips to spend weekends with my girlfriend, who attended Skidmore College in Saratoga Springs

Howard's senate district also included rural Greene County and he took me to a meeting of the New York Farm Bureau, which was quite a stretch for a kid from Roxbury. It was a subtle way for Howard to provide context for me outside my urban experience. The Farm Bureau officials explained how farmers produced the food we needed in New York State and beyond, and how they were essential to a strong state economy. There was also a bit of self-interest on Howard's part. His support of bills that supported farmers meant, in turn, that the Farm Bureau and farmers in his district supported him. I am grateful to Howard to showing me early on how Albany operated and his sharing of knowledge would be helpful to me in the future. I also was pleased that I made friends with rural folks and farmers, a new development for me.

Our friendship extended beyond state politics and I assisted Howard politically when he challenged Albany's "mayor for life," Erastus Corning 2nd, who was first elected in 1942 and served eleven terms, until his death in 1983. It was the first and only primary challenge against Corning, the longtime Democratic incumbent. I met with Black leaders in Albany and introduced Howard to Black pastors and their congregations around the city. One day, several weeks into the primary campaign, I got a call from Mayor Corning's office assistant who said the mayor would like to see me at City Hall. I met the mayor at the appointed time and he proceeded to give me a stern lecture about staying in my lane, and that he didn't meddle in Harlem politics and I should not meddle in Albany politics. He tried to intimidate me with a tone that was quiet and urbane, but definitely threatening. He made a strong suggestion that he had good friends in high places in the legislature who could be detrimental to my political career if Corning chose to unleash these forces upon me. I also should note that Dorothea "Polly" Noonan, a machine operative who controlled the women's wing of the organization, was also in the mayor's office at the time and Corning clearly had invited her to reinforce his message. In fact, she chimed in and told me I ought to listen to the mayor's sage advice and she, too, had an intimidating tone. Unlike Corning, a Yale-educated patrician, Noonan was not concerned about decorum and did her verbal arm-twisting with a string of expletives. She seemed to be a world-class curser and passed on some of that fierceness to her granddaughter, United States Senator Kirsten Gillibrand, Democrat of New York.

I listened without interrupting Corning or Noonan, whom everyone understood was his confidant. When they had finished, I thanked them for their time and the friendly advice. I said I would return to my work in the state legislature and get back to campaigning for my friend, Senator Howard Nolan, in the primary race for mayor of Albany.

I felt that I had done my best to live up to my campaign promises. I felt like I did help plant the seeds of real change among the independent newcomers, particularly legislators from Brooklyn, led by maverick assembly members Al Vann and Roger Green, and Major Owens in the senate. Meanwhile, the Brooklyn Old Guard, led by Senator Vander Beatty, liked things exactly the way they were because they had a strong hold on power over the long run and did not want an influx of newly registered voters to upset their winning streak. The assembly passed a bill, with wide support, to establish a state holiday in honor of Reverend Dr. Martin Luther King Jr. The bill stalled in the senate, where Beatty tried to pass his version of the bill.

Beatty said that he had spoken to King's widow and family members and that they supported his legislation that would make the MLK day on a Sunday. He floated this compromise because it would not require a paid day off during the week for state workers or create another paid holiday for private employers. Assemblyman Seymour Posner from the Bronx, chairman of the Labor Committee, was a member of the hospital workers' union that had worked with Dr. King to plan the March on Washington. He was outraged by Beatty's venture. He called Mrs. King and reported that she never heard of Senator Beatty, never talked to Senator Beatty, and the King family opposed a Sunday holiday. Everyone walked away from the Beatty proposal.

Not long afterward, Beatty got caught up in a corruption scandal and was forced to resign after being sentenced to a prison term. In the end, the MLK holiday was passed by Congress in 1983 and became a federal holiday.

What my experience in Albany taught me was that Black legislators had only limited influence and remained, more or less, outsiders when it came to the true power brokers—white suburban and rural legislators and white urban representatives. Percy Sutton led the counter forces by encouraging Black legislators to work together and he helped establish a program at the City University of New York, CUNY, that provided additional state funding for students with financial hardship. It was initially called SEEK. A similar program to provide financial assistance for minority students was named the Educational Opportunity Program, or EOP. The programs provided counseling, academic support, and financial assistance to help low-income and first-generation college students gain access to education and support services to help them fully succeed and earn a degree. I continued to support the creation of EOP and it has functioned for more than fifty years at the City University of New York and State University of New York campuses and far, far beyond. It was the legendary Assemblyman Arthur Eve, a Democratic member of the assembly from 1967 to 2002, who brought EOP to the SUNY system and I was proud to call Arthur a friend. The EOP program has functioned well and with demonstrated success for six decades.

Arthur Eve influenced me in other ways. I still remember that Arthur often used a quote from civil rights leader the Reverend Jesse Jackson, who said: "You need two kinds of leaders, the tree shakers and the jelly makers." I loved that quote. Arthur was truly a tree shaker and his chief of staff, Norman McConney, an Albany legend, was the jelly maker who made legislation out of the demands Arthur made to legislative leaders. McConney was a product of the EOP program at the University at Albany and he joined Eve's staff after graduation. McConney stayed in Albany for the rest of his long and distinguished career—working with legislators of the Black and Puerto Rican Caucus—in support of policies to benefit needy and neglected communities in New York.

One of Arthur's significant contributions was when he mounted a vigorous impeachment effort against Governor Rockefeller following the state's disastrous response to the Attica prison uprising, which had been spurred by inmates who demanded improved conditions. The four-day revolt in September 1971 at the maximum-security Attica Correctional Facility near Buffalo turned into a horrific massacre. Following a hail of gunfire, Rockefeller directed hundreds of state police troopers to storm the prison complex. It was the worst prison riot in US history and a total of thirty-nine people were killed in the assault, including twenty-nine prisoners and ten prison guards. A number of employees who were held hostage at the beginning of the uprising were injured.

I knew my time in Albany had lost its luster after I was less than enthusiastic about being reelected to a third term in 1978. The culture of Albany, despite our efforts to change it, was hidebound and entrenched. It was a closed system that kept newcomers, minorities, and mavericks at a great disadvantage and largely incapable of making inroads to disrupt or reform it. It was hard to maintain enthusiasm for the legislative process when it was painfully clear that my vote and the votes of the minority party really didn't make any difference. One bright spot was that I managed to hold on to my coveted Capitol office, which was spacious and inviting and caused a twinge of envy when I brought my legislative colleagues there. But the nice office could not make up for feeling defeated and demoralized and essentially irrelevant as a member of the minority party.

On the home front, things were also strained and became more so. My wife Cecilia never acquired an interest in politics, not even by my third term in the senate. Her resentment deepened when I was away from home three or four days a week when we were in session in Albany. The absences also diminished my relationship with my daughter, Marci, who wanted me to be a steadier presence in her life. At least Cecilia had her career goals to focus on. She earned a master's degree and a PhD in education from New York University. For these reasons, as well as my dissatisfaction with my limited role as a legislator, I decided not to run for a fourth term. I wrapped up my career in the senate in 1980, after five largely frustrating years in Albany.

By then, our marriage was badly damaged and ultimately could not be repaired. We stayed together awhile longer for our daughter, who was still in high school. Cecilia was promoted to a faculty position at Baruch College and our paths diverged irrevocably. Fortunately, our breakup was free of acrimony and I deeply appreciated how she had supported me and made sacrifices as I pursued my political career, and especially recognized what a wonderful mother she was to our daughter. We did not fight or harbor grudges. Rather, we had slowly but steadily grown apart and were no longer compatible. The legal term is "irreconcilable differences" and that did not exactly describe our split, but it came close. It was more a compatibility problem and a wide chasm between our interests. We vowed to work together and to do what was best for our daughter even after we ceased to be a couple. At seventeen, Marci went off to college at Skidmore in Saratoga Springs.

As I prepared to finish my tenure in Albany, an air of disappointment clouded my memories of my time in the state senate. I learned a lot about government service and got schooled in the realities of politics. I still believed that elected officials could enact reform, create important and lasting change, and make the world a better place. Perhaps that was naive, but my time in the legislature did not knock all the idealism out of me. It was, above all, a great learning experience and it toughened me up, inured me to failure and rejection, and set the stage for the next phase of my career. I felt I had grown and matured and was ready to take on something exciting. What that next chapter would be was not yet clear to me. As I considered new opportunities, I was struck by how transitory things had become. My political career and my marriage were both over. It was at difficult times like that when I leaned into my faith, dug deep into my spiritual reserves as an ordained minister, and prayed to God to show me the path for what I might do next. I wanted above all to make a positive impact and create change that helped the less fortunate. I still had the fire in my belly. I still wanted to change the world. It took five years to determine that Albany was not the place where I could make that happen. I reflected and read the Bible and kept myself open for the next opportunity to serve the Almighty and the greater good.

Chapter 13

International Opportunities

O ne quality I managed to cultivate in myself during a long and varied career is resilience. My faith grounds me and makes it easier for me to put disappointment, failure, and professional and personal setbacks behind me. I was able to move past my frustrating tour of duty as a state legislator in the dysfunctional culture of Albany and to quickly look ahead to the next chapter. There was also something exhilarating, and slightly frightening, about those interstices when I was between jobs and about to strike out in an entirely new direction. This was the situation I found myself in after completing three terms as a state senator.

My friend and mentor Charlie Rangel knew of my disappointment in Albany and that I was looking for a new professional challenge. He contacted me and suggested there might be something worth exploring in Washington in Jimmy Carter's administration. Rangel had been a strong supporter and campaigned for the peanut farmer from Plains, Georgia. The underdog Democrat pulled off an upset of incumbent Republican president Gerald Ford in a very tight election. Rangel was growing in stature and influence as a congressman and Carter knew the value of rewarding loyal supporters on his side of the aisle on Capitol Hill.

Charlie arranged a meeting at the White House for me with Louis Martin, a former labor leader from Detroit whom Carter had made an adviser responsible for outreach to the Black community. The meeting was cordial and direct. Martin indicated that he was looking in particular for accomplished Black leaders with varied careers in both the public and private sectors who would like to be considered for positions as American ambassadors to African countries. I listened intently and said I was looking at a range of opportunities, but I would give serious thought to an embassy posting in an African country.

I had a long-held interest in Africa, maintained by keeping up on news reports and developments on the continent, and by reading books on the subject. My first opportunity to visit the continent came in 1977 through the Africa-America Institute. AAI, as it was known, was founded in 1953 as an international organization "dedicated to strengthening human capacity of Africans and promoting the continent's development through higher education and skills training, convening activities, program implementation and management," according to the group's mission statement. In addition, AAI fostered business, cultural, and educational relationships between the United States and Africa and they also provided scholarships to low-income students. This allowed scholarship students to attend leading African universities and other programs that focus on increasing the skills of the next generation of young Africans so that they could become competitive globally.

When I learned that AAI was sponsoring a cultural trip to Africa for ten African American state legislators, I applied. I was proud to be the first state senator selected from New York. Our group of ten included interesting and accomplished Black legislators, two of whom I developed a bond with during the trip and remained connected to throughout our careers. The first was Julian Bond, a state senator from Georgia who was active in the civil rights movement of the 1960s. He began his activism while he was a student at Morehouse College in Atlanta. In 1960, he helped establish the Student Nonviolent Coordinating Committee, or SNCC, an influential student civil rights group. He was an eloquent and effective spokesman for SNCC as its communications director from 1961 to 1966. He led voter registration drives, organized demonstrations against racist Jim Crow laws, and became a notable figure in the movement. In 1965, Bond was elected to the Georgia House of Representatives along with eleven other Blacks, following passage of the Civil Rights Act of 1964 and Voting Rights Act of 1965. In a racial backlash, Georgia state representatives voted overwhelmingly not to seat Bond because he had publicly opposed the US involvement in the Vietnam War as a SNCC officer. After court challenges, the case went all the way to the US Supreme Court and Bond won on the grounds that his opposition to the Vietnam War was a matter of free speech, protected by the US Constitution, and he finally cleared that legal hurdle and was formally seated in the state legislature.

After four terms in the house, Bond was later elected to serve six terms in the state senate and he completed a successful twenty-year career in state government. Bond became the first president of the Southern Poverty Law Center in 1971 and much later ran for the US House of Representatives from Georgia's 5th Congressional District in 1986. He lost the Democratic nomination that year in a runoff with rival civil rights leader John Lewis in a bitter campaign marred by unsubstantiated allegations of Bond's drug usage.

I was proud to call Julian Bond a friend and a colleague. He was also a noted writer, educator, and political commentator who served from 1998 to 2010 as chairman of the National Association for the Advancement of Colored People, or NAACP. He died in 2015 at the age of seventy-five.

Another colleague and friend I connected with on the state legislators' African tour was George "Mickey" Leland, a state representative from Houston, Texas. He was an antipoverty activist who was elected to the US Congress in 1978 as the successor to the highly respected Barbara Jordan. Leland was a powerful Democrat who became chair of the Congressional Black Caucus in Washington. Leland was a well-known and effective advocate on hunger and public health issues. In 1984, he established the House Select Committee on Hunger and was appointed chairman of the group assigned to comprehensively study the problems of hunger and malnutrition. This led to Leland overseeing a humanitarian mission to deliver aid to refugee camps in Ethiopia and he died in a plane crash during a relief mission to Fugnido, Ethiopia, in 1984.

Our group's trip to Africa with the Africa-American Institute was led by Walter Carrington, a staff member with AAI who would later be named US ambassador to Nigeria. Our in-depth tour started in Sudan and traversed eight countries. Fortunately, we traveled during a time of relative political stability, despite the fact that Nigeria was under military rule. It was a vital, transformative experience for me and it offered a solid introduction to the history and politics of African countries, while also forging lasting friendships. I made it a point to attend annual AAI conferences, where we networked with political and business leaders from African nations. One of the highlights was developing a lasting connection to Andrew Young, who served as US ambassador to the United Nations under President Carter, followed by a successful campaign for mayor of Atlanta.

Our tour of the African countries left me with indelible impressions of Sudan, Nigeria, Ivory Coast, Ghana, Senegal, Zambia, Botswana, and Lesotho—a kingdom within the borders of South Africa. The situation in Lesotho, which declared its independence from the United Kingdom in 1966, made for some challenging travel. We flew to the Johannesburg Airport in South Africa early one afternoon and had to stay in a dormitory at the airport and wait for a flight to Lesotho the following morning because we were not granted visas to visit South Africa. I recall that a young and nervous aide to the US Embassy was assigned to be our minder in Lesotho—we complained about the confinement and said we were eager to visit Johannesburg. He called the embassy and reported that those Black men were getting restless and making demands, which was an exaggeration. It turned out that eventually we were allowed to spend a few hours in the city to explore. It was an experience I will never forget because I came face-to-face with the oppressive regime of apartheid. We tried to talk with Black people in the streets, but many were too fearful to be seen speaking with us and they avoided us. The Black people that we did encounter were laborers who left by train, bus, or van at the end of the workday and they traveled to the impoverished townships where they lived under grim conditions far different than where they worked in white districts.

When our group of Black men went into a gift shop to purchase some souvenirs and handicrafts, the embassy aide assigned to keep watch on us began to get flustered. He apologized to the white female shopkeeper who said it was alright. "I know they are not our boys," the shopkeeper said. "Our boys know better."

It struck me immediately that this was a different form of systemic racism compared to the overt form that Blacks experienced in the Jim

Crow South. There were no signs that designated "Whites Only" drinking fountains or areas that proclaimed that Blacks were not allowed. In the rigid system of apartheid, Blacks knew their place and what they could and could not do. That small incident in the gift shop underscored that this was a nation of white supremacists and that Black people understood their place in the social order. At that point, Blacks had not tried to challenge and overthrow apartheid. It was an unforgettable trip to my roots, the African homeland, and it left me emotionally drained. I vowed to return to explore African history more deeply.

Andrew Young, the civil rights leader and minister, had been executive director of the Southern Leadership Conference. Young was a close friend and strategist for Reverend Dr. Martin Luther King Jr., and he was with King in Memphis, Tennessee, when King was assassinated in 1968. Young ran as a Democrat for Congress from Georgia in 1970, but lost. He ran again two years later and this time he won. He was the first Black congressman elected in Georgia and he had become a close ally of President Carter's when he was governor of Georgia. Young introduced Carter to Black leaders around the country during his presidential campaign and Young's involvement was critical in delivering a strong Black voter turnout for Carter.

In turn, Carter gave Young a high-profile position as ambassador to the United Nations, the first Black person to hold that position. He quickly came under pressure given the very tense relations between the Israelis and the Palestinians. Our foreign policy had been supportive of Israel and dismissive of the Palestinian Liberation Organization. The PLO was established in 1964 with a goal of the liberation of Palestine through armed struggle. The PLO was considered to be a terrorist organization by Israel and the US. Still, since 1974, the PLO had been given observer status at the United Nations and that put Young in the middle of a long, simmering hatred between Israelis and Palestinians. In an attempt to find a solution, Young agreed to meet with a representative of the PLO in a secret meeting. When somebody leaked to the press that the clandestine meeting had taken place, the Israelis expressed outrage and put pressure on Young, who was forced to resign. This left the US contingent at the UN demoralized and in disarray.

Young had hired four excellent deputies, including Donald McHenry, a Black diplomat with broad experience in both international affairs and as an academic. After Young's ouster, Carter promoted McHenry to fill Young's position and at the same time promoted William vanden Heuvel, who had been a key aide to US Attorney General Robert F. Kennedy. McHenry and vanden Heuvel were expected to do damage control and to get the office back on its feet after the disruption of Young's departure. This left the third deputy position open after McHenry and vanden Heuvel were both promoted. I had followed closely all the turmoil because I knew Young and several people in his office. Around this time, I had another meeting with Louis Martin, who once again got right to the point. He asked if I would be interested in the opening at the UN left by the two promotions, and I said that I was interested and that I thought it was a better fit for me than to take a posting at an embassy in Africa.

Martin moved quickly. My initial meeting at the State Department went well and I also met with McHenry in New York City, and that too went very well. I found McHenry to be smart, well informed, and personable. He supported me for the position and made the offer. I said I would take the job. President Carter appointed me to the position of Alternate Representative of the United States of America for Special Political Affairs in the UN, with the rank of ambassador. I had to try on that mouthful of a title for a few moments and wished my mother were still alive to know that her son, a kid from Roxbury, was about to become a US ambassador. I know she would have been thrilled.

The next step was to be confirmed by the senate, which was not always a sure thing given partisan politics. I was informed that the common practice was to win endorsements from the New York senators. I booked a flight to Washington, DC, and had meetings scheduled with Democratic senator Daniel Patrick Moynihan and Republican senator Jacob Javits. I did not know either of New York's US senators well, but I was familiar with Moynihan's fraught relationship with the Black community. The bad blood stemmed from Moynihan's controversial 1965 report, published when he was assistant secretary of labor, titled *The Negro Family: The Case for National Action*, which became known as the "Moynihan Report." The report gained notoriety and changed the trajectory of Moynihan's political career, helping him rise from the academic ranks at Harvard to a four-term United States senator from New York.

Moynihan hoped to persuade White House officials that President Lyndon Johnson's civil rights legislation, the Civil Rights Act of 1964, would not alone produce racial equality. Within weeks, the report sparked heated debate. The Johnson administration distanced itself from Moynihan's report, which seemed to many critics to be contradictory and ambiguous. Hardline conservative commentators used the report to reinforce racist stereotypes about loose family morality in the African American community. Moynihan was criticized widely among Black people for "blaming the victim" and for mischaracterizing and misunderstanding the matriarchal structure of Black families, and the role of Black women as heads of households. Moynihan claimed his aim with the report was to advocate additional policies to alleviate race-based economic inequalities, and he wrote in the introduction that "the racist virus in the American blood stream still afflicts us: Negroes will encounter serious personal prejudice for at least another generation."

Moynihan added: "The gap between the Negro and most other groups in American society is widening. The fundamental problem, in which this is most clearly the case, is that of family structure. The evidence—not final, but powerfully persuasive—is that the Negro family in the urban ghettos is crumbling. . . . So long as this situation persists, the cycle of poverty and disadvantage will continue to repeat itself."

I had read the report and it was widely discussed and harshly criticized among my circle of Black friends. I took special offense because I knew extraordinary Black women like my mother, who represented the best of the matriarchal African American family structure. As a result, Moynihan had very few supporters among politically active Blacks, myself included. Moynihan did manage to get strong support for his US Senate candidacy from Bernard R. "Bernie" Gifford, a leading Black educator and deputy chancellor of the New York City Public School System at the time. I knew that Gifford was looking for something in return from Moynihan since he was a candidate then for president of City College of the City University of New York, or CUNY, which had a strong presence in Harlem and a long relationship with Black political leaders. Gifford lacked the widespread support of his Black colleagues, but Moynihan supported Gifford for the CUNY presidency.

Moynihan pressed me on why I was not supporting Gifford. I informed the senator that Harlem's Black political leaders, including myself, supported instead Dr. Alvin F. Poussaint for the CUNY president's opening. Poussaint was a medical doctor and noted professor of psychiatry at Harvard University. His books included *Why Blacks Kill Blacks* and *Raising Black Children*, coauthored with James Comer. He is an acclaimed authority on race relations in America, the dynamics of prejudice, and issues of diversity. Poussaint was born in East Harlem and from 1965 to 1967 served as Southern Field Director of the Medical Committee for Human Rights in Jackson, Mississippi. In that role, he provided medical care to civil rights workers and demonstrators during major marches, including the 1965 march from Selma to Montgomery, Alabama, led by Dr. Martin Luther King Jr. Poussaint walked the entire march route to tend to the injuries of marchers who clashed with police and racist crowds. For all these reasons, we felt Poussaint was a much better fit than Gifford. As it turned out, neither man got the job, but the contest stirred controversy nonetheless.

I needed Moynihan's support and could not afford to lose his endorsement for the ambassador opportunity. During our meeting, Moynihan said he had heard the Black leaders were not supporting Gifford because he "was too close to the Jews." I was shocked and said I did not understand where he would get that notion.

I was saved by the bell, as it were, because just as our conversation had stalled, Senator Javits strode into the office. He was friendly, mentioned that he had known me for some time, and that he would endorse me for the position in the senate confirmation hearing. Moynihan told him about the Gifford issue and his belief about the reason for the lack of support from Black leaders. Javits, who was Jewish, dismissed Moynihan's remark, and said he knew that the Jewish comment had nothing to do with me and that it did not reflect my position on Gifford.

After I left the meeting with Moynihan and Javits, I reported back to Charlie Rangel and he was very upset. He called Moynihan when I was in his office and Charlie yelled, cursed, and had a very heated discussion with Moynihan. After Charlie hung up the phone, he paused and said that I would have Moynihan's support in the confirmation hearing. The Republicans controlled the senate and Richard Lugar, Republican of Indiana, was chair of the Foreign Relations Committee and a key figure in my confirmation hearing. Lugar presented a letter from the Lilly Foundation, which mentioned that I had worked with them and supported charitable work with churches in Indianapolis. Lugar cited it as a very important document regarding my fitness for the office and he gave me his full support. That was the key endorsement I needed, and everything else fell into place.

I was approved without lengthy debate or any Republicans trying to hold up my nomination, which is a common tactic in partisan politics. I was grateful to Lugar, as well as to Moynihan and Javits. I got my title of ambassador and began an entirely new kind of job in 1979, one that marked a very interesting new phase of my career at the age of forty-four. Our office was in the United Nations Headquarters on 1st Avenue across from the UN complex. I was fortunate to come into a position with a seasoned staff of good, committed people already in place, each of whom had expertise in their State Department specialty area. That saved me a great deal of time and worry in getting up to speed on my core responsibilities, which included handling host country relations. That meant that I helped UN delegates from other countries navigate the nuances and challenges of living in New York City, including assistance with housing and other issues where I could be helpful. I developed good working relationships with representatives from African countries as well as the UN Trust Territories in the Pacific, a group that I assisted as they worked through the process of gaining their independence.

There were elements that I immediately liked about my UN position. I interacted with some brilliant people because countries from around the world sent their best and brightest to the UN, along with those who possessed great leadership potential. One of those up-and-coming diplomats I got to know was Kofi Annan, from Ghana, who rose through the ranks and served as the seventh secretary-general of the United Nations from 1997 to 2006.

During my time with the UN, I enjoyed the travel and learning about new cultures and traditions, particularly when I had the opportunity to travel abroad. I made two work trips to Africa, visited the South Pacific and Caribbean on assignment, and met the presidents of seven countries. There were a lot of formal dinners and receptions, as well as meetings and conferences. I made a point of going out of my way to invite Black people from Harlem and other parts of New York City to offer them the opportunity to interact with diplomats and foreign service staff members from around the world. I knew from their comments afterward that my guests learned a lot and thoroughly enjoyed being invited to join me at UN events. It was a small way that I could promote diversity and level the playing field for people of color who normally did not have access to the kind of opportunities found at the UN.

I was impressed with the quality and commitment from our staff. For each of my international trips, staff members traveled ahead as an advance team to map out logistics, and to develop talking points in consultation with local officials. As a result of their early ground work, they were well-orchestrated visits of several days. I was always warmly welcomed and leaders of the areas I visited were very happy to see me. The seven presidents I met rolled out the red carpet for our diplomatic fact-finding and engagement mission. They felt valued that a UN ambassador from the United States would make a special trip to meet with them, to learn about their needs, and to discuss how we might be of assistance. Fortunately, there were no major conflicts such as civil wars or violent uprisings in any of the countries I visited. I especially enjoyed encounters with new cultures and people, and the opportunity to leverage the resources and wealth of the United States to support programs and initiatives in developing countries.

I returned to Washington after a trip to Africa in September 1980 and attended the Congressional Black Caucus and Conference in the nation's capital. There was a private reception at the White House hosted by President Carter, followed by an evening reception at the Kennedy Center. I was tired and thought of skipping the second reception, but I am very glad I reconsidered and attended. It changed my life because at the Kennedy Center I met Dr. Joyce F. Brown, a brilliant, beautiful, and dynamic young woman. Both of us were attending solo and we have two different recollections about the first meeting between myself and the woman who would become my wife. The way I remember it, Joyce walked past, I was attracted to her, realized she was alone, and followed her to a buffet table where I introduced myself and asked her name. Joyce's version was that when I met her, I introduced myself and she showed no recognition when I said my name, and I was a bit miffed that she did not know who I was. Memories can often have various versions, but the fact remains that we started talking, it was a comfortable and warm conversation, and we discovered that we had much in common. The more we spoke, the more surprised we were that our paths had never crossed before in New York City.

Joyce attended the conference representing the faculty union at Borough of Manhattan Community College, where she was director of instructional testing and research. Joyce grew up in New York City, attended Catholic schools, and earned a bachelor's degree in psychology at Marymount College in 1968. She earned a master's degree in counseling psychology at New York University. In 1980, she completed a PhD in counseling psychology at NYU, which she completed by taking night courses while also working full-time at Borough of Manhattan Community College.

The conference was held at the Hilton Hotel in Washington, where most of us were staying. I played tennis with David Dinkins at eight the next morning and met Joyce for breakfast following our tennis match. The conversation was as easy and comfortable as the night before and we just kept talking. It was the beginning of a wonderful relationship. Three years after we met, Joyce and I married in 1983 and I'll have more to say later in the book about Joyce and how she has enriched my life across four decades. I was so grateful I decided to attend the Kennedy Center reception and the conference. That decision and my chance meeting with Joyce changed the trajectory of my life. Joyce made me a better person, she has been a tremendous partner, and is my best friend.

My tenure as an ambassador at the UN was ended by the 1980 presidential election, when Ronald Reagan defeated Jimmy Carter. Reagan was sworn in as the fortieth president of the United States during his inauguration on January 20, 1981. The new administration wasted no time in cleaning house. The very day of his inaugural celebration, I received a telegram from President Reagan that thanked me for my service and also told me to surrender my diplomatic passport because I was no longer employed by the US Department of State. It was not unexpected, but it was the most abrupt firing I had ever experienced. We were not sore losers, and we cooperated and assisted the incoming staff. We had a few meetings with Jeane Kirkpatrick, Reagan's appointment as ambassador to the UN. Her foreign policy sharply diverged from our strategy under President Carter. Kirkpatrick was a former Democrat who became a neoconservative and switched to the Republican Party in 1985. She was a strong advocate of authoritarian regimes around the world if they supported Washington's policies. Liberal commentator and author Noam Chomsky referred to her as the "Chief Sadist-in-residence of the Reagan Administration" for her support of brutal military regimes that had no regard for human rights or the democratic process.

I managed to make some important connections during my year at the UN. For instance, I worked for Carter's secretary of state, Cyrus Vance, and made a lasting association. I had previously known his wife, Grace, from her work as a board member of the New York City public television station. Grace Vance reached out to me after I was terminated by the Reagan administration and she informed me that the public television station, WNET, Channel 13, was looking for a senior executive and she thought I would be a good fit for the job. I told her I was interested and gave serious consideration to the opportunity. I also was contacted by a representative of the Rockefeller family, who asked me to consider the position of president of the American Committee for UNICEF, the UN agency that supports children in economically depressed countries around the world. I interviewed for the position and learned that it was primarily fundraising work, with no real policy involvement in UNICEF programs. I decided to pass on that job and instead looked at the public TV position. Following a satisfying interview process, I was offered the job and I took it.

I started at Channel 13 in February 1981, just two weeks after I was relieved of my duties at the UN by the Reagan administration. What I liked best about the TV job was that I would be working with a staff of creative people who were eager to produce additional local programming that took an in-depth look at issues important to New York City residents as well as topics that resonated with people all across the state. Today, the station has branded itself as THIRTEEN, part of the WNET group, and it is widely considered one of America's most respected and innovative public media providers. It was then, and is still, a unique cultural and educational institution that harnesses the power of television and electronic media to inform, enlighten, entertain, and inspire.

From the moment I stepped into the main office and studios of Channel 13 on West 57th Street in Manhattan, I found the work interesting and creative, and it demanded a partially new skill set I would develop as I hit the ground running. I was particularly impressed with the leadership style of John Jay Iselin, who had come from the publishing industry. He was vice president of Harper & Row publishers and a senior national affairs editor at *Newsweek* before being named president of WNET, a position he held from 1973 to 1987. He left WNET to become president of the Cooper Union, the college in the East Village, and died in 2008.

At the station, I was able to stay involved in particular areas of interest of mine, including politics and international affairs. With the rise of the oppressive apartheid Afrikaner regime in South Africa beginning in the late 1940s, and still entrenched after several decades of activity, I wanted to get involved in ending this racist political and social system of white supremacy and minority rule. In apartheid, laws were enforced to ensure segregation and to keep Blacks marginalized as second-class citizens, although they represented the overwhelming majority of the population of South Africa. It was an abhorrent system of racial injustice that was starting to get attention in the US, particularly on college campuses, beginning in the early 1980s. I experienced it up close on my day in Johannesburg in 1977 during my first Africa tour with other elected officials.

My interest in South Africa grew out of learning about Nelson Mandela, an imprisoned leader and symbol of strength and resilience of the opposition African National Congress. While I was getting settled into my new job at Channel 13, I got to meet Randall Robinson, a Black attorney and congressional staffer in Washington, DC, who founded TransAfrica to push for an end of apartheid in South Africa. The group previously was known as the Black Forum on Foreign Affairs, which was established in

1975. Two years later, he renamed it the TransAfrica Forum and it was later shortened to TransAfrica. Robinson had gained a following when he organized demonstrations at the South African Embassy and went on a hunger strike to draw attention to the plight of Black South Africans under Afrikaner rule, and he pushed for an end to the long racial oppression and policy of discrimination.

Robinson's group developed an effective strategy of lobbying members of Congress—he knew many top aides and lawmakers personally—and he used TransAfrica to impose sanctions and boycotts on multinational companies that continued to do business with South Africa. Robinson borrowed the tactics of Dr. Martin Luther King Jr. and the civil rights movement, including civil disobedience and nonviolence, to try to urge action from Congress against the South African regime. Robinson encouraged the opening of TransAfrica chapters in several major US cities and I agreed to lead the effort to open a chapter in New York City. I solicited friends and coworkers to join me and I also used my connections among Black churches throughout Harlem in order to gain more involvement and commitment to TransAfrica's work. It was a completely volunteer initiative and I was successful in fundraising and building a volunteer network as I helped open the New York City chapter of TransAfrica.

It is telling, perhaps, that I was most passionate about my outside work on behalf of TransAfrica and the dismantling of apartheid in South Africa, even more so than working on the latest cultural programming at Channel 13. The issue with the job was less about it not being a good fit and more about the pull of the political sphere that never left me. Working to rally interest and to open the New York City chapter of TransAfrica reminded me that I had a special talent for community engagement, grassroots organizing, and creating support for an idea or a particular program. I had been at Channel 13 about nine months and I was already getting restless. I was infected by the bug to get back into politics. Someone once told me that politics is like a virus and once it gets inside you, you are infected and no vaccine or treatment can get the political bug out. That is how it was with me. Guilty as charged. With less than a year at the public TV station, I had a conversation with Arthur Eve, the dynamic and highly regarded assemblyman from Buffalo who had become a sounding board and supporter. He heard me talk about how I was itching to get back into politics and he invited me to a meeting at which, he promised me, details would be laid out of a political opportunity he felt would both excite and interest me.

I had considered my work at Channel 13 as a form of public service since it was a public TV station, but the TransAfrica work had reignited my passion for organizing and building a new venture through the political process. I came to believe that I could make the greatest contribution and have the most significant impact on my community by moving back into the arena of public policy. I told Arthur that I was restless and the end of my marriage had taken a toll. The divorce settlement between Cecilia and I was finalized, we divided our assets, and I remained in the Upper West Side apartment. I was now ready to move on to the next chapter, personally and professionally.

Chapter 14

Lieutenant Governor Campaign

I consider Arthur O. Eve the most dynamic Black leader of the New York State Legislature in the modern era, or any era. He was a pioneering politician who broke racial barriers, attained success as a self-made man, and became a beloved institution of representative politics in Buffalo, New York. Born in New York City, of Dominican heritage, he was raised in Florida, studied at West Virginia State College, and ended up in Buffalo in 1953 with a few dollars in his pocket and limited prospects. Following a two-year tour with the US Army in Germany, he returned to Buffalo in 1955 and worked in an automobile plant. He married Constance Bowles the following year, 1956, and joined the Democratic Party yet remained a fiercely independent voice not beholden to machine politics. He became an activist on behalf of minority rights and racial justice. A decade later, having built a base of support in Buffalo, Eve was elected to the New York State Assembly, the first Dominican American elected to public office in the nation.

His thirty-five-year career in the state legislature was one of the longest and his Buffalo constituents kept reelecting him so he could do the people's business in Albany. I got to know Arthur during my time in the state senate. I saw that he could actually get legislation passed since he was in the majority, and his dynamism and ability to galvanize public opinion made him a force for reform. In 1968, as a freshman assemblyman, he managed to delay construction on the State University of New York at Buffalo's campus by negotiating an agreement that Black and minority workers would be hired by the unions for the campus work and other taxpayer-funded construction projects in his Buffalo district. He gained national renown for serving as an observer and negotiator in the wake of the bloody 1971 Attica prison riots, because the inmates respected Eve. He had visited the prison on a regular basis, exposed the poor conditions, and introduced prison reform legislation in the assembly. I especially respected Arthur because he stayed true to his roots. He cut his teeth in activism as a young, vocal leader during Buffalo's civil disturbances over racial inequality in the 1960s. He became a leading voice in pushing for access to education, one of my key issues, among Black and minority students.

I always enjoyed my discussions with Arthur because the fire of idealism still burned bright in his belly and he was respected as a statewide advocate for the advancement of Black people. He was a leader of the Black and Puerto Rican Caucus in the legislature, where he was the highest-ranking Black leader as the assembly's deputy speaker. I always liked how he wore a typical legislator's conservative business suit but accessorized it with a vibrant, colorful scarf in an African motif with political buttons. When he spoke, he possessed a preacher's passionate prose.

Arthur became a good friend who also supported me in my political campaigns. I always referred to him as a force to be reckoned with, which is why I did not hesitate to make room in my schedule when he requested a meeting in the spring of 1982. After eight years in office, Governor Hugh Carey decided not to run for a third term and Democratic leaders began to discuss who would be the best candidate to run to succeed him. Carey's lieutenant governor was Mario M. Cuomo, a Queens Democrat who was known as a talented orator and brilliant lawyer, but he lacked statewide name recognition. The Democrats did not want to lose the governorship to the Republicans again. Carey was the first Democrat to hold the office in more than a decade, following four terms of Republican governor Nelson A. Rockefeller and one year to fulfill Rockefeller's unexpired term by his dutiful lieutenant governor, Malcolm Wilson.

The leading Democratic candidates were Cuomo and Ed Koch, mayor of New York City. The Black and Puerto Rican Caucus was divided over whom they should support. Some were in favor of backing Cuomo, but others wanted Koch, although he had disappointed them in the mayoral race since his administration offered only small victories for Blacks and sometimes failed to keep its promises. Koch had vowed to save a private hospital in Harlem from closure, but he failed to do so, and its loss was a major blow for low-income Black residents as well as Black physicians who struggled to get admitting privileges to affluent, white hospitals in New York City.

The meeting that Arthur Eve called was held at the Manhattan offices of 1199 SEIU, a powerful union of healthcare workers. The agenda was to discuss the gubernatorial primary, to organize Black leaders and the Black community, and to reach consensus on whether to endorse Koch or Cuomo for the Democratic nomination. But another pressing issue that Arthur wanted to settle at the meeting was to pick a Black candidate to run as lieutenant governor with Cuomo because it was becoming clear in the run-up to the meeting that Arthur and the Black power brokers had soured on Koch. The idea of putting up a Black running mate with Cuomo was that it would bring out a large Black vote for Cuomo's bid for governor and it would also build a foundation of statewide Black activists that would pay future dividends as a way to empower, organize, and mobilize Black voters and increase Black voter registration for future races even if Cuomo ended up losing.

There was only one shortcoming to Arthur's plan: They did not yet have a Black running mate for Cuomo. About fifty people filled the conference room at the 1199 offices and I suddenly felt the room grow silent and many eyes were staring at me. After some perfunctory discussion, Arthur turned to me and said they thought I would make an ideal lieutenant governor candidate on the ticket with Cuomo. I had sort of suspected this when Arthur called me the day before and wanted to make sure I was coming to the meeting. And the way the other attendees had interacted with me, as if they knew a secret I did not, also made me feel a little wary that I was being set up for something. Indeed, I was. They put me on the spot. I suddenly felt the room get very warm and the walls seemed to close in on me, and I got a bit flushed. I did not say anything at first. And then I said I was flattered and I was about to say I would need time to think about it, but I was surrounded by these Black leaders

I admired who had helped me in many ways, and I agreed to run right then and there, on the spot. I wished I had a chance to talk it over with my family and friends and political allies, but I made the commitment in front of that group and the decision was made.

Of course, that meant that I would have to go into campaign mode and I would have to leave my job at Channel 13 because that position would be a conflict of interest for a candidate for statewide office. That did not cause me much concern because my job at the television station wasn't really fulfilling my larger ambitions to put myself in a position to make a difference and to lift up the Black community by helping them gain access to higher education, for instance, and to achieve racial equality in other ways. I also had been itching to get back into politics and they provided that opportunity on a level that was one step up from the state senate since this was a statewide position, and the Number Two job in state government. I had always intended to get back into public service. My relationship with Joyce Brown was continuing to develop and I was pleased that she was very supportive of my desire to return to politics. In fact, she said she wanted to play an active role in the campaign. Timing is everything, as they say. Making sure I did not pass on Arthur Eve's meeting created another one of those unexpected career turns, just as attending the event where I met Joyce had been.

I submitted my resignation at the station and threw my hat into the ring as the Democratic candidate for lieutenant governor in the 1982 campaign as the running mate with Mario M. Cuomo for governor.

I was in a familiar position once again. I started off with no money, no fundraising operation, and no campaign staff or structure in place. This was not unlike the start of my state senate campaign. And, once again, I was familiar with the notion of being an underdog even before the race began. That was because New York City mayor Ed Koch had more name recognition, more money, and a much larger and more powerful political organization than Cuomo did. Koch chose Alfred DelBello, the Westchester County executive, as his lieutenant governor running mate. I knew DelBello would be a formidable candidate because his position in affluent Westchester County gave him access to a lot of deep-pocketed donors who would contribute large sums to his campaign.

It was June when I agreed to be the lieutenant governor candidate and the primary race with Cuomo and McCall and Koch and DelBello was set for early September, which only gave me three months to create a campaign and develop some momentum. I had a few senate staffers and former volunteers I could call on, but DelBello was a current county executive of a large county with a lot of resources and people at his disposal. I understood from the outset that I was on the bottom of the ticket, which meant that I was there to boost and bring Black voters to Cuomo's gubernatorial bid. The truth was that I did not know Mario Cuomo very well and had only met him a few times. The other fact, which we didn't publicize, was that I had supported Koch over Cuomo in the bitter and bruising New York City mayoral campaign that left both angry with each other.

Primary campaigns are vastly different than a general election, because primaries pit two or more candidates from the same political party against each other. It's been described as a civil war and it almost always ends in anger, recrimination, grudges, and retribution. My name was on campaign buttons and posters with Cuomo, but truth be told we rarely interacted at campaign events, we communicated only occasionally, and in essence we ran two separate campaigns. I was in the race to help Cuomo, but it turned out that he did not offer my campaign much at all in terms of financial support or campaign volunteers. It was up to me to create my own team. During the entire three-month primary, Cuomo and I only shared the stage a couple of times, which occurred at campaign events supported by organized labor since we both received strong support from the unions.

In short order, I managed to put together a statewide campaign since we had to cover exponentially more territory than during the race for my senate district. Our campaign manager was Barbara Fife, who was a volunteer along with all of our campaign workers. Barbara was terrific and she brought along some enthusiastic supporters from the New Democratic Coalition where she was a key figure. She ran my campaign very well. I was impressed with her skill set. I was also grateful to my good friend Jim Capel, a political adviser and also a driver who shuttled me all around the state. Since we did not have the budget to rent a plane to crisscross the state, we drove thousands of miles from Manhattan to Buffalo and all across the state. No matter how exhausted I was from barnstorming the state by automobile, Jim got me where I needed to go. He was a godsend.

My major campaign issue was education and I had plans to improve access to higher education for Black and minority students and also to improve the quality of kindergarten to twelfth grade public school education through hiring more teachers and offering incentives to retain top educators. I positioned education investment as an economic development tool and how better schools and a better-educated citizenry would create more economic opportunities. I also visited a lot of rural communities and discussed my plans to support the agricultural sector of New York State's economy and, in particular, to help the struggling dairy industry. We received the best reception in rural areas and small upstate towns because it was a big deal when the candidate for lieutenant governor came to make a speech. To the contrary, when you show up in a large city, like New York, Buffalo, Rochester, Syracuse, or Albany, your presence garners almost no attention from the news media—because they have plenty of big-city stories to cover. On many of my stops in rural communities, they said they had not seen a Black candidate since Basil Paterson passed through in 1970 when he was the lieutenant governor running mate on the Democratic ticket with US Supreme Court Justice Arthur Goldberg.

During my campaign stops in rural upstate New York, some of my supporters in those areas made an unusual request to my campaign. They wanted campaign literature and posters without pictures. They said since my last name was McCall, voters would assume I was Irish and that would gain votes. In politics, if that works, you go with it.

We had a fundraising committee, but they always fought headwinds because Koch had already locked up a lot of the big donors. I did get some financial contributions from labor unions, but it was a tough fundraising environment. I received some nice checks from personal friends, business associates, and former clients. Ted Kheel, a prominent labor attorney, served as finance chairman. But no matter how hard we worked on raising money, we were way behind what DelBello had raised and there was nowhere near enough in our campaign account to be competitive. It was clear, based on our respective campaign war chests, that it would be an uphill battle to mount a serious challenge to DelBello.

I was able to help Cuomo cut into Koch's strong support in New York City by turning out Black voters who might have otherwise gone to Koch if I was not Cuomo's running mate. I was very upset by the Cuomo campaign's nasty exploitation of Koch's sexual identity when "Vote for Cuomo Not the Homo" signs were spotted around the city. Both Mario Cuomo and his son, Andrew, the future governor and his father's top campaign aide in the 1982 race, disavowed any involvement in creating the antigay slur signs and they condemned it. Still, it tainted Cuomo and I had always worked hard to be inclusive and supportive of the LGBTQ community—that underhanded and deplorable smear tactic bothered me deeply.

I was not the only one who was surprised that Cuomo defeated Koch in the hard-fought primary and became the Democratic nominee for governor. I felt like I had done my part to seal Cuomo's victory by turning out a strong Black vote, but I had not been so lucky as his running mate. I lost to DelBello, which I attributed in large measure to the fact that he outspent me by a large margin. I was disappointed, of course, because nobody likes to lose an election, but I put it in perspective and considered it a learning experience. I had made a lot of solid statewide contacts and my supporters praised me for running a good, strong campaign that chose dignity and decorum over any mud-slinging or dirty tricks. I was proud that I kept my campaign on the high road, I held my head high, even in defeat, and my supporters vowed they would come back and work for me whenever I decided to run again for elective office. That vote of confidence helped soften the blow of my loss to DelBello.

I had no time to lick my wounds or take a break from politics because the general election loomed and the Democrats took Cuomo's Republican opponent, Lewis E. "Lew" Lehrman, very seriously. Lehrman was a wealthy businessman who had been an investment banker and economist and had been president of the Rite Aid pharmacy chain before he stepped down from the company's executive committee in 1981 to prepare for his run against Cuomo. I was a good Democrat who signed up to support Cuomo, although I felt less than supported by him during our primary race. I moved into an office in the Cuomo campaign headquarters in Manhattan and offered my services. I was there for just a couple of weeks when Herman Daniel "Denny" Farrell Jr., the longtime Harlem assemblyman and early supporter of Cuomo, came to see me in my office accompanied by Mario's son, Andrew Cuomo. They told me they needed that space and essentially evicted me, even though I had been a loyal supporter and did not cut and run after my own election defeat. I was not happy with what I considered shabby treatment, so I retreated to my apartment, where I said I would continue to support Cuomo's bid against Lehrman. It was clear that they had no official or central role for me and I was disappointed and miffed, although they did occasionally invite me to attend campaign events and fundraising receptions. I swallowed my pride and continued to work as an unpaid volunteer on behalf of Cuomo.

As expected, it was a tight race and when Cuomo defeated Lehrman—by a narrow margin of just two percentage points—I was elated and I congratulated the governor-elect, and I felt my efforts as a loyal Democrat and a good soldier would be rewarded. I expected I would get a call from Farrell or Andrew informing me I would get a position in the Cuomo administration. I had indicated I was interested in working with Governor Cuomo. This began a period I came to call The Long Wait. I expected I would get a phone call, but the call never came. I was not being invited to join the inner circle of the Cuomo administration as I had anticipated. I felt used and abused by the Cuomo camp. I went from angry to depressed. It marked a real low point in my professional career. I had not worked since June, when I resigned my position at Channel 13 to run for lieutenant governor. That meant no paychecks for six months and I had severely depleted my savings because I had to pay for my normal living expenses and I was also paying Marci's college tuition. It was a very challenging time for me.

When Governor-elect Cuomo started announcing key appointments, I was pleased that three Black commissioners of state agencies were named. I was pleased to see the inroads Black political leaders had made, but I was also upset to find that there was nothing in it for me after all I had sacrificed and done to help Cuomo beat Koch in the primary. I had run through my savings, and I really needed a job and was getting sick and tired of waiting for the Cuomo folks to do the right thing.

It was mid-January when some angry rumblings started coming from Black ministers, who complained that I should have gotten a job in the Cuomo administration. The message got through and in late January, I got a call from Tonio Burgos in Cuomo's appointments office. He said they were going to offer me the job as commissioner of the Division of Human Rights, the one job I did not want. I felt like it was a token offer because that position was seen as the Black person's job. I also knew it was a dysfunctional office with a tremendous backlog of cases and a poor reputation for failing to resolve discrimination complaints regarding housing and employment. People were disappointed with the agency; it didn't get much attention or interest from the public or the press. To add insult to injury, the salary for the Human Rights commissionership was less than other similar agency heads—another indication of how it was regarded by the Cuomo administration.

All things considered, this was not a job offer that I found in any way appealing, but I needed a job. They appointed Liz Abzug, Bella's daughter, as deputy commissioner and Esmeralda Simmons, a brilliant lawyer and an associate of Assemblyman Al Vann, as general counsel. Abzug and Simmons were not my choices, but they were quality hires and they would at least be allies in trying to reform the agency. In the end, I had no other options. I needed a job and although this was not the position I wanted, I decided I had to take it and I intended to make the best of it. My office was on the ninetieth floor of the World Trade Center, which offered a stunning panoramic view. I also had an office in Albany. One other positive aspect was that I was able to negotiate for a job on behalf of my friend and campaign leader Jim Capel. I got him appointed assistant commissioner for financing and administration and he was pleased with the position. I felt good that I had managed to win at least that concession from Burgos and could reward Jim for his loyalty and hard work for me. I did not regret helping my friends and the people who helped get me there.

The work itself was demoralizing because everything I had been told about the Division of Human Rights beforehand turned out to be accurate. We were not getting results, there was a long backlog of cases, and the agency was not nimble enough to move quickly to resolve discrimination complaints. I managed to make inroads and to turn things around a bit by solving cases whenever possible through mediation because the court process took too long and contributed to the long backlog. I put in place mediation training for our lawyers, set up advisory councils around the state, and raised the division's profile and the public's perception of our work. I was not successful in getting any additional support from federal government programs and we got very little out of Washington and its US Equal Employment Opportunity Commission, or EEOC. President Ronald Reagan appointed Clarence Thomas as chairman of the EEOC in 1982, just as I was beginning as commissioner of the New York State Division of Human Rights. I hoped that the two of us, both Black leaders, would be able to work together and come to some sort of accommodation. I tried many avenues, but Thomas ignored me and would never agree to a meeting with me. In the end, I came to realize Thomas did not really believe in equal opportunity, and he has demonstrated that as a US Supreme Court Justice.

After two years as commissioner of the Division of Human Rights, I resigned. Despite my best efforts and new initiatives, we had failed to move the needle significantly on reforming the operation. We were not making significant progress on the case backlog and I was not professionally fulfilled. I decided it was time for me to move on and to do something else.

In an ironic twist, DelBello made headlines and surprised political observers when he announced that he was resigning from his position as Cuomo's lieutenant governor, with just two months' notice, effective February 1, 1985. DelBello did not pull punches. He said he had very little interaction with Cuomo and that he was bored with the job because the governor did not give him enough to do. He went into private business after quitting on Cuomo.

DelBello's experience, it appeared, was not much different than mine was when it came to Mario Cuomo. Essentially during our campaign, although we shared the same ticket, Cuomo went his way and I went mine. He did not know me well and did not go out of his way to get to know me. I served my function by helping to get out the Black vote for his primary against Koch and he was a pragmatic political opportunist. When I was of no more use to him, he moved on. I have no idea to this day how Mario felt about me. He was known to be something of a political loner, as DelBello found out. I definitely left state service with a conflicted feeling about Mario Cuomo, the fifty-second governor of New York, that I am not sure can ever be resolved, especially since his death on January 1, 2015. I also had an interesting and somewhat complicated relationship with his son, Andrew, who was elected the fifty-sixth governor of New York in 2011 and about whom I will have more to say in a later chapter.

Once again, not unlike my tenure in the state senate, government service had offered more disappointment than uplift. I felt like I was not using my talents to the best of my ability in my second go-round with Albany politics. I was tired of it and decided to look where I had been effective in the past, the private sector. I had done this dance before, from the public to the private sector, and back again. I knew the steps. I felt comfortable making the move because I refused to let myself stagnate or become bitter over the situation. I always had the utmost faith in my ability to land on my feet and to author my own destiny.

One reason why I felt comfortable about my next move into a new and challenging position was because I had a partner who would provide support and guidance as we faced whatever lay ahead for us.

Joyce and I married in August 1984. At that same time, we both were invited to join a group of elected officials, educators, and community leaders from New York City at a conference and tour of Israel, sponsored by the Jewish Community Relations Council of New York. I had visited Israel in 1977 with a group of Black elected officials. This would be a first visit for Joyce. We coordinated our wedding plans around this trip.

Our wedding ceremony took place at the Episcopal Cathedral of St. John the Divine in Manhattan, a historical and architectural treasure, which was also the largest cathedral in the world. James Morton, the charismatic dean of the cathedral, officiated at our ceremony. I had first worked with him in support of the cathedral's community service programs while I was in the state senate. The cathedral was in my senate district on the Upper West Side of Manhattan. In 1980, Dean Morton designated Andrew Young, Marian Wright Edelman, and myself as Fellows of the Cathedral, an honorary position in recognition of our public service and support of religious institutions and principles. I considered it a great honor.

Our wedding ceremony was attended by family and a few friends, followed by a reception. Later that evening, as newlyweds, we boarded a flight to Israel.

Our group met with Israeli and Palestinian leaders and visited the extraordinary Jewish, Christian, and Muslim holy sites. These visits are inspiring. They make history come alive. They are powerful places that have shaped our faith, our history, and our culture.

The trip to Israel also solidified my political and personal relationships with two influential elected officials: Congressmen Major Owens and Chuck Schumer. Owens, who represented Brooklyn, was a friend from when we had served together in the state senate and we enjoyed a close relationship during his long and distinguished career in Congress. We were joined by Schumer, a young member of Congress from Brooklyn, and his wife, Iris. Our time together on that trip fostered a strong friendship and deep political connection. I supported all of Chuck's political contests and he supported mine. His endorsement in my Democratic gubernatorial primary race against Andrew Cuomo was very significant.

I appreciate Chuck Schumer's vital role in the US Senate as a national leader shaping a diverse, inclusive, and progressive democratic society.

After five days of tours, meetings, and networking in Israel, Joyce and I departed for our actual planned honeymoon in Greece and Paris. Those were memorable, happy days together in a magical place that we will always cherish.

Chapter 15

The Private Sector

O ne thing I always managed to do, even in disappointing and unfulfilling work situations, was to make good friends and build up my strong network of professional colleagues. That is how it was with Howard Nolan. He and I were both Democrats elected to the New York State Senate in the same year, 1975. We spent time together at the Saratoga Race Course because he owned thoroughbreds and it was fun to be there as his guest and to soak up his knowledge of the thoroughbred racing industry. We also socialized and were supportive colleagues in legislative battles. Howard was a successful attorney, he owned real estate and was a savvy businessman who had acquired wealth. I had confided in Howard about my dissatisfaction with the position I was appointed to in the Cuomo administration and he was sympathetic with my decision to quit after two years. He told me he would keep his ears open for opportunities and, good friend that he was, Howard proved true to his word.

Howard was a major client of Citibank and at a golf outing he was paired with Citibank chairman John Reed. Howard brought up my name during the round of golf and extolled my attributes and skills. He said my contacts in state government in Albany, among powerful Black political leaders in New York City, and international experience with my trips to South Africa as a UN ambassador might be an asset to Citibank. After Howard talked me up on the golf course, John Reed arranged a meeting at Citibank headquarters in New York. I found Reed to be a very interesting and astute business leader and we had a good discussion about South Africa and the growing movement to divest from the country in order to protest its apartheid policy. Citibank had banking assets and operations in South Africa, which we discussed. Our meeting ended very favorably and Chairman Reed indicated that a job offer would be forthcoming.

I was no stranger to moving easily from the public sector to the private sector and this seemed like another one of those moments where I was willing to try a new endeavor and see where this unexpected opportunity might lead. I was forty-nine years old, still young enough to take some career risks and to recover if it did not work out. In the end, I decided there were no compelling reasons for me to turn down a position with a prestigious international financial institution such as Citibank. It seemed like a way to round out my career portfolio and I agreed to join the team at Citibank. I was put into contact with two leading executives to determine what job might be best suited to my skill set. I met with Rick Braddock, who was in charge of retail operations, bank branches, and real estate, and also Charlie Long, who handled government relations and who was responsible for Citibank's operations in South Africa.

After our meeting, it was decided I should start out on Braddock's team and oversee some branches, study loan units, and get a better sense of the Citibank culture and to observe its financial operations from the inside. After a number of months in that role, they said I would transition to government relations with a focus on states where Citibank had no presence and we needed to seek permission to operate. Braddock was a fellow Dartmouth graduate and we shared a love of New York City. I really enjoyed working for Rick, but after about one year, I was moved to government relations under Long. I had started working out of a regional office in Queens, but with this new assignment, my office moved to Citibank headquarters on Park Avenue in Manhattan and the location alone felt like a promotion. I could not complain about the compensation, which was roughly double what I had made during my best year's salary in the public sector.

It was clear from my previous meetings with Charlie Long that I had some work to do to bring him around to my position, which was that the South African regime and its policy of apartheid was blatantly racist and indefensible and that it must be changed. My feeling was that apartheid's days were numbered as the movement to force companies to divest took root and spread aggressively. But Charlie and most other top executives at Citibank remained committed to their investments in South Africa because they were profitable operations and they made sense from a purely business standpoint. It would be my role to inject the metric of racial inequity as a way of assessing Citibank's financial commitments in South Africa, and its government system, which was built upon a philosophy of white supremacy and oppression of the Black majority. I brought up my deep concerns about apartheid with Chairman Reed, and he responded with transparency and indicated that he and the Citibank board were open to at least listening to the arguments of the anti-apartheid movement and that they might be open to a gradual divestment.

During the interim weeks before I joined Citibank, I was still advocating for change in South Africa and working on behalf of TransAfrica. The organization sponsored a luncheon for Bishop Desmond Tutu of South Africa, the internationally renowned human rights activist and one of the most prominent figures in the anti-apartheid movement. Bishop Tutu was a South African Anglican bishop and later archbishop who received the Nobel Peace Prize in 1984 for his work opposing apartheid in South Africa. I was seated next to Bishop Tutu and he was warm and funny, with a warm laugh. He asked me about my work, and I said I was about to join Citibank and that I would encourage them to change their relationship with South Africa. He seemed very interested, said he would like to meet with Citibank officials, and asked if I could set up a meeting. I arranged for a lunch with Chairman John Reed, Charlie Long, Bishop Tutu, and myself the following week in Manhattan. It was a private meeting at the Waldorf-Astoria Hotel. The Citibank officials did not want the press learning that they had met with Tutu, so it was kept below the radar.

Bishop Tutu was a very effective and persuasive speaker and he was at his most forceful when he was talking about the moral failing and the social and racial injustice created by the apartheid system. They had not heard such forceful and authoritative views before on the racist system in place in South Africa. The Citibank brass left the secret lunch somewhat softened and perhaps swayed by Bishop Tutu's heartfelt condemnation of apartheid. I got a call from Charlie Long a few days later and he was not pleased. He said that Bishop Tutu had spoken publicly about the meeting with Citibank upon his return to South Africa and it put unwanted strain on the delicate negotiations. I felt that they were impressed that I could make the lunch with Bishop Tutu happen, but I am sure they were disappointed with the breach of confidentiality.

I liked my new work in government relations, particularly learning the arcane banking laws and how each state had separate regulations when it came to banking. Since Citibank was expanding into new states across the United States, this kept me busy as I had to become a quick study of the variations of banking laws in each state in which we planned to open branches. I worked with a platoon of lobbyists, with a separate unit for each of the fifteen states we were eyeing. My position overseeing state government relations meant that I traveled frequently to be in touch with our lobbyists and state officials. I worked hard and we started getting results. We eventually succeeded in helping to change banking regulation to a uniform national banking code instead of each state making their own laws. That was a major win for Citibank.

I had also negotiated Citibank's approval of allowing me to continue my public service, since the bank saw this as good exposure for them and a net gain. I recalled a class in government at Dartmouth and a guest speaker, Austin Tobin, the impressive executive director of the Port Authority of New York and New Jersey.

The Port Authority is a unique governmental agency created by Congress that permits the transportation infrastructure of two states to be managed by a single agency. It operates all the international airports in New York and New Jersey, all the bridges and tunnels connecting the two states, and also manages economic development projects in both states. Tobin was an advocate for regional governmental agencies in order to effectively manage activities that transcend the boundaries of a single state.

In the case of the Port Authority, the governors of New York and New Jersey each get six appointments to the Board of Commissioners that oversees the system. I learned that there was an opening for a Port Authority commissioner from New York and after I cleared it with Charlie Long, I let Governor Mario Cuomo's appointments office know that I was interested. I was appointed by Cuomo and became the first Black commissioner on the Port Authority Board from New York. It helped me feel better about the strained relationship I had with Mario after the lack of attention he gave me when I was his running mate and that my loyalty to him and hard work during the campaign was not rewarded with a significant position in his administration.

I was just learning how the Port Authority operated when Governor Cuomo called me to register his displeasure at what he considered an exorbitant salary of $160,000 offered to Steve Berger, who had been tapped as Peter Goldmark's successor as Port Authority executive director. It was not a lavish salary in the private sector, but Mario had a hardline stance when it came to compensation for public servants. He believed a public-sector salary should be much lower than the private sector because public service was a calling and demanded a financial sacrifice because it was the taxpayers' money. Cuomo was quite upset when he called me and railed at the $160,000 proposed salary, which also was slightly more than he earned as governor at the time. I listened to the governor intently and with respect. And then I joined a near-unanimous decision by the Board of Commissioners and voted to pay Berger $160,000. I enjoyed my board work with the Port Authority, which was not paid, and I held that position for six years while working at Citibank—all the while with the blessing of my bosses.

The Reverend Jesse Jackson, the noted civil rights leader and close associate of Dr. Martin Luther King Jr., declared his candidacy for president in the 1988 campaign, which became a suddenly serious situation to weigh for myself and all Black government officials. Jackson also ran in 1984, but he did not gain much traction. Still, it was historic for a Black man to run for the highest office in the land and he was a legitimate candidate because of his considerable talents, his charismatic quality, and his strong record as a civil rights leader. My mentor Percy Sutton threw his support behind Jackson's candidacy and he asked me to help build a statewide organization to assist Jackson's candidacy. Percy also got Arthur Eve and Al Vann to join us. My role was as Jackson's state finance chairman and I ended up going to Atlanta to attend the Democratic National Convention, my first, as a Jackson delegate. The Omni Coliseum was packed and the atmosphere was electric because Jackson had challenged front-runner Michael

Dukakis of Massachusetts in every state and he took Dukakis all the way to the final primary in California before Dukakis edged him in delegates. Jackson generated a lot of excitement with his stump speech of wanting to create a "Rainbow Coalition" of African Americans, Hispanics, Asian Americans, Middle Eastern Americans, Native Americans, small farmers, the poor and working class, and LGBTQ people. He became a champion of the underclass and the oppressed and his message of unity and lifting up the downtrodden resonated widely as Jackson ended up winning 6.9 million votes, seven primaries, and four caucuses. I was impressed with Jackson, based on several meetings and listening to his powerful speeches. I was proud to cast my vote for Jesse Jackson at the Atlanta convention. His results proved that a Black candidate could compete and hold his or her own in a campaign for the highest political office. Jackson ended up beating out the veteran political candidates Dick Gephardt, Joe Biden, and Al Gore. His impressive showing was a watershed moment for Black pride.

The Jackson presidential run was thrilling and it gave me a lift. Meanwhile, at Citibank, I was doing well and felt respected and settled. It was 1990 and I felt like I had made the right move to return to the private sector. I was invited to a dinner by two friends, Charlayne Hunter-Gault and her husband, Ron Gault. In 1961, Charlayne Hunter integrated the University of Georgia with another student, Hamilton Holmes. They sued the university for discrimination and they won. They broke the color barrier and the court forced university officials to admit them. Charlayne majored in journalism and moved from a television station in Washington, DC, to the *New York Times*, where she covered the urban Black community as a metropolitan reporter. She worked for nearly two decades as an award-winning correspondent for *The MacNeil/Lehrer Report*. Charlayne's husband, Ron, had worked for the Civil Rights Division of the United States Department of Justice and the Ford Foundation before he became a banking executive. They were a power couple and they used their positions to advocate for divestment in South Africa. I felt energized, empowered, and optimistic when I met with them because they had so much passion and energy for making sure that the long arc of the moral universe bent toward racial justice in South Africa.

The dinner I attended was with Thabo Mbeki, a powerful South African leader who had served as an ambassador and organizer of Nelson Mandela's African National Congress. When the ANC was banned, Mandela and the leadership decided it would be best for Mbeki to go into exile and in 1962 Mbeki made a daring escape with a group of friends, traveling in a minibus disguised as a soccer team. He was an outspoken opponent of apartheid while in exile in England and he developed global contacts whom he enlisted in his long struggle for divestment in South Africa. We had a very interesting discussion at dinner with Mbeki, whom I found to be eloquent and sophisticated, with a diplomatic style that commanded respect and attention. In 1989, F. W. de Klerk replaced P. W. Botha as South African president following Botha's stroke. De Klerk took the dramatic step of removing the ban on the militant Black opposition groups, including the ANC, led by Mbeki in exile, and imprisoned leader Nelson Mandela. De Klerk's National Party began to negotiate with the ANC and preparations for the first democratic elections took four years before they were finally held in 1994.

For context, in the 1990 New York City mayoral election, David Dinkins defeated Ed Koch and became New York's first Black mayor. Joyce and I had strongly supported David and we were thrilled by his victory. At the dinner, we expected Mbeki to say he planned to urge Dinkins to impose sanctions on New York City banks doing business in South Africa. We were surprised when Mbeki said he was optimistic about a major change in South Africa just underway that would eventually bring about democratic rule and open the door for the African National Congress, a once-banned Black political organization, to begin to prepare to play a governing role in the new South Africa free of apartheid.

Mbeki discussed how there would be a great need in this emerging South Africa for a significant number of educated Black men and women to fill positions in private corporations and government agencies. There was an immediate need to begin to create a pipeline of training in order to prepare young people to seize the new opportunities and leadership roles in the new South Africa. Mbeki made a proposal that Dinkins should arrange for New York companies to provide training for Black

South African professionals in order to be ready when leadership positions opened up to them.

It was an exciting idea that we heard for the first time that evening as Mbeki sketched it out in his discussion. I sat with Charlayne and Ron at their dining room table with a future president of South Africa—and none of us, including the guest of honor, had an idea at that time that we would one day address him as President Mbeki. That dinner conversation planted the seeds for what would become a formal professional training project called the United States and South Africa Professional Development Program. The plan called for companies based in New York City to offer six-month internships to South African emerging executives. The American companies would pay for the interns' lodging and meals at International House, a residence affiliated with Columbia University. In turn, the South African companies would continue to pay the salaries and travel costs of these young men and women executives during their New York internship, so that they could continue to support their families in South Africa.

Based on our dinner conversation with Mbeki and the program he sketched out, Ron and I presented the international exchange proposal to Mayor Dinkins. He immediately responded positively, agreed to all the elements as outlined, and said he would place no restrictions on the companies while the program was in progress. Ron and I also reached out to a coalition of government relations executives who represented companies concerned about divestment in South Africa. Ron and I next traveled to South Africa to solicit companies there to participate in this international exchange and we received many positive responses and commitments to get involved.

At this time, Ron was an executive for an investment firm, First Boston, and he had a lot of contacts in the financial industry. Those we approached saw this, as we did, as a win-win situation with no restrictions or obstacles placed on their businesses. There was a growing recognition that significant changes were coming to South Africa and that there were harbingers that the end of the racist system of apartheid was just ahead. There was also consensus that this opportunity would represent positive public relations for the participating companies and progressive firms wanted to be known as contributors to social change. The business leaders we approached also understood the need to develop a pipeline of talent, that these interns would be in positions of influence in the near future and making decisions that would affect their industries and the bottom line for companies.

Ron and I worked hard to get solid corporate buy-in and we built a strong program rather quickly. From 1992 to 1996, a total of 106 men and women from South Africa came to New York City and completed the program. There were twenty-six companies participating, including Citibank, Chase Bank, Consolidated Edison, IBM, Goldman Sachs—who contributed $2 million to the program and also sent Black executives to mentor the South African participants. On the South African side, a total of thirty companies took part.

We had a process for evaluating the program and the participants said it gave them confidence and new skills, and helped to advance their careers. We kept in touch when they returned to South Africa and they told us they were given greater responsibilities, and several informed us that they had received promotions. Moreover, several of those graduates of the program hold important positions in South Africa today, including a government minister, senior bank executives, CEOs of government agencies, and successful entrepreneurs.

As the program grew and advanced and I took on new responsibilities, Ron assumed greater leadership of the program, along with Nomsa Daniels, a young South African woman who had completed her studies at Hunter College of the City University of New York. Eventually, she was appointed executive director.

My wife Joyce made a significant contribution to the program. She was recruited by Joseph Murphy, chancellor of City University of New York, to serve as assistant to the chancellor and she was soon promoted to vice chancellor for student affairs for the entire CUNY system. Joyce's career path shifted in 1991 following racial discord at Baruch College that led to the president's resignation, and Joyce was appointed interim president while a national search for a new president was conducted. Joyce created a Saturday academic program for the South African interns, led by faculty from Baruch College's business school—a helpful addition.

At this time, Joyce left her position as interim president at Baruch College and returned to her position in the Chancellor's Office at the City University of New York. When David Dinkins's deputy mayor Bill Lynch left his position, the mayor called Joyce and offered the job to her. She decided she could not turn David down. She took a leave from CUNY, accepted the offer, and became Deputy Mayor for Government and Community Relations. It was Joyce's first time in government service and it was a difficult transition, although she ended up enjoying her time on David Dinkins's staff and the challenge of the work.

Not long after that, David reached out to me because he faced a crisis at the New York City Board of Education, and he asked if I could help. I also succumbed and could not turn David down. The mayor got two appointments on the seven-member board and the other five were appointed by the borough presidents. A Republican on the board, Michael Petrides, was a politician from Staten Island and an associate of Rudy Giuliani, who made a name for himself as the federal prosecutor who took down some Mafia bosses in the 1980s. He was gearing up for a challenge to David for the mayoral seat, even as David was still in the first year of his first term. Petrides got support from Ninfa Segarra, who gained popularity for leading the fight in championing Latino rights and she was appointed in 1990 to the Board of Education by Freddie Ferrer, Bronx borough president. Segarra became a problem. She seemed to have no party loyalty and, although she was a Democratic appointee, she soon began siding more with Republicans Petrides and Giuliani. She made a connection with Petrides and the two of them formed a league of opposition and they attacked any substantive reforms David tried to work through the Board of Education. In fact, Petrides and Segarra were extremely obstinate and disruptive in meetings and ushered in a very tumultuous period for the board. The president was losing control of the board, and the mayor could no longer advance his educational agenda through the board as he and previous mayors had done in the past.

David called me greatly concerned about the troubled state of affairs at the Board of Education. He said he needed a strong ally running the board and asked if I could help. My term at the Port Authority had ended and this represented a new opportunity. I called Rick Braddock, my boss at Citibank, laid out the situation, and told him I really wanted to be of service to Mayor Dinkins. I said being president of the Board of Education would be a much greater commitment of my time and would take away from the hours I could put in at Citibank. Rick understood what was at stake politically and he gave me generous leave time so that I spent half of my time on Citibank business and the other half handling Board of Education duties. There were plenty of challenges facing the board, including education funding, getting the cooperation of board members, and agreeing on operational changes. It was a long and difficult two years, but I felt that I had done my part to stabilize the dysfunction on the board and to prove my loyalty and commitment to the administration of Mayor David Dinkins. As a Black man, I felt that it was important to support his agenda because he would be judged harshly as the first Black person to hold the office.

Another very challenging issue we tackled on the Board of Education was mental health and sex education programs. It took some heated debate and a series of contentious sessions, but we finally agreed to pass a policy that would allow students to get condoms from medical professionals at public high schools as a way of halting unwanted teen pregnancies, halting the spread of sexually transmitted diseases, and also being proactive in trying to stem the deadly tide of AIDS. I was also proud that I played a large role when it came to increasing diversity among the schools' teachers and administrative staff, and we hired more minority principals and district supervisors than ever before. We made a big push and achieved some success in getting parents more engaged in their child's education. Eventually, after David finished his single term as mayor, the Board of Education ceased to exist. It was allowed to dissolve and to be replaced with the New York City Department of Education, reporting to the mayor, which is what exists today.

As I was preparing to step down from the Board of Education after two years of service, something unexpected happened. New York State Comptroller Edward V. "Ned" Regan, a Republican, who was first elected in 1979, announced that he was resigning after fourteen years in the comptroller's post. It was a shocking development because Regan knew the job was his for as long as he wanted it. Prior to serving as comptroller, he had been a Buffalo city councilman and Erie County executive. He was not leaving the state comptroller's post for a different position and he never explained his sudden departure. He had achieved mixed results as comptroller and had been criticized for some of his policies, including refusing to divest from South Africa over the issue of apartheid and other issues. Even after more than two decades as comptroller, he remained something of an enigma. What I knew was that his resignation caught my attention and I weighed whether I wanted to put myself in position to become Regan's successor.

I had stayed at Citibank for nine years, longer than I expected, and it was the longest period of time I had spent in any single job throughout my career. They had been a kind and generous employer, always supported my outside activities, gave me half-time leave when I was taking charge of the troubled Board of Education, and, throughout my tenure there, they had been supportive and accommodating. I felt that I had done good work, had learned a lot, but the pull of elected office and getting back into the political game became a strong force drawing me back. I considered my greatest accomplishment at Citibank was helping convince the bank to divest from South Africa. I had a lot of help in making that happen, but I felt that my voice was one of the loudest and strongest in the divestment movement among the Citibank leadership.

President F. W. de Klerk's gradual dismantling of apartheid progressed from lifting the ban on the African National Congress to suspending executions to ordering the release of political prisoner and anti-apartheid leader Nelson Mandela in the winter of 1990. On February 11, 1990, after twenty-seven years of imprisonment, Mandela was released and apartheid was over. Joyce and I traveled to South Africa with Charlie Long, who had been the leader of Citibank's business ventures in South Africa. He and Citibank had opposed divestment until it became clear that there would be a new South Africa. Long had actually never visited South Africa and Joyce and I introduced him to Mbeki and other emerging leaders who would be influential members of the new government. Long wanted to meet those people because Citibank planned not only to continue its financial services in the country, but to expand its business operations in South Africa's new era of openness and racial reckoning. After sessions we set up with the emerging leaders, Long—a conservative Republican—reported that his most interesting and productive meeting was with Chris Hani, the leader of the South African Communist Party.

Hani was charming, smart, passionate, and outspoken about his vision for a free South Africa. He enjoyed a reputation as a heroic leader in the Black community's long struggle for freedom. Hani received military training in the Soviet Union, fought in wars in Zimbabwe and Rhodesia, and led the armed wing of the ANC before being forced into exile during the apartheid era. He also had worked as a clerk for a law firm and was a dynamic force who clearly would have been an important leader in the new government. Hani was assassinated by two Afrikaners on April 10, 1993, in the driveway of his home in a suburb of Boksburg. The killing was a signal that violent opposition to a new regime would continue and there were fears the country would erupt in violence. Mandela addressed the nation and appealed for calm in a now-famous speech that had the gravitas of a president, even though Mandela would not become president until May 10, 1994.

That trip to South Africa with Joyce and Charlie Long felt like the end of an era for me personally, even beyond the dismantling of apartheid. I had a very good run of nine years at Citibank, which helped restore financial stability for Joyce and myself after I had given up a lot of earning power in various unpaid public service and political campaign positions. But more importantly, I had been able to manage my personal moral convictions as a Black man and to maneuver successfully in a white corporate structure. I had been able to raise the issue of systemic racism in South Africa, to convey my perspective, and to convince the corporation to adopt my position. That was an outcome that gave me lasting satisfaction and sense of accomplishment. I carried it with me as I prepared, once again, to make a shift from the private to the public sector.

Chapter 16

New York State Comptroller

The question that hung in the air that I had to answer for friends and associates, as well as for myself, was this: Why would I give up a satisfying and lucrative position at Citibank for the uncertainty of running for a political office after I had my heart broken and spirit defeated by dysfunctional Albany? I must concede that I could not articulate an immediate and overwhelmingly convincing argument for the choice I was about to make. Then again, one might say I had made career decisions impulsively in the past and this time was no different.

I could have remained at Citibank and settled into a comfortable, well-compensated position as a senior executive. But I had been with Citibank for nine years, I had accomplished more than I had hoped, and there was a certain sense of routine and sameness that had set in. I had stayed with Citibank longer than any other job in my career at that point and at fifty-eight years old, I felt like sixty was just around the corner and I wanted a new challenge and to push myself for at least one more professional test of my talents and skill set before I began that slow descent into retirement age. I also was never interested in just coasting and Citibank was starting to feel like gliding easily without having to pedal fast or push against any headwinds.

What made this rare opportunity for statewide elective office especially appealing was that I could throw my hat into the ring for the New York State Comptroller opening without the arduous grind and crushing expense of running a statewide political campaign, which I had learned from experience could bankrupt a person both financially and emotionally. Regan, the top-ranking Republican in state government, had quit so abruptly on February 1993 that he stunned his staff and Capitol insiders, and also triggered a special appointment process involving a vote by state legislators rather than a traditional election by registered voters. It would be up to the state legislature, with the overwhelmingly Democratic assembly and the senate, which was narrowly controlled by Republicans, to select Regan's successor.

The state constitution stipulated that the 211 members of the legislature, sitting in a joint session, would select someone to fill the comptroller's unexpired term. Because 127 of the 211 lawmakers at the time were Democrats, the election of a Democrat was essentially certain. This major political advantage made Assembly Speaker Saul Weprin the deciding factor, since the Queens Democrat held sway over 101 Democrats in the majority in his house. Democratic governor Mario M. Cuomo, also of Queens, expected to run for reelection in 1994, would have major influence in the decision because he would be looking for a comptroller who could help him pull Democratic votes onto his ticket in the statewide elections.

Regan announced he would step down at the end of April 1993, although his term ran through the end of 1994. His official statement at a news conference in Manhattan did not fully explain Regan's reasoning as to why he would quit his job in the middle of his term. Moreover, Regan, at age sixty-two, was leaving the powerful comptroller post for a relatively minor and obscure position, president of the Jerome Levy Economics Institute based at Bard College at Annandale-on-Hudson, New York. The nonpartisan research center was founded in 1986 and sponsored economic conferences and scholarly papers, supported scholars-in-residence, and issued economic forecasts. Regan had served on the advisory board for two years and the institute's founder, Leon Levy, was a contributor to Regan's comptroller campaigns.

While Regan's sudden departure caused a lot of head-scratching around the Capitol, would-be candidates wasted no time in declaring their candidacies for comptroller. Those who jumped into the race the same day as Regan's announcement included Carol Bellamy, the former New

York City Council president who ran against Regan in 1990 and nearly won. She would be a formidable candidate, and she was the first one to get out front by calling an afternoon news conference in Manhattan to declare her candidacy. State Senate Minority Leader Manfred Ohrenstein, a Manhattan Democrat, gave her a strong endorsement. What came next caught me off guard, but also did not surprise me because Bellamy was fast and aggressive and laser-focused. Mayor David Dinkins also said publicly that he would support Carol Bellamy for comptroller.

Bronx Democratic assemblyman G. Oliver Koppell said he was considering the race. Assemblyman Alan G. Hevesi, a Queens Democrat, said he planned to continue to vie for the New York City comptroller's position and would not switch to the state comptroller's opening.

I was not ready to make a final decision and had indicated to my inner circle that I was seriously considering contending for the seat. Several prominent Black legislators, led by my friends, Assemblymen Clarence Norman Jr. and Albert Vann, both from Brooklyn, held a news conference in Albany to say they demanded a minority candidate to be selected for the first time to a statewide office. They said they had unified behind me as their first choice, they would push for a McCall appointment, and they cited my work as a state senator, at Citibank, and as the current president of the New York City Board of Education. I was flattered by them taking this initiative, but I was not yet ready to declare myself all in and I instructed the Board of Education spokeswoman, Linda Scott, to respond to reporters by saying I had not yet made a final decision on whether I would seek the job. This bought me a little more time, but I could not use this delaying tactic for very long or it would backfire. I wanted to spend a little while longer consulting with Joyce, my family, and my closest friends and political advisers, although I knew which way I was leaning.

I was drawn to the office, formally known as the Office of Audit and Control, for a variety of reasons. The state comptroller was one of just four statewide elected officials in New York State, alongside the governor, lieutenant governor, and attorney general. I also felt my job experience and skill set aligned well with the requirements of the state's chief fiscal officer, who approves all state contracts, pays all state expenditures, and oversees the audits of public entities within New York, including towns and cities. One of the most important roles for the state comptroller is to serve as the sole trustee of the New York State Common Retirement Fund—commonly referred to as the State Pension Fund—for all present and future state retirees. No other state, to my knowledge, placed so much trust and responsibility in the hands of its comptroller. Today, the total value of the state pension fund is about $200 billion, up from about $60 billion in 1993.

The comptroller position has a storied history from the earliest days of the republic. New York State's first comptroller was Comfort Sands, who took office on July 24, 1776, and left office on March 23, 1782. The title in that era was auditor-general. In previous centuries, the position was seen as a stepping-stone to higher office, such as governor, US senator, or the US Supreme Court. Political luminaries held the position, including Millard Filmore in 1848, the first comptroller by general ballot, who went on to become the thirteenth president of the United States. In the modern era, the legendary comptroller was Arthur Levitt Sr., a Brooklyn Democrat and World War I veteran, who was first elected comptroller in 1955 and held the office for six terms until 1978—a total of twenty-four years, the longest-serving comptroller in state history. I met Arthur once, not long before he died in 1980, and he was regarded as a sage of Albany. He was given a lot of credit for creating an atmosphere of reverence for the powerful role of comptroller and the office's extraordinary fiscal responsibilities. I learned in my conversation with him that he served on the New York State Board of Education for two years just before he was elected state comptroller. Now, I was contemplating trying to make a similar move, from the New York City Board of Education to comptroller, all because Ned Regan suddenly and surprisingly stepped down from a position that he likely could have held for a couple more four-year terms since he was well regarded and he won reelection fairly easily.

After I spent time soul-searching and consulting with my family and closest advisers, I decided that I would jump in to the campaign for comptroller. I felt I had an advantage in the sense that it was clear that the majority Democrats in the legislature and Assembly Speaker Saul Weprin in particular would end up making the final decision. From my two terms in the state senate, I had forged strong and relationships with many Democratic lawmakers in both the senate and assembly, especially among the Black and Puerto Rican Caucus in which I was active. I also realized that I could not afford to appear to waver or delay, because Carol Bellamy was already in campaign overdrive from day one. I had served with her in the state senate and I knew she would be a formidable challenger. Carol, like me, was out of politics at the moment and working for a bank so we had similar qualifications.

Even before I could make a public announcement, I received two important phone calls urging me to run, one from Denny Farrell, chair of the Banks Committee in the assembly, and the other from Clarence Norman Jr., longtime state assemblyman and chairman of the Kings County Democratic Party. They were two of the state's most influential Black leaders and they pledged their full support of my candidacy. I realized it would be a hard-fought race with candidates who would break various barriers for the Office of Comptroller: Bellamy running as the first woman who entered the race; Fernando "Freddy" Ferrer running as the first Latino; Joel Giambra of Buffalo running as a western New Yorker; and myself running as the first Black candidate vying for statewide elected office.

I scheduled a news conference and declared my candidacy in New York and Albany, only to find at several turns that Carol Bellamy had beat me to the punch. I had known Saul Weprin tangentially and also his son, David Weprin, a banker. But by the time I reached out to the Weprins, the son informed me that he had already endorsed Bellamy. I was pleased to learn that Saul's wife, Sylvia Weprin, an educator who had worked with me at the Board of Elections, had pledged to back me. So, it seemed, the Weprins were a household divided and the biggest question, the one that would decide our political futures, was which way was Saul Weprin leaning: Bellamy or McCall?

It was a very interesting and unusual campaign, unlike any other I had participated in. It was a low-key and brief venture that lasted less than two months, late February to early April. I put together a campaign committee, we had a few receptions and fundraisers and raised some money for my candidacy, but there were no TV or radio advertisements and no marketing per se because the public was not voting and we were not trying to persuade the electorate. Rather, it was the majority Democratic lawmakers we needed to persuade. Each week, I'd go up to Albany and spend a couple of days, systematically visiting the offices of legislators in the Legislative Office and the Capitol. Whenever I managed to buttonhole an assembly member or senator, I would make my case on why I was the best candidate for comptroller and invariably they would ask: "If you become comptroller, will my per diem be processed on time?" That was the most common comment and complaint I got, that the per diem checks for legislators—less than $100 to cover daily meals and lodging while they were in session in Albany—were routinely late in being sent out. I promised that if I was selected as comptroller, I would make sure that their per diem checks would be issued in a timely manner.

I made a strategic hire when I brought Lisa Linden on board, a highly respected media strategist and political campaign public relations executive with the firm Linden Altschuler & Kaplan, later known as the LAKPR Group. She was a young and energetic protégé of Howard Rubenstein, one of the top PR executives in New York. Linden was interested in working on political campaigns and Rubenstein did not do political work, so she left to start her own firm. She did some outstanding work on the unorthodox campaign I waged for comptroller.

One of our biggest wins was receiving the endorsement of the *New York Times*, which was very influential and helped me catch up to Carol Bellamy. Two important developments followed. Sheldon Silver, chair of the powerful Assembly Ways and Means Committee and the future assembly speaker who was sent to prison in 2020 in a corruption scandal, asked all four candidates to come to Albany to make a presentation in front of his committee. My campaign team and I prepared a binder that highlighted my pertinent professional experience and laid out my goals and plans for the Comptroller's Office. I also did a lot of prep work with the help of an advisory group of Wall Street executives. Wanda Henton, Bill Hayden, Jake Walthour, Glen Sergeon, and Joel Moser advised me and walked me through topics Silver's committee members might ask me and helped me become well versed in front-burner issues confronting the comptroller. I felt relaxed and confident in front of Silver and his committee. I made what I felt was a very solid and convincing presentation before the committee and I left each member with the McCall binder of accomplishments and well-organized strategies for the office going forward.

It was exactly what was called for, because I won over the legislators and Speaker Weprin, and I was officially informed that I had the job. I was sworn in on May 7, 1993, as the fifty-ninth comptroller of the state of New York since the position was established in 1776. It had all happened so quickly and now it was starting to sink in that I had just made history as the first Black person to serve as comptroller in more than two hundred years of the state's history. I celebrated very briefly and got right down to work.

My first task was to build a team of competent people. I had the power to keep people who were working with Regan or to replace them with my own people. I decided to keep John Hull in his role as chief investment officer, which he had held under Levitt and Regan. It was a critical position and everyone I spoke with praised Hull as an outstanding public servant and a highly skilled fiscal officer. I also thought it was important to show that I was not beholden to party status since he was a Republican. Retaining John Hull also sent a strong signal to Wall Street and the investment community that I valued stability and continuity, traits that were important to investors. I called John personally and asked him to stay. He was grateful for the call and agreed to continue as chief investment officer.

Next, I hired Comer Coppie as first deputy comptroller, essentially a workhorse who runs day-to-day operations. Comer had served as senior assistant postmaster general of the US Postal Service and also as budget director under Washington, DC, mayor Walter E. Washington. Comer was extremely well organized and a detail person who would stay on top of even the smallest issues as my first deputy. I also needed a communications director and I hired Steve Greenberg, whom I had known from my time in the senate and who was a highly regarded veteran of the state assembly and of many Democratic political campaigns. It was also imperative to me that my inner circle reflect the diversity and inclusion that I valued, and I hired Paula Chester, a very talented Black woman, who had been a senior executive in the New York City Comptroller's Office and who would serve as my chief counsel.

I had barely unpacked boxes in my New York and Albany offices when early challenges arose. A group of activists led by state employee labor unions and retiree organizations mounted a challenge against the comptroller's traditional role as the sole trustee of the state pension fund, which is one of the largest in the country with roughly one million members, retirees, and beneficiaries. Sensing a vacuum of power after Regan's hasty departure and the fact that I had not even had a chance to get acclimated and to meet my staff, they pushed an idea of having a pension fund committee to make investment decisions rather than having the fate of tens of billions of dollars resting entirely on the Office of the Comptroller. I had our staff do some research and made the case that the state pension fund had been highly regarded under the sole trustee system, was well funded, and earned excellent returns that outperformed other similar large funds. Compared to the New York City Pension Fund, which is controlled by five boards and is underfunded and underperforming, the state pension fund was a model of transparency and efficiency. I also received strong backing from Arthur Levitt Jr., the longtime comptroller's son, who at the time was chairman of United States Securities and Exchange Commission, the SEC, and someone held in high regard by Wall Street. He became a vocal supporter of the sole trustee model, which his father had endeavored to keep intact. In the end, despite some rocky early weeks from the activist reformers, we weathered the challenge and as comptroller, I remained the sole trustee of the state pension fund.

That was an early win that set a tone of my independence and reputation as a strong guardian of the state pension fund at a time when state operations were under financial strain and both Governor Mario Cuomo and the state legislature were searching for an influx of revenue to fill a deficit in order to balance the state budget. They attempted an old Albany tradition of trying to raid the state pension fund. It was true that the state was experiencing deep red ink, but there was also a lot of waste and excessive spending that could have been trimmed instead of dipping into the future pension checks of dedicated public servants. I pushed back and reiterated the solemn vow I took as the sole trustee to protect the state pension fund. At the same time, I was called upon to make another annual announcement by the Office of Comptroller, an actuarial statement showing how much New York State contributes to the pension fund. We hired outside actuaries who crunched the numbers and determined the amount that the state should deposit in order to keep the fund financially sound. The governor and the legislature got their own actuaries, separate from ours, and they determined that their contribution in 1993 should be reduced from approximately $420 million to $3.1 million. It was an outrageous and egregious raid on the pension fund masquerading as mathematics. I immediately declared that their accounting was erroneous and indefensible and I also announced that the Office of the Comptroller would be suing the Office of the Governor—Democrat versus Democrat—because we would not agree to their actuarial assessment and planned to challenge it in court.

We retained the law firm Paul Weiss, which specialized in financial and pension matters, and we also had the advantage that the retirees we served included all the judges and retired judges across the state who had benefited from strong performance and excellent returns on the fund—which in turn allowed for increases in their pension checks. "Do you think we can win this?" one of my staff members asked me in confidence. I reiterated the fact that every judge and retired judge would be on our side. In the end, we received a unanimous decision from the Court of Appeals, the state's highest court, which affirmed our position and the numbers our actuaries had determined. It was a powerful victory and, while it did not endear me to Governor Mario Cuomo, it established myself and our office as fiercely independent and that we would stand up to attempts to tap into money earmarked for state employee retirees.

The next major provocation came following the New York City mayoral election of 1994, when David Dinkins was defeated by Rudy Giuliani and I lost my friend and strong ally in Gracie Mansion. Instead, I now had to attempt to get along with a hard-nosed and aggressive Republican, a brash former prosecutor whom I did not know well and with whom I had only had a few brief contacts during my career. None were particularly pleasant. Rudy was abrasive and he made no effort to hide it. Giuliani was newly elected as mayor when he proclaimed that the New York State Comptroller could not audit New York City municipal agencies. It was an outrageous and totally baseless assumption with no standing in the law and I said just that. It was established fact and legal precedent that the state comptroller was charged with the responsibility to audit every municipality across the state. Giuliani alleged that my audits as a Democratic comptroller would be politically biased against his Republican administration. I had demonstrated political independence by suing Governor Cuomo and vowed to continue to be fair and balanced with the Republican in the mayor's seat. But Giuliani persisted, hoping to score political points, and we ended up in court once again.

We hired the firm of Paul Weiss once again, given their track record of success. We started in state Supreme Court, where the judge ruled that we had both the right and the authority to audit New York City agencies. This might have been enough for another mayor to cede defeat, but not Giuliani. He doubled down, dug in his heels, and had his lawyers do everything possible to delay and drag it out. Giuliani appealed to the Appellate Division and a four-judge panel declared that we had the right and the authority. That was two defeats for Giuliani, but he was not finished yet. In the bulldog fashion that he enjoyed projecting, he took the case all the way to the Court of Appeals and we received a unanimous opinion in favor of the state comptroller. In the end, Giuliani's pathetic political ploy cost us one full year of distraction and a considerable sum paid to the Paul Weiss law firm. Both were strains and stresses that I certainly did not need as I began my first full year in the office. After the legal brouhaha cleared, we resumed auditing New York City agencies; there were no complaints and the audits were considered fair, accurate, and necessary. In fact, we were frequently praised in New York City newspaper editorials for bringing oversight and transparency to municipal spending in New York City.

I had served the unexpired eighteen months of Regan's term and now had to face a general election in the fall of 1994. Fortunately, the Democrats unified behind me and there was no primary opponent, but the Republicans had been huddling to see who they might run against me in the November general election in the hopes of recapturing the office that had been theirs for fifteen years. They selected John Faso, a young Republican lawmaker and lawyer who had risen quickly to the position of minority leader in the assembly. He was popular and energetic and lived in Kinderhook in Columbia County. There was a twist in this election and the Republican and Conservative parties did not align behind a single candidate as they traditionally did in statewide elections. Instead, the Conservatives selected Herb London, an author, academic, and commentator with a hardline Conservative stance in his writing and his political activism.

Earlier, behind the scenes of the state GOP, Republican and Conservative leaders wanted to support a single gubernatorial candidate to challenge Cuomo in order to avoid splitting the conservative vote as they had done in their disastrous performance in the 1990 campaign for governor. That year, London was the Conservative Party nominee and they declined to cross-endorse Republican nominee Pierre Rinfret, a Canadian-born businessman and political neophyte. Rinfret's support for abortion had angered Conservatives and they stuck with London over Rinfret. In the end, London and Rinfret split the vote and Cuomo was reelected easily to a third term; Rinfret received 865,948 votes and London tallied 827,614 votes. If they had put up a unified ticket, the Republicans might have seriously challenged Cuomo, who received 2.1 million votes.

This was the backstory behind London and Faso both vying for the comptroller position on two different party lines. As the November election approached, Faso, who was early on considered the frontrunner, was displaced by London to unify the Republican and Conservative political parties.

I knew we would need a strong media strategist and political consultant as part of my campaign team. I interviewed a couple of candidates and was most impressed by David Axelrod, a former *Chicago Tribune* political reporter and columnist who left journalism to serve as communications director for US Senator Paul Simon in 1984. A year later, he formed his own political consultancy firm, Axelrod & Associates. They helped Harold Washington, Chicago's first Black mayor, win reelection in 1987. Axelrod's firm was known for its success in working for Black politicians. Of course, Axelrod would become best known for serving as the chief strategist for Barack Obama's presidential campaigns and as a senior political commentator on CNN since 2015.

I liked Axelrod's knowledge, energy, and confidence. I offered him the job and was pleased that he accepted. He got right to work and laid out a media strategy for a very spirited race for comptroller against London. He had me out on the campaign trail at an exhausting pace, crisscrossing the state to pick up Democratic support from political leaders and voters alike, as well as holding fundraising events from Long Island to the Adirondacks, and from Buffalo to New York's border with Massachusetts.

We tried to take the high road and I ran on my respective records in political office and the private sector, but the campaign turned ugly when race and religion got interjected beyond our control. My campaign did not start the fire or fan the flames. On the contrary, we were forced to defend ourselves after we could no longer ignore the racist attacks that London's camp launched against me. London was Jewish and his team sent an email to Jewish voters across the state that included a link to a recording of a controversial Black Nationalist figure spewing anti-Semitic hatred. The fellow was a crank to whom I do not wish to give any more credence than he already received. The London campaign never identified the voice of the lunatic on the recording, but it mentioned my name in the email message in a clearly racist tone and the clear inference was that I had spoken the vile words on the recording because I was Black and a supposed Jew hater. In fact, it was not me, I did not know anything about the speaker, I condemned his diatribe, and I had worked well with Jewish lawmakers and business people throughout my career. That was not the end of it, though.

Calls from the media and political colleagues poured in and they expressed shock and outrage and wanted to know if it was me on the recording and if I had said those terrible things. I explained the situation, denied any involvement or knowledge of the anti-Semitic remarks, and denounced the words in the strongest language possible. I was upset and angered by the entire episode. I dispatched a team to investigate it and they traced the recording to a studio where a member of London's staff paid to duplicate the audio recorded at a radio station that catered to conspiracy theorists and promoted hate speech.

At the same time, I worked hard to counter the damage from these underhanded tactics by the London campaign. This controversy continued to undermine my attempt to run on my record and it clouded and overshadowed the actual issues in the race and our differing viewpoints on how the Office of the Comptroller should operate. Fortunately, people who knew me understood that the recording could not have come from my mouth and they accepted that it was a political dirty trick. Furthermore, I received strong backing from Jewish leaders in the legislature, including Senator Roy Goodman and Assemblyman Dov Hikind. Goodman and other Republicans from Manhattan withdrew their support from London and they threw their backing to me. We scheduled a major press conference at City Hall in Manhattan and we released a statement condemning London for launching racist attacks against me, and for staging a ginned-up recording to slander me. More importantly, my statement was endorsed and signed by fifty leading members of the Democratic Party in New York. All condemned London for the racist attacks against me. Nonetheless, Rudy Giuliani doubled down, continued to support London, and refused to withdraw his endorsement as Republican legislators like Goodman had done.

All my hard work on the campaign trail paid off. I won the election and defeated London by a margin of 52 percent to 47 percent and I was now, officially, the first Black candidate elected to statewide office in New York. I was very proud of my election victory and much of my win had to do with the fact that I outraised and outworked London. My campaign war chest crushed his, with $3.6 million raised by our team compared to just $543,000 for London.

Political pundits credited my victory over London in part to his attack ads against me and the anti-Semitic remarks maliciously attributed to me—a smear campaign the voters saw through.

The unexpected outcome was that I was the only Democratic statewide candidate to emerge victorious. Mario Cuomo suffered a shocking defeat by Republican newcomer George Pataki, which nobody saw coming. Pataki denied Cuomo a fourth term as governor in a stunning upset on November 8, 1994, after Cuomo had been leading in the polls by as much as ten points. Pataki ran on reinstating the death penalty, which was red meat to conservatives, and it set him apart from Cuomo, a longtime vocal opponent of capital punishment. Pataki also promised to slash income taxes by 25 percent at a time when Cuomo had few new proposals to stem rising red ink in an economic downturn. That eroded

Cuomo's support further and Pataki's team hammered Cuomo on the Arthur Shawcross case, a murderer who was paroled and who, after his release, committed additional murders on the watch of Cuomo, who was portrayed as soft on crime.

Cuomo unsuccessfully sought a fourth term after he had gained a national reputation as a powerful orator praised for his soaring political speeches. Cuomo had a strong record and Pataki was a relative unknown who came from Garrison, a small hamlet in Putnam County in the lower Hudson Valley. He had been a staff member for Senator Mary Goodhue and he ended up running against her and capturing her seat. Pataki's margin of victory was viewed as a combination of factors that conspired against Cuomo. Cuomo was against the death penalty and Pataki was in favor of it, as were about 70 percent of New Yorkers. The electorate had grown tired of Cuomo after three terms, his approval rating was dropping, and Pataki was seen as a fresh, new face who would not be beholden to the past and the old ways.

It was a tight contest and Pataki won by just three percentage points, 2.53 million votes for Pataki to nearly 2.36 million votes for Cuomo. Political pundits struggled to explain the victory from a little-known Republican state senator and essentially settled on citing Cuomo fatigue after twelve years of the Queens Democrat's oratorical grandiosity alongside a paucity of practical accomplishments. In the end, the electorate delivered more of a negative vote against Cuomo than a sweeping mandate for Pataki, who had no record.

In the statewide attorney general's race, Democrat Karen Burstein, of Long Island, a former state senator, narrowly lost to Dennis Vacco, former United States Attorney for the Western District of New York, a Buffalo Republican. Staten Island borough president Guy Molinari caused a controversy when he stated Burstein would not be qualified to serve as attorney general because she was a lesbian. That salacious remark hurt Burstein's candidacy and the *New York Times* railed against Molinari and the smear tactic he used as "gutter politics." Burstein publicly identified as a lesbian in 1994.

As the lone Democrat standing with my win against London in the comptroller's race, I tried to put the nasty racial politics behind me. I also had a role to play not only as the first Black person elected to statewide office, but as the standard-bearer for Democrats across the state. I was called upon to support Democratic candidates and enlisted to help lead the efforts to rebuild the defeated and depleted Democratic ranks of up-and-coming office holders. I was fortunate to be able to partner with a newly chosen chair of the New York State Democratic Party, Judith Hope, a dynamic woman from Long Island with extensive fundraising experience. That is exactly what we needed after losing the governor's office to the GOP's Pataki. Ms. Hope was a force to be reckoned with, a Southerner by birth, daughter of the speaker of the Arkansas legislature. I wanted to be seen as a team player and also to do my part to bolster efforts to expand our Democratic Party base of support in New York, and I went on the road occasionally with Party Chair Hope to headline fundraisers and attend galas, political breakfasts, and all manner of party functions.

In the assembly, Sheldon "Shelly" Silver, a streetwise Manhattanite, replaced Saul Weprin as speaker after Weprin's death at age sixty-six on February 11, 1994, following a debilitating stroke. Weprin was a revered Queens political figure who brought stability and a feeling of camaraderie following the disarray caused by the conviction of his predecessor, Mel Miller, on federal fraud charges.

I realized quite soon that it was going to be a different culture in the assembly with Silver, compared to the easygoing and approachable Weprin. I learned how to do things outside the speaker's purview, almost in spite of Shelly, who could be an obstructionist if one failed to win his trust and get his approval for any Democratic Party initiative.

I had to gain mastery of the operation of the Office of Comptroller, which employed about 2,200 people at five offices around the state. It was a large and complex agency. I already understood the grind of an upstate-downstate commute, which I had done while I was a state senator. This was a similar situation and I divided my time between offices in Albany and New York City. Typically, I was in Albany on Mondays and Tuesdays to coincide with the days the legislature was in session, because my job required frequent interaction with lawmakers, particularly those who chaired committees pertaining to state employees, the pension fund, and financial matters. When legislators were hammering out a budget or passing a flurry of end-of-session bills, I often spent three days in Albany, Monday through Wednesday, so I would be accessible to them and so we could schedule meetings easily. Thursdays and Fridays were reserved for working in the New York City office because those were important days for the financial markets and for executives in the financial industry. The analysts and investment specialists who managed the state pension fund were, by and large, headquartered in New York City. Some weeks, I would spend the entire week in either Albany or New York City, as the work demands dictated. Joyce and I had purchased a condominium on the outskirts of Saratoga Springs, overlooking Saratoga Lake, which we enjoyed, but its location was more convenient for me than for Joyce, who was appointed in 1998 as the sixth president of the Fashion Institute of Technology in Manhattan. We enjoyed unwinding at the Saratoga condo on the weekends after stressful weeks in our jobs. In addition to traveling constantly between New York City and Albany, I traveled frequently around the state as part of my duties.

The heavy travel schedule did take a toll on me physically, but fortunately I had a state vehicle and a state driver assigned. I was in good physical condition, but the countless hours in the back seat of a sedan definitely did not help my issues with back pain. I was fortunate in the quality of my staff, who kept things running smoothly when I was on the road, and they also gave me immediate updates when I was traveling—in case I needed to handle a particularly challenging situation.

I was proud of the strides we made in my first full four-year term as comptroller. First of all, we made the office more visible and accessible to the public and state officials. Through our printed materials, our improved website, and my public appearances, we did a better job of explaining what our office did and its importance for retired state employees and all New Yorkers who wanted to make sure their tax dollars were being properly spent—which we accomplished through our audit function. I also made it a hallmark of my tenure to increase diversity by hiring more Blacks, Hispanics, women, and people of color in management-level positions. We maintained the same rigorous requirements, application, and vetting process. We managed to lower barriers to minorities on a management track without lowering standards or sacrificing the quality of our employees. In my speeches and in practice, I made sure that we were removing obstacles to potential minority financial managers and I gave them opportunities to prove themselves through exceptional performance. We demonstrated that we could increase diversity and the quality of our outcomes through precise metrics and solid data. I was very proud of that success in particular.

I also was happy to set the tone for our office and to become recognized statewide and nationally as a progressive leader in corporate governance. Since our pension fund was one of the nation's largest, with tens of billions of dollars in investments, we could exert influence on how corporations behaved and we could try to shape the stances of some corporations. Similar to what I had managed to help Citibank do in South Africa, as the sole trustee of the state pension fund, we could divest of certain companies' stock if they were involved in practices that we found objectionable. For example, our exposure to investments in tobacco companies was often a point of debate and contention from our stakeholders and pensioners. We had to balance their objections over health concerns with the performance of our large investment portfolio and how divesting from certain industries might unduly harm our return on investment. We had intense discussions and negotiations about our investments in tobacco companies and we eventually reached a compromise: We would not increase our shares of tobacco companies, but we also would not fully divest ourselves. Instead, we would make a pledge that we would not purchase any new shares of tobacco stock. It was often a delicate balance and I took my role as sole trustee very seriously. At times, my inner circle of advisers was so sharply and evenly divided on either side of these contentious issues that I had to do my best to take in everyone's concern and make the investment moves that best served both sides.

One principled stand we took that I was very proud of concerned Swiss banks and the role they played during the Nazi occupation of European countries during World War II. I was a leader of a group of public pension fund managers who focused on documented and widespread looting of Jewish assets in Swiss banks and the Swiss banking authorities who turned a blind eye and did not try to intervene to stop this illegal and immoral activity. The World Jewish Congress provided evidence that Swiss banks were complicit in Nazi theft of Jewish assets and we demanded a full accounting, access and transparency of all records, and full reparations with interest for the stolen funds. They did not immediately comply, but we refused to do business with these banks until they eventually capitulated and restored the money to descendants of the Jewish families from whom they had helped the Nazis steal assets during the war.

Given the heavy travel schedule, and the complex and substantial demands of the job, my efforts to bring diversity and inclusion and other systemic adjustments to the office and its culture made for an intense workload. Since I was the lone Democrat elected to statewide office, I had to learn how to work with the Republicans. To get things done, I needed to reach across the aisle and work hard at consensus and compromise on some issues. One example of a bipartisan success was the implementation of the 529 College Savings Plan, which allows families to save money for higher education costs with tax advantages so that the college account grows with funds federally tax-deferred. New York was not the first state to adopt this federal program, but it took a lot of work with my team and Governor Pataki's Republican administration. The program was well received and our cooperation across political lines was praised. We had managed to rise above politics to get it done, despite some pushback and criticism I faced from Democratic loyalists. I shrugged off this internal party squabbling and kept my eye on the fact that it would serve a greater good by working together. Similarly, we worked in a bipartisan way to achieve a cost-of-living adjustment, or COLA, for elderly state pension fund beneficiaries that required negotiations with Pataki and the Republican-controlled senate. We managed to get the COLA passed through consensus and putting party politics aside.

I also had to battle the Republican governor on occasion and I was not afraid to do so. For instance, I had to exert my influence as comptroller when Pataki and IBM announced they were moving a substantial number of state jobs from Albany into abandoned IBM facilities in Kingston and Poughkeepsie, which conveniently happened to be GOP strongholds. I felt this was a purely political relocation, not based on data or saving state funds, and it was disruptive to the families of the workers who lived in Albany. I also did not want to simply look the other way when Pataki was making such a blatant move as shifting these stable jobs out of a Democratic area to a Republican one. I spoke at rallies, encouraged the opposition forces, and in the end, we stopped Pataki and IBM from making those unnecessary moves.

The job of managing such a large workforce also taught me important lessons about state employees. I learned that civil servants by and large were good, hardworking people who had earned their position through merit and taking fair and open examinations that rewarded the person who performed the best. If they came to work for the Comptroller's Office, they made a good salary and received excellent benefits, and they felt secure in their jobs until retirement if they showed up and did a competent job. Some people, I discovered, took advantage of this comfortable situation and made a career out of doing only what they were asked to do. My sense was that about 80 percent of the staff did the bulk of the work of our office and about 20 percent just showed up, hung around, collected their paycheck and benefits, and rarely offered to lift a finger unless prodded. Although I understand its advantages and I supported civil service, in practice, as a manager, I found it very difficult to get rid of the nonperforming employees whom I could not get to produce much work. The civil service rules and union protections leaned in favor of employees and I found it discouraging at times. Trying to let go of an unproductive or difficult employee was very difficult and we learned our lesson when some of those we had terminated ended up suing the state. Our lawyers often advised us to settle because it would be less costly in terms of legal fees and the waste of our time at a trial. It was also a truism that juries usually decide in favor of the employees in those cases. In rare instances if it was an egregious case, I dug in and refused to roll over, and I fought back with our own lawsuits. Regardless of the outcome, it cost time and money and if we ended up losing, it was a double defeat and made us gun-shy in the future. One veteran manager even advised me to let the slackers remain, give them very little responsibility, and let more conscientious employees do their work.

My first four-year term passed in a snap and soon I had to focus on my reelection campaign. While I was gearing up again, I received a very strange phone call from Senator Alfonse D'Amato, the powerful three-term US senator from New York. D'Amato said he was calling me confidentially to let me know that I should not worry about my reelection because the Republicans intended to put up a weak candidate, a sacrificial offering of sorts, in the form of Bruce Blakeman, majority leader of the Nassau County Legislature on Long Island. D'Amato essentially told me I could coast and still beat Blakeman easily because he was not a strong candidate. I did not depend on D'Amato and went about my usual strong campaigning and all-in effort to win the race. I did, and in convincing fashion. I ended up defeating Bruce Blakeman by a wide margin, what might be dubbed a trouncing. I got 2.9 million votes to Blakeman's 1.4 million, and I garnered 65 percent of the vote versus his 32 percent. I guess D'Amato had given me sound advice, after all. I was grateful to be overwhelmingly returned for a second term.

One of the actions I took that received the most scrutiny was my decision to move the Office of the Comptroller out of the cramped, outdated, and poorly maintained Alfred E. Smith Building and into a location that represented a seriousness of purpose and a strong faith in the future of the office and its function.

We used the pension fund with the collaboration of the Dormitory Authority of the State of New York to leverage a real estate investment that helped stabilize a derelict stretch of State Street just a block from the Capitol, and we were part of Albany's ongoing downtown revitalization. Some criticized the fifteen-story office building at 110 State Street, which cost a total of $84 million and was opened in 2002. It was a 470,000-square-foot building with a 350-car parking garage, which was badly needed for our employees. I considered it a sound investment for the work of the Comptroller's Office for generations after me and I was glad we got the project done. We did come in for criticism because some observers considered it overly lavish by state government standards, but it was nothing out of the ordinary for a Class A office building. Still, it earned a nickname that stuck: Taj McCall. It never bothered me. I had developed a thick skin by that point and remained convinced that we had done what was necessary and right for the office and our large staff. My response to all the critics was this: Is there a law that says state employees are not supposed to have a nice office in which to work?

We let our results speak for themselves. For instance, the state pension fund value rose from $75 billion in 1996 to $120 billion in 2001. We earned annual returns as high as 30 percent in 1998, which was one of several years when we outperformed the stock market. By comparison, the Standard & Poor's stock market index was 28 percent in 1998. And we often did better in the down years when the market was in negative territory, such as in 2001, when the state pension was –8.7 percent for the year compared to –11.89 percent for the S&P that year.

When I was first elected, much was made of the fact that I was the first Black person to hold the position of comptroller, as well as the first Black person elected to a statewide office. I felt good that I had acquitted myself well and achieved success on many levels during my tenure. I spent nine years as comptroller, including two full terms in which I was elected and completing one year of Ned Regan's unfinished term at the outset. That was the same amount of time I had spent at Citibank and both positions represented the longest span of years that I had stayed in the same position. My experience was that there were pros and cons to both the private and public sectors. One challenge in the public sector was limited flexibility in hiring and firing employees because of all the civil service and union regulations that had to be followed. At the same time, there was often a pursuit of more noble ideals in public service beyond the profit motive, which was generally the first consideration of private industry.

One issue I would have liked to reform was the exorbitant cost of running for statewide office. I spent $3.6 million to run for comptroller in 1998 and there was no public campaign financing available so we had to raise the vast majority of that large sum. That meant accepting contributions from the financial community that the comptroller oversaw, a situation Regan had been criticized for allowing as a "pay to play" system. I would argue that regrettably this is partially true for all state and federal elections. I did my best to walk that fine line and to make it clear that a campaign contribution did not buy influence or special favor or a state contract—despite what citizen activists might contend. I would refer the skeptics to an in-depth *Wall Street Journal* investigation into my campaign donors and whether they were given special favor or gained contracts. In other words, they dug into whether there was a quid pro quo situation. What the *Journal's* investigation concluded was that campaign contributors received no special favors and the dozens of financial executives they interviewed confirmed this fact. There was not a single person interviewed who said they assumed that they would gain access and business by making a campaign contribution to my office—conceding that was random speculation with no basis in anything they had personally observed. I felt that for myself and my office, we brought honor and dignity and distinction to the Office of the Comptroller. I successfully carried out my duties as the sole trustee of the state pension fund by helping it grow through wise investments and careful stewardship, and we had left the office with a Class A office building in the shadow of the Capitol that helped improve downtown Albany and made the 2,200-member staff of the office proud and comfortable with their work environment.

As I looked back over my tenure as comptroller, I thought of my various interactions with Senator Moynihan, following our contentious discussion during my senate confirmation. Most of my contacts with him occurred when I called the senior senator from New York for information or assistance from Washington. It was always an interesting exercise to telephone the senator because I never knew what to expect. Someone once jokingly warned me that a call to Moynihan about a thorny budget issue would likely segue into a long lecture about the marathon twenty-six-year Peloponnesian War, which finally ended in 404 BC after Athens surrendered to Sparta—with the assistance of the Persian Empire. Moynihan's exegesis carried a professorial tone and rolled along at great length until it reached a kind of conclusion in which the senator said he had been thinking about this ancient conflict and that he wanted to share some fresh insights on the clash of the Greek titans.

Over time, our conversations became less didactic and more friendly and casual, as he offered useful information and useful political advice. At one point, Senator Moynihan invited me to Washington and I was ushered into his private office in the Capitol for a five o'clock meeting. He promptly opened a bottle of sherry and began steadily sipping the dark ruby liquor. I was never a drinker, with my consumption limited to an occasional glass of white wine. I did not want to disappoint my host and I lifted the glass to my lips but barely drank anything. The senator continued to drain and refill his glass and by the end of our nearly three-hour meeting, the bottle of sherry was empty and he had traversed a lot of ground that included history lessons, political wisdom, and his achievements. It was a very pleasant monologue. I listened intently and pretended to sip my sherry. All my meetings with Moynihan followed that same pattern: He talked and I listened.

In 1998, Moynihan declared that he was not going to seek reelection to another term. To my surprise, at his announcement he endorsed me to succeed him. He cited my ability to be elected statewide, and my record as comptroller. He also highlighted the fact that there was not a single Black member in the US Senate at the time. This glaring inequity had to be addressed. It was racial inequality writ large. I decided for that reason and others that I had to give the campaign some serious thought. The bottom line was this: Did I have a desire to try to go to Washington or continue my public service in New York? My decision was settled when two important visitors to my office, wise counsels both: Congressman Charlie Rangel and Dennis Rivera, president of Local 1199 of SEIU, the Service Employees International Union, a powerful union of more than two hundred thousand members who work in the healthcare industry.

There had been some speculation that First Lady Hillary Rodham Clinton might consider relocating to New York State in order to be able to run for Moynihan's senate seat. Rangel and Rivera both confirmed to me that Clinton was interested and they had both committed their support for her. Rangel was quietly developing support for her possible candidacy among the members of the New York congressional delegation. As dean of that delegation, Rangel could be very persuasive and he was receiving positive responses in his effort to line up support for Clinton. Rivera told me that he was already lining up support from labor leaders and he, too, as a political power broker, was getting interest and gaining traction on behalf of a Clinton candidacy. My two visitors delivered the message loud and clear: I could not even think about a run without Charlie's backing. He had been a strong backer of every one of my political campaigns and without the blessing of Charlie and Dennis and the support of the New York congressional delegation and labor unions, I would not have a strong base from which to challenge for Moynihan's seat.

I made my political calculus and decided that I should try to get something for declining and leaving an open path for Hillary. I took a bold step and called the White House and asked for Mrs. Clinton, despite the fact that I did not know her personally. In my favor, though, was the fact that I had gotten to know her husband, President Bill Clinton, fairly well over the years and we developed a friendly relationship. My legislative colleague Arthur Eve's son, Eric Eve, who had worked for me and left to work as a political director for President Clinton, helped me make the connection. When President Clinton came to New York for events, Eric made sure I was invited and introduced me to the president. We had a nice one-on-one conversation. I made an impression.

My call to the White House was answered, but not by the first lady. I left a message with my name and number and Mrs. Clinton called me back within an hour. She was very pleasant, warm and cordial, obviously well briefed, and she acted like she had known me forever. I urged her to seek Moynihan's senate seat and I let her know that I would support her. She told me she appreciated my support and she suggested that she would be contacting me.

The Clintons had a practice at the time that had generated quite a bit of criticism. They had been inviting large donors to the White House to spend the night in the historic Lincoln Bedroom. A couple of weeks after my call to the White House, Joyce and I received an official invitation to visit the White House and to stay in the Lincoln Bedroom. Of course, we accepted. It was a lovely visit. We were invited into the president's personal dining room, and Bill and Hillary welcomed us, along with Dennis Rivera and his companion, and Harold Ickes, a friend from the Basil Paterson campaign who was now serving as deputy chief of staff for President Clinton. I recall over dinner that we had a lively conversation about the prospects of Hillary's senate campaign. It was abundantly clear that the Clintons and their advisers were serious about her run and they definitely wanted it to happen.

After a delicious meal, we moved to the White House theater and were treated to a movie—I forget which film—but it was a very pleasant way to conclude an exceptional evening. The Clintons were gracious hosts and the staff was wonderful and service impeccable. In order to comply with government transparency rules, the names of White House overnight guests were publicly disclosed and I was asked by the media when I returned to New York if we were major donors to President Clinton. I replied, "No, we went to the White House on scholarship." My quote made the newspapers.

This was just the beginning of our relationship with the Clintons. Joyce and I were invited to several White House events over the next year. I clearly saw an opportunity developing. If I was going to help her, I decided, she could help me. This is as it ever was and will be in politics.

Meanwhile, back in Albany, nine years passed rapidly, but I was also beginning to feel that familiar pull to move on and to look for a new opportunity and a new challenge. After Moynihan announced late in 1998 that he was not going to seek reelection after four terms, the maneuvering began quickly among those who were considering a run for the seat in 2000. Giuliani, who was prevented by term limits from running for mayor of New York City again, was the first to say he was interested in running. Giuliani became the presumptive Republican nominee and he formed an exploratory committee, but Congressman Rick Lazio, of Suffolk County on Long Island, was raising money and talking about challenging Giuliani in a primary. After months of positioning, Republican governor George Pataki endorsed Lazio and convinced Giuliani to step aside in the name of party unity.

Among Democrats, Congresswoman Nita Lowey was interested in the position and, as a well-liked, hard-working veteran of the House, she was presumed to be the frontrunner. Of course, Hillary Clinton already had a powerful, first-class campaign operation set in motion and Lowey could not match the Clintons' broad support, deep pockets, and major resources.

As 2002 approached and I was completing my ninth year as comptroller, my mindset was more a matter of seeking a bold new challenge rather than simply riding a comfortable position for another decade or so. I was not the kind of person to hold on to a job if it did not interest me deeply or make me feel like I was making a significant contribution. I wanted to leave the job of comptroller on a high note and to use my success in the office as a stepping-stone to a position that was even more challenging. There was only one statewide elected office higher than the one that I had held for nine years. I was prepared to take that next big step, the biggest of my political career.

Chapter 17

Campaign for Governor

Throughout my tenure in politics, I understood when the time was right for me to run for a particular political office and I was a very patient man when it came to waiting for the best opportunity. That is why I decided not to jump into either the US Senate race or the New York City mayoral race in 2000, even though many people tried to convince me to run, including a group of New York City banking executives. The group took me to dinner at the 21 Club in Manhattan and said they would raise money for my mayoral campaign and urged me to run. After several other entreaties, I decided I would not run primarily because I did not think it was the right time or the right office for me.

There were three major Democratic candidates running for New York City mayor in 2001: City Comptroller Alan Hevesi, Public Advocate Mark Green, and Freddy Ferrer, the Bronx borough president. I considered all three friends, making my decision about whom to support a difficult one. I endorsed Ferrer because I considered him very capable and he had a good record of public service. In my experience he always focused first on the needs of New York's minority citizens and he was deeply committed to social justice and racial equality. Also, thinking strategically, I realized that Freddy's support from the Hispanic community could be helpful to me in any future political campaign I entered.

And then, the terrorist attacks on the World Trade Center on September 11, 2001, changed everything instantly. Two hijacked planes were intentionally flown into the Twin Towers, causing both towers to collapse.

The cataclysmic event killed 2,753 people, injured thousands more, and caused an estimated $60 billion in damage to the World Trade Center site and an economic loss of at least double that amount, estimated at $120 billion or more. The attacks reverberated around the world and not only transformed airport protocols and homeland security but altered the political landscape irrevocably. Rudy Giuliani made his mark and gained immense popularly as the New York mayor who helped stabilize the crisis and console residents of the wounded city after the attacks, but he could not run again due to term limits. The Democrats needed a tough, savvy manager who could take charge of the immense work to be done in the aftermath of the devastating attacks. The Democratic Party's leaders began shifting away from Ferrer and toward Mark Green after the mayoral primaries, scheduled for September 11, which were postponed two weeks until September 25.

Green was a progressive Democrat who had the backing of the Working Families Party, an important voting bloc that carried a lot of weight. Green narrowly defeated Ferrer in a heated Democratic primary that left Green badly bruised and nearly broke. After Green won the primary election, I endorsed him for the general, although he had difficulty consolidating a coalition of the disparate political factions of the Democratic Party in New York City—particularly among Blacks and Latinos.

Meanwhile, I was already a declared candidate for the 2002 gubernatorial election. I made my announcement at the Plaza Hotel in Manhattan in February, 2001. The 9/11 attacks caused me to pause my campaign as we grieved for the dead and focused on the long, sad litany of funerals and memorials as well as the grim task of trying to recover and identify bodies—a horror that continued for years.

The mayor's race took a dramatic turn when billionaire businessman Michael Bloomberg, a lifelong Democrat, changed his party affiliation and ran as a Republican. He spent an estimated $90 million of his own money, exponentially more than Green had at his disposal. It was an unheard-of outcome when Bloomberg defeated Green and there were now back-to-back Republican mayors in New York City, where Democrats held a five-to-one enrollment margin over Republicans. In my view, the amount of his personal wealth that the billionaire spent on his mayoral campaign was obscene. It always bothered me that Bloomberg was a super-wealthy person who essentially bought the office. The way he won the mayor's position never sat well with me.

On July 7, 1999, Hillary Rodham Clinton traveled to Moynihan's farm, named Derrymore in Pindars Corners in rural Delaware County, about seventy miles west of Albany, and announced an exploratory committee for her senate run. Afterward, Clinton began a "listening tour" throughout the summer, a term that was mocked by some in the press, and she systematically started visiting all sixty-two counties across New York State and met with small groups of state residents to hear their concerns and issues. She was not always well received, particularly in upstate counties that were the domain of rock-ribbed Republicans. She faced criticism as a "carpetbagger" because she had never lived in the state before her campaign. To blunt some of the opposition, she and her husband, President Bill Clinton, purchased a Dutch Colonial home in Chappaqua, an upscale town in Westchester County. They paid $1.7 million for the eleven-room residence, which made her a target as both carpetbagger and wealthy elite—although the house was considered relatively modest compared to the estates surrounding the Clintons' house.

The New York State Democratic Convention in 2000 was going to be not only the site of the nomination of Hillary Rodham Clinton, but it would also be the first public event where Andrew Cuomo and I would appear together. I had some rather conflicting personal experiences with both Cuomos, father and son, thus far in my political career and I was wary. At the time, Andrew Cuomo was the secretary of the Department of Housing and Urban Development, or HUD, in Washington, DC. He had been appointed an assistant secretary in 1993 by President Bill Clinton and in four years had risen to the top position and was then leading the massive agency. He was forty-three years old in 2001 and, with a growing national reputation, he was considered a rising star in the Democratic Party. I knew he would be a formidable candidate for governor because he had the support of his powerful family and the Cuomo name still carried weight. He also had the backing of the Kennedy family, America's most popular political dynasty, because he was married at the time to Kerry Kennedy, whom he divorced in 2005.

Since Cuomo was still secretary at HUD through the official end of Bill Clinton's presidency on January 20, 2001, he could not declare his candidacy for governor until then. I got a call from Andrew a week before the New York State convention in June of 2000. Andrew wanted to make a pact that we would not discuss the gubernatorial race at the convention. The idea was we would only focus on Hillary in order to make sure the spotlight shone only on her and we did not create a distraction talking about the primary between the two of us. I reluctantly agreed because it seemed like the gentlemanly thing to do and because I was supporting Hillary and did not want to take anything away from her moment. A few days later, our campaign committee learned that Andrew had reserved a large yacht anchored in the Hudson River in Albany, with a planned performance by musical legend Tony Bennett. It was a high-priced promotion for his gubernatorial candidacy that he had not yet announced, after he had expressed such concern to me about upstaging Hillary at the convention. How were Tony Bennett and a party yacht docked near the convention site playing it low-key and keeping the focus on Hillary? That was another Andrew sleight of hand. I did not call him out on it, but I made a mental note and pledged that I would not be so trusting next time when dealing with my opponent.

The *New York Times* coverage of the convention made note of the fact that I received a spontaneous, thunderous applause when I took the podium to offer remarks. These were the Democratic Party workers and loyalists whom I had gotten to know during my years as comptroller and I had attended their fundraising dinners and rallies and conventions from one end of the state to the other. They appreciated my support and they hardly knew Andrew, who had spent the past eight years as a Washington bureaucrat. The statewide party leaders he had known when his father served as governor two decades earlier had largely moved on, retired, or passed away. Andrew came to the podium after I spoke and he received tepid applause, according to the *Times* coverage. The contrast between the reception I received and Andrew's was obvious to anyone at the convention.

I was pleased when Hillary was elected as the first female senator from New York in November 2000 and I liked that one of her earliest and most forceful efforts was to demand medical benefits for first responders following the September 11 terrorist attacks. Their health had been severely damaged by smoke and ash and burning piles of building rubble and twisted metal and they deserved assistance.

I began my campaign in earnest in February 2001 and we had a list of five hundred supporters and a solid base of backers who included county Democratic chairs, union leaders, and other political figures. Our gala at the Plaza Hotel in Manhattan to announce my candidacy was an elegant affair with high energy and passion from my supporters. We had strong support from public employees and state worker retirees, as well as Black and minority voters. I had grown the state pension fund considerably in my years as comptroller and the financial community had given me high marks for how I ran the office and the fiscal successes we achieved. In my campaign announcement speech, I emphasized that I believed deeply, from personal experience, that quality education was the most important factor in lifelong success and achievement. I stressed that my campaign would be focused on providing opportunities for higher education to minority and underserved communities.

My campaign attracted support from Black elected officials, civil rights leaders, activists, and ministers from across the state. We had a unified and energized Black community behind us. The Reverend Al Sharpton, who supported every earlier campaign of mine, brought in many people who did not always vote in elections. Many of these supporters focused on the historic aspect of the campaign: electing the first Black governor of New York. They wore buttons with the words "Make History."

Andrew had an interesting response to counter my Black support. He tried to attract Black voters by selecting a Black attorney, Charlie King, as his lieutenant governor. King had one notable position: He was a Cuomo loyalist beginning with Mario and continuing to the present with Andrew. What he did not have was any significant relationship with Black folks. He brought nothing to the campaign. Andrew also promoted his Kennedy connection to deliver Black voters to him. He told the following ludicrous anecdote. "Every Black family has three pictures on the wall, Andrew would tell people, Jesus Christ, Martin Luther King, and a Kennedy, John or Robert." Now that he had married into the Kennedy family, he thought that would attract Black support. I wonder if Andrew has ever been in a Black home. Neither King nor the Kennedys delivered for Andrew.

I attracted support from former officials in Mario Cuomo's administration who had negative experiences with Andrew. Former lieutenant governors Al DelBello and Stan Lundine, former secretary of state Gail Shaffer, and Superintendent of Insurance James Corcoran endorsed me and were active in my campaign.

Three prominent Democratic mayors had negative experiences with Andrew when he was secretary of HUD. Mayor Willie Brown of San Francisco, a longtime friend, organized a robust financial campaign for me in California. Two other mayors, whom I did not know, also endorsed me: Tom Menino of Boston and Richard Daley of Chicago, who hosted a fundraiser for me in his city.

I was grateful for a groundswell of support, including backers I had not expected, such as Jerry Finkelstein, father of Andy Stein, former assemblyman and Manhattan borough president. Finkelstein was a political operative who brought in Joseph Flom, managing partner of the powerful Manhattan law firm Skadden Arps. Flom had chaired David Dinkins's successful mayoral campaign. We were not able to retain the services of David Axelrod as campaign strategist because Axelrod's string of high-profile successes placed him in high demand. I was most concerned about fundraising against the Cuomo-Kennedy forces.

There was also a Donald Trump situation that came into play, long before the flamboyant New York real estate developer was considered a presidential candidate. A Trump staff member came to my office near the end of my time as comptroller with a proposal for a real estate project. My staff and our real estate consultants vetted Trump's proposal, and they didn't like the terms of the deal and rejected it. Shortly after that, a friend of Trump who was supporting me, Jerry Finkelstein, said although we had rejected Trump's proposal, he would like to help raise money for my campaign. We formed a committee with Trump as co-chair, along with two friends: Ed Lewis, founder and publisher of *Essence* magazine, and Frank Savage, an international banker and financier. They were heavy hitters and I was honored that they would serve as co-chairs in organizing a major fundraiser for my campaign.

They purchased a block of tickets for a concert at Radio City Music Hall with Whitney Houston, the pop icon and hugely popular entertainer, followed by a fabulous dinner at the iconic Rainbow Room on the sixty-fifth floor of 30 Rockefeller Center in the NBC Building adjacent to Radio City with panoramic views of the city. We got a big turnout, no doubt because of the efforts of Finkelstein, Trump, Lewis, and Savage, and it was very successful. After the event, Trump hired our chief fundraiser, Clyde Butler, and she joined the Trump team and prepared a second proposal to me as comptroller. Once again, we did not feel it was a sound investment and we turned it down. Two months later, after we had twice rejected Trump, he fired Butler. She did not deliver.

To their credit, the Clintons stayed officially neutral during the primary campaign, although senior staff members indicated to me they were leaning toward supporting my candidacy. I had no idea what they were telling Andrew's team. I read in the *New York Post* that Andrew Cuomo and his wife, Kerry Kennedy, had been guests of the Clintons at the White House and the *Post* article speculated that the first couple was leaning toward the Cuomo campaign. Bill Clinton called me personally the following day, unexpectedly, to tell me that the *Post* article was inaccurate. Bill told me that there had been no discussion about our gubernatorial primary and certainly no endorsement of Andrew. The president reiterated that he and Hillary intended to remain neutral in our contest.

I got a nice bounce in the summer of 2001 at the New York State Fair in Syracuse, a major event for central and upstate New York. As a highlight of the twelve-day fair, the state comptroller traditionally hosted a luncheon for invited guests, both political and civic leaders from the area. I called Ickes and invited Hillary Clinton, New York's new senator, and Bill Clinton, the former president. It was an opportunity for her to connect with people from that area of New York State. She and President Bill Clinton accepted, which suddenly made it the hottest ticket in New York State. We got a huge turnout, standing-room only, and the roughly three hundred guests heard warm remarks about me from both Bill and Hillary and I gave them a tour of the fairgrounds. This was not just some brief photo op because Bill insisted on tasting the specialty foods from nearly every vendor we passed. That man had an appetite. The Clintons as my guests touring the State Fair proved to be a huge boost for my campaign because it showed they supported my candidacy rather than Andrew's. Their appearance also drew major national media coverage, which also boosted my exposure and name recognition.

Our campaign sought a third-party endorsement to gain another ballot line. Traditionally, Democratic candidates aligned with the Liberal Party, which was founded in 1944 by leaders of the moderate wing of the American Labor Party and by union leaders. The Liberal Party had endorsed FDR and JFK for president. In 1976, Ray Harding, an immigrant from the Balkans and a lawyer, became the leader of the Liberal Party and he gradually transformed the party from its ideological roots to a personal enterprise based on patronage and nepotism. Its critics coined an expression: "The Liberal Party is neither liberal, nor a party." Harding was a resourceful power broker who will be remembered for having the Liberal Party endorse Rudy Giuliani over David Dinkins for New York City mayor in 1993. It was well known that Giuliani did not possess a liberal bone in his body, but that did not stop Harding's calculating style.

By backing Giuliani, Harding enjoyed personal benefit and one of his high-ranking officials, Fran Reiter, was appointed deputy mayor by Giuliani. Moreover, Harding's two sons were rewarded with important positions in Giuliani's administration despite not having any discernible qualifications for those positions. Harding became a leading adviser to Giuliani and a major lobbyist who served as the conduit to Giuliani for individuals and companies seeking business from New York City or to curry favor with the mayor.

I had accepted the Liberal Party support and endorsement in my earlier campaigns for comptroller and state senate and Harding offered me the Liberal Party endorsement in my gubernatorial bid. But I declined, concerned about Harding's transactional nature and his penchant for quid pro quo. Frankly, I was worried about what he would request and expect if I were elected. Instead, I preferred the emerging Working Families Party, a progressive group composed of unions and community organizations and, as an alternative to the Liberal Party, I sought their endorsement. Cuomo also appealed for their support. As a new organization, the Working Families Party needed a candidate who could attract fifty thousand votes to their line during the general election in order to gain a permanent ballot line.

The Working Families Party convened to select a candidate for governor. If either candidate received 25 percent of the votes, they would face a primary election in order to win their endorsement. I had an advantage because Bertha Lewis, a legendary organizer, came to the Albany convention with a group of women from Brooklyn. I did not know how they pulled it off, but their dogged efforts yielded an overwhelming plurality in my favor. I ended up receiving more than three-quarters of the votes cast, and I immediately received the Working Families Party endorsement over Cuomo without the need for a primary.

Cuomo accepted the Liberal Party endorsement since he was not the Democratic candidate on the ballot for the general election. He could not help them attract the required fifty thousand votes, while I pulled eighty thousand votes for the Working Families Party and won them a permanent ballot line. One of the achievements of my campaign that I was proud of was the fact that I established a ballot position for the Working Families Party and I put the Liberal Party out of business. Ray Harding later became enmeshed in the pay-to-play scandal that imprisoned State Comptroller Alan Hevesi. Harding was convicted of accepting $800,000 from a financial firm to arrange a contract with the state pension fund. He pleaded guilty and cooperated with the prosecutors in order to avoid prison time. Harding in the end managed to keep the money, but he was disgraced and he died in 2012.

My game plan was to be a very visible presence on the campaign trail and I visited every county in the state, except for Madison County. That was not an intended omission. We were scheduled to fly to Madison County for a campaign stop, but high winds prevented us from landing. Well, we actually got within about ten feet of the runway and the pilot of the small private plane we had chartered aborted the landing and lifted up and away from the tarmac at the last moment. We flew on toward the next stop and, thus, Madison County was the only county we missed during the campaign.

As with any political race, I also endured my share of disappointments. A big setback was the fact that I did not receive the endorsement of the New York State United Teachers union. I had a long relationship with NYSUT's senior leaders, Randi Weingarten and Sandy Feldman, and despite their best efforts they were not able to get their members to go along in the form of an endorsement of me. In the end, NYSUT did not endorse any candidate, but they contributed significant financial support to the incumbent, Republican governor George Pataki.

In the primary race, I had considerable support from another large public employees' union, Civil Service Employees Association. The CSEA president, Danny Donohue, supported me and I also had strong backing from CSEA's New York City chapter and prominent labor organizer Lillian Roberts. A turning point in the primary campaign was when Donohue sent CSEA delegates who backed me to county Democratic conventions and I received support from CSEA chapters in Queens, Brooklyn, Manhattan, and the Bronx.

Westchester County turned out to be a battleground and pundits predicted it would go in favor of Cuomo, a resident of the county. I had campaigned hard in Westchester and had refused to cede the county to Andrew. We had a good organization and a lot of support there, and at the Westchester County convention something strange happened. I was nominated and seconded as the candidate. No one nominated Andrew, even though David Alpert, the county chairman, supported him. I was the unanimous choice. I won. The outcome was a serious blow for Andrew and a huge win for me. A week later, something similar happened in Queens, which was where Andrew grew up, and it was expected to go in Cuomo's column. The key was the support I had won from Queens leader Thomas Manton. Assemblyman Anthony Seminerio nominated Cuomo at the convention and when Manton called for a second, nobody responded and the nomination went to me, which sent a very strong signal that I was leading the race for the Democratic primary for governor.

Leading up to that summer's New York Democratic Party Convention, polls confirmed that I had a sizable lead over Andrew and he decided to try to get on the ballot by an unconventional method that involved bypassing the convention and seeking petitions to win a place on the ballot. I did not object, despite Andrew's bad-mouthing of the party leadership, whom he referred to as "hacks." It sounded like sour grapes to me, or that Andrew was sulking. The harsh reality was that if Andrew had managed to get 25 percent of the votes at the convention, he would have been on the ballot. He appeared to not have enough votes, but he was trying to avoid the embarrassment of a landslide with me winning by a margin of, say, 70 percent to 30 percent.

And yet, a primary victory was not a lock for me by any stretch of the imagination. Our campaign was not complacent and we always viewed polls with a healthy dose of skepticism and knew that our opponent was a wily political veteran about whom we should neither feel casual nor turn our backs. In the private polling our campaign did through Tom Kiley, we had a strong lead among Black and Latino voters and a sizable lead overall. Andrew Cuomo was going to go down swinging, though. Six days before the primary, he called a press conference and stood alongside former president Bill Clinton and longtime congressman Charlie Rangel and said that he had decided to pull out of the race "in the interest of party unity." It was political trickery that I did not appreciate and, despite everyone urging me to attend Andrew's little concocted drama, I declined to be part of the charade. My victory in the primary was a hollow one because I beat nobody. It was the sound of one hand clapping. Since Andrew undercut my win by dropping out, it was an awkward victory celebration. His ruse of party unity had done me more harm than just about anything he could have pulled off. Instead of gaining huge momentum by soundly defeating Andrew, we ended up looking awkward without any opponent and it amounted to a form of back-stabbing on his part. The timing was against us, as well, since primary day was September 10, one day before the one-year anniversary of the 9/11 terrorist attacks and the city was filled with somber remembrances. Overall, my landslide victory was completely overshadowed and, in the end, it was nothing like it should have been if Andrew had done the right thing and stayed in the race—or, better yet, not challenged me in the first place.

The aftermath of Andrew's disingenuous dropping out of the primary at the last minute left my campaign in a terrible situation financially because we had spent nearly all our money taking on Cuomo in the primary that evaporated. It was a very costly mirage. My opponent in the general election, two-term Republican governor George Pataki, did not face a primary.

Pataki had the power of incumbency and he had something on the order of $30 million in his campaign war chest. We had essentially gone broke fending off the Cuomo challenge and we were finding it difficult to raise money from donors who already had contributed or to attract new donors with whom we did not have a strong relationship. The good news was we had enough to make payroll for our campaign staff, but we did not have a fraction of what we needed to compete with Pataki in New York City—the most expensive media market in the nation.

We called an all-hands-on-deck fundraising meeting in mid-September, one week after the primary. We did not sugarcoat our financial dire straits. We got a jolt of optimism when former president Bill Clinton joined us and said he wanted to help. We got a good bounce of interest as an FOB, Friend of Bill, and it gave our fundraising an instant boost. We prepared to take on George Elmer Pataki and the GOP. I considered Pataki, unlike Andrew Cuomo, a bland opponent who would be difficult to counterpunch because he had taken credit for popular measures such as reducing property taxes and for being a steady hand at the side of Mayor Giuliani during the grief-filled months and steady march of funerals and memorial services following the 9/11 attacks. Pataki never missed an opportunity to appear at a Giuliani press conference. Even though he often did not have an official role because Giuliani was a take-charge leader, the governor was getting the kind of press coverage and national TV exposure money could not buy.

One of Pataki's secret weapons was Charles A. Gargano, an Italian-born businessman who grew up in Brooklyn and established a successful construction company. He was a major Republican donor and fundraiser who helped George H. W. Bush get elected president in 1988 and was rewarded with an appointment as ambassador to Trinidad and Tobago. Governor Pataki appointed Gargano chairman of the Empire State Development Corporation and vice chairman of the Port Authority of New York and New Jersey. Those powerful twin appointments earned Gargano the title as the state's "Economic Czar." Gargano was a financial wizard who set up a PAC, or political action committee, in Virginia for Pataki's gubernatorial campaign because that Southern state had a low bar for disclosure and allowed unlimited donations at the time, compared to New

York's tough PAC rules. It allowed Gargano and Pataki to shield his big donors and to thwart reporters trying to follow the money. Another factor working against us was the candidacy of Thomas Golisano, the billionaire founder of Paychex, the payroll services and human resources firm. He was a founding member of the Independence Party and had twice run for governor before, in 1994 and 1998. Golisano spent an estimated $93 million on the three campaigns, he increased his vote tally each time he ran, and broke the fifty-thousand-vote threshold each time so that he got a line on the ballot as the Independence Party candidate. Golisano was essentially buying his way in and he took a slice of support away from me in upstate counties and in Rochester and Buffalo, where he had bases of business operations. He also drew some political fans who liked hockey because he once owned the Buffalo Sabres of the National Hockey League.

As the incumbent, Pataki could call a lot of the shots and he demanded that all the minor party candidates be part of any debate with me, which meant that I was one of five challengers and my presence was diluted by Golisano and candidates from the Green Party, the Marijuana Party, and others. I also faced an uphill battle with the media, since the *New York Post* was an extension of the Pataki campaign, and I was attacked by Fred Dicker, the Albany bureau chief for the *Post* and Bob Hardt, the *Post*'s political reporter. I set up a meeting with Dicker, myself, and Steve Greenberg, my communications director and campaign strategist. Dicker was an equal opportunity mud slinger. He made it clear that if we had negative stuff to traffic about Andrew, he was interested. He said his forte was negative coverage and if I had dirt on Andrew, I should pass it along to him and he would do the story.

At one point, Dicker let our campaign staff know that he was going to write a negative story about my lieutenant governor running mate Dennis Mehiel. Dennis wasn't going to play that game and in order to thwart Dicker, our campaign leaked the story to Marc Humbert, the Albany bureau chief for the Associated Press. This infuriated Dicker. In turn, Dicker went even further out of his way to write negative stories on my candidacy and his colleague Robert Hardt Jr. found ways to pile on as well.

It was Hardt who did the most damage by a series of front-page investigative stories in the *Post* in October 2002 that became known as the letterhead controversy. Hardt broke the story regarding numerous letters I had written on state comptroller letterhead to heads of companies recommending job-seekers whom I knew, including relatives. Two among the dozens of letters were written on behalf of my daughter, Marci, and a cousin. The leak came from the research arm of the Pataki campaign, who did a deep dive into the New York State Archives from my years as comptroller and their operatives found this cache of letters. At the outset, we did not know where Hardt and the *Post* got the letters because he would not reveal his sources and this kept us rocked back on our heels and clumsily trying to counter the stories from a very weak position. We did not do a good job of stemming the bleeding and the *Post* stretched the story out for a full week. This steady drip of negative coverage did irreparable harm to my campaign. The *Post* made the inference that the state pension fund had large blocks of stock in the companies to whom I wrote and that it was a quid pro quo arrangement. It was not. I strongly defended my right to send letters of endorsement to support people I knew, a routine matter for political figures at any level as well as people of influence outside politics. It was accurate that my daughter Marci was hired by Verizon. It was not accurate that it was because this was a stock that the state pension fund owned. No improprieties existed and none were ever discovered. I issued a statement regretting the appearance and impression of a conflict of interest and released to the press on my own accord all of the reference letters that the *Post* was using to attack me. In an effort to be transparent, we put all the letters out on the table to take the leverage away from the *Post*. I wrote in the statement that I never sought to leverage my public position or mix my government role with my personal and professional relationships. The letters were simply standard but heartfelt letters of reference..

But the damage was already done. A Quinnipiac University poll released on October 16 found that two-thirds of likely voters were aware of the letterhead controversy and of those, more than 20 percent said they were less likely to vote for me as a result of the situation and the appearance of an abuse of power. That was a critical juncture of the gubernatorial election and I could feel the energy and confidence that had been part of my campaign begin to leak out, like air from a punctured balloon.

The main regret I had was that I had used official letterhead instead of personal stationery. I did not regret my efforts to assist individuals seeking employment.

The final tally of the general election was a resounding defeat for me. I received just 33 percent of the vote, compared to about 50 percent for incumbent governor George Pataki and 14 percent for Golisano on the Independence line. It was a poor showing and I was upset, but I understood the confluence of events that doomed my candidacy: the power of the incumbency, the overwhelming money advantage of Pataki, the letterhead controversy, Golisano's Independence Party line, and also the matter of race.

I consciously did not want to make race an issue during the election, but as a Black man and the first African American candidate for governor, there were obviously racial attitudes at play. The final tally for Pataki and lieutenant governor candidate Mary Donohue was 2,262,255 votes or 49.4 percent; McCall and Mehiel 1,534,064 or 33.5 percent; and Golisano-Donohue 654,016 or 14.3 percent.

The lopsided Pataki victory was also influenced by the fact that there was a low voter turnout of less than 50 percent of eligible voters. Furthermore, Terry McAuliffe, chair of the Democratic National Committee, did not provide the level of financial and logistical support I expected. Near the end of the campaign, the DNC made a contribution, but it was an embarrassingly small number and it was too little, too late. I was also hurt by the fact that the *New York Times* editorial board, who endorsed me in the primary over Andrew Cuomo, changed course and endorsed Pataki over me in the general election. This also broke *Times* protocol, as I was led to believe, because I sat down for an extensive interview and grilling by *Times* editorial board members while Pataki snubbed them and refused to make himself available. By tradition, the *Times* should have endorsed me, but instead they gave their backing to a no-show candidate for the first time. It did not go unnoticed or unmentioned that there was some suspicious timing in the *Times'* Pataki endorsement, which coincided with negotiations between the *Times* and Gargano, Pataki's economic czar, regarding state subsidies for the *Times'* new office building on 8th Avenue in Midtown Manhattan. Political observers called it a conflict of interest and suggested that the *Times* should have at the very least endorsed nobody for governor instead of muddying the waters with its support of Pataki. I was not pleased with my shabby treatment by the editorial board executives of the Gray Lady.

Former governor Mario M. Cuomo and his son Andrew did host one fundraiser and formally endorsed my candidacy. I was honored that Bill and Hillary Clinton participated in a significant way, attending major fundraisers and attending my rallies in Harlem and Washington Heights. I was grateful for the support of the former president, and first lady and US senator from New York.

I was proud of the fact that there was no quit in my campaign staff and we were working fourteen to eighteen-hour days, seven days a week, in the final two months of the race even though our polling was showing we trailed Pataki by a large margin. We went down swinging.

It was a hard loss to swallow and it took me some time to get out of the funk and depression the defeat put me in. I would not say I was bitter. Perhaps disappointed is a better word. The fact that I am a Black man who faced this sort of treatment from Andrew caused some discussion. The next Democrat Andrew challenged for governor was another Black man, David Paterson. Pundits once more raised the issue of race, but I did not. I felt that David was unseasoned as governor and he performed poorly during his time in the office. In fact, I did not endorse David, who was Black like me and a personal friend. I stated that the contest was not about race for me and I actually endorsed Andrew over David. I appreciated the fact that Andrew and Mario Cuomo and family members thanked me personally for doing that. At the same time, I never considered the Cuomos friends and I did not maintain any sort of relationship with them. They reached out to me when they needed something from me.

People often ask if Andrew and I have buried the hatchet. I feel I did. Privately, at least, Andrew was always cordial, although we did not have many interactions after our primary battle for governor. Andrew did appoint me as the chairman of the board of the State University of New York, for which I expressed gratitude. It was a complicated relationship I had with two generations of Cuomos, father and son. Andrew and I were cordial when we overlapped at public meetings or political events for SUNY, but he never scheduled a private meeting with me as governor. At the outset of my time at SUNY, I met with Andrew after he was elected the fifty-sixth governor of New York on January 1, 2011. I let it be known in Democratic circles that I was interested in chairing the board. He told me he wanted to appoint me to the New York State Commission on Public Ethics, or JCOPE. I said I was not interested in the JCOPE position and that I wanted to contribute to SUNY through the unpaid board chair position because access to education for minorities and the underserved was my most important cause throughout my political career. He ended the meeting by saying he would appoint me to the SUNY board. He was as good as his word.

Chapter 18

Freedom

My long career taught me that we never say never when it comes to politics, but I was feeling burned out by the grueling campaign for governor and the disappointment of losing—which never gets easier as you get older, no matter what anyone says. After I completed my second and final term as comptroller at the end of 2002, I was essentially a free agent. Aside from exhaustion, the strongest sensation I carried inside me was a feeling of freedom. For the first time in eight years as comptroller and the past year as a gubernatorial candidate, I was not beholden to the tyranny of schedulers, a jam-packed calendar that daily went from before sunup to late into the night, and a staff of assistants and advance people and logistics specialists. For a decade, I was told from my team where I should be every day, whom I should meet, what I should say in prepared remarks, and on and on. Every facet of my political and professional life, and my personal life as well, was scheduled every single day—generally in thirty-minute blocks.

I recalled a meeting with David Dinkins after he left office as mayor of New York City. He took out his schedule book and showed me that he had six events that day. I told him it looked like he was as busy as when he was in office. He told me there was one big difference between being mayor and a private citizen. "I go where I want to go," he told me. "I make the decision, not a staff member." He was speaking about the freedom that he and I both felt after leaving elected office.

There was hardly time for me to pause and ponder my next career move when some interesting and attractive job offers came in from the private sector, including consulting work and positions on corporate boards. I was approached by executives with Tyco International, which was founded in 1960 by Arthur Rosenberg as an investment and holding company. The Massachusetts firm focused on high-tech materials science and energy conservation products. By the end of the 1970s, with savvy acquisitions, sales topped $500 million, and its aggressive acquisitions continued into the 1980s. Dennis Kozlowski became CEO in 1992 and in the next decade, Tyco acquired hundreds of small companies related to electronic components, fire and safety services, flow control and health-care products.

Kozlowski spearheaded several billion-dollar acquisitions and revenue soared to $35 billion in 2002. Scandal hit the high-flying company when Kozlowski got caught up in a massive scandal, he was convicted of steal-ing more than $150 million from the company, and served an eight-year prison sentence. "It was greed, pure and simple," Kozlowski told a New York State parole panel. He was released in 2013—widely considered a poster boy for the corporate excesses of the 1990s bull market. A couple of board members were caught up in Kozlowski's criminal scams and they, too, were found guilty of grand larceny, securities fraud, and other charges.

In the wake of the scandal, Edward Breen was appointed president, CEO, and chairman of Tyco and soon named John Krol as lead director of the Board of Directors with a priority of improving Tyco's corporate governance. Krol, who was known as Jack, was the former CEO of DuPont. Bruce Gordon, a Black man who had served as an executive at Verizon, also joined the new board. This was a period of major restructuring on Tyco's part following the Kozlowski scandal. The restructuring was a massive effort that touched all facets of Tyco's vast workforce of 260,000 people. I accepted the offer to join the board and the opportunity to be involved in the restructuring. Tyco had acquired the security company system busi-ness ADT, whose portfolio included a significant amount of home security business in South Africa. In contrast to the business model in the United States, police officers often are not responsive to being called to a home theft in South Africa. In most instances, ADT sent armed employees to homes where security alarms had sounded. The problem was that there were occasionally violent confrontations and shootouts between ADT security personnel and the criminals. When reports surfaced of some ADT employees being killed during botched robberies, the board intervened and raised serious concerns about whether ADT should continue to do business in South Africa because of the liability and litigation risks.

I was a voice of opposition to the proposal that ADT should pull out of South Africa. My position was that South Africans needed economic development and a strong and viable private security firm to provide a sense of protection and comfort for tourists, homeowners, and businesses. I recommended that a delegation of Tyco board members travel on a fact-finding mission to South Africa. Our group included myself, Bruce Gordon, retired US Admiral Dennis Blair, and Jack Krol. Our trip took place in 2004. We had fruitful discussions and reached an agreement that ADT would send two employees on a security call, rather than just one, which would make them less likely to be challenged in shootouts and violent confrontations at scenes of home burglaries. In addition, President Mbeki gave us assurances that the police would be more responsive and cooperative in answering burglary calls. Our mission was significantly aided by my friends Ron and Charlayne Gault, who had introduced me to President Mbeki. The Gaults now lived in South Africa, where Ron served as an executive responsible for J. P. Morgan's operations in the country and Charlayne was CNN's South Africa bureau chief. They were very helpful in scheduling meetings with Mbeki and other officials. I felt good about the workable solution I had helped broker; we returned to the US and reported to the full Tyco board about our success, and the company decided to continue to support ADT's operations in South Africa.

I also had an interesting and rewarding experience as a board member with Ariel Investments, the largest minority-owned investment company, with more than $10 billion under management. It is headquartered in Chicago and was established in 1983 by John W. Rogers Jr., chairman and CEO. As comptroller, I had invested in the company. I liked Ariel's investment philosophy of focusing on patient value-investing within small- and medium-sized companies. I found the company to be very well managed and a first-class company, a stellar example of a Black-owned business that competed successfully with much larger investment firms. I was also impressed with Ariel's co-CEO and president, Mellody Hobson, a very good manager and communicator. She is a prominent Black businesswoman who was named one of the "100 Most Influential People" in the world by *Time* magazine in 2015. In 2020, Starbucks Corporation appointed her chair of the board, making her the only Black woman to chair a Fortune 500 company. Hobson previously served as chair of DreamWorks Animation and was a longstanding board member of Estee Lauder Companies. She is married to George Lucas, the billionaire filmmaker of *Star Wars* fame, and the couple have become major philanthropists.

I learned many valuable lessons during my time on the board of Ariel Investments and made lasting professional and personal relationships with the two CEOs. Mellody contacts me if she has a question about investment issues involving public funds. Mellody contributed to the McCall scholarship program. The entire team at Ariel is a high-quality, hard-working, and extremely talented group of people and I was proud to be associated with them.

Another important involvement in this period was my work as a member of the board of the New York Stock Exchange. While I was serving as state comptroller, I was the first public official appointed to the NYSE since its founding in 1817, which I took as a vote of confidence from Wall Street due to my leadership as comptroller. I was invited to join the NYSE board in 1999 and remained after I left public office, with a four-year stint that ended in 2003. My service on the board was marked by a tumultuous period for the New York Stock Exchange, which was consumed by a scandal and long-running legal battle over what many considered the excessive compensation of Richard A. Grasso, chairman and CEO of the NYSE from 1995 to 2003. He began his career at the stock exchange in 1968 at age twenty-two as a floor clerk and worked his way to the top of the nation's best-known and most revered stock exchange that had an international cachet, as well. Grasso worked tirelessly during his thirty-five-year career with the NYSE, rose up the ranks, and became president and finally CEO in the early 1990s. His tenure as CEO was marked by a string of successes and he became the leading cheerleader for the exuberance and wealth created by the long-running bull market. Grasso was lionized for how he led the effort to reopen the New York Stock Exchange after the terrorist attacks of 9/11 and the symbolism turned Grasso into a hero of capitalism. For myself and other board members of the NYSE, Grasso was a well-regarded, tested, and deeply committed leader who had a track record of success.

The game-changer was Eliot Spitzer, first elected as attorney general in 1998. He took an aggressive stance and launched multiple investigations into the financial industry. He vowed to clean up corruption in the securities industry and became known as the "Sheriff of Wall Street," a tough-guy image he relished. As Wall Street's most recognizable face, Grasso soon found himself in Spitzer's crosshairs. Spitzer easily won reelection to a second term as attorney general in 2002 and doubled down on his pledge to clean up what he considered widespread abuses on Wall Street. Grasso, after eight years running the Big Board, surely sensed that he and Spitzer were heading for a showdown.

In 2003, according to records that came to light in Spitzer's long-running legal battle against Grasso, the New York Stock Exchange CEO made an inquiry about cashing out some of his retirement benefits. This set off further scrutiny. Although I was not aware of any such exchanges, some directors later said that Grasso had expressed concern that any future board would be less willing to give him the money to cash out benefits—a charge that Grasso vehemently denied. The issue was all the accumulated unused sick time and bonuses included in retirement benefits Grasso had stockpiled during thirty-five years at the NYSE.

With pressure ratcheting up on the matter of Grasso's compensation, the directors decided to examine corporate governance practices in the securities industry and, although a relatively new member, I was appointed chairman of the Nominating and Governance Committee in light of my years as comptroller. The other board member assigned to the committee with me was Leon Panetta, a former congressman from California who had been chairman of the US House Committee on the Budget during his nine terms in the House. He left to serve as director of the Office of Management and Budget, followed by serving as White House chief of staff for President Bill Clinton. In 2009, President-elect Barack Obama appointed Panetta as director of the Central Intelligence

Agency. Panetta led the CIA for two years before Obama appointed him secretary of defense in 2011—an extremely demanding job he held for two years. I was impressed with Panetta's skills, which I observed at close range. We were handed this delicate job and we conducted a major study and ended up issuing a report that included significant recommendations on how to shore up and improve the governance practices of the New York Stock Exchange.

That was a helpful blueprint for the future of the NYSE, but it did nothing to resolve the scandal that embroiled Grasso and all of us. Kenneth Langone, one of the most active board members, is a billionaire investor who financed the establishment of the Home Depot. He is also a major philanthropist and key donor to the Republican Party. He chaired the compensation committee from 1999 to 2003, when his term expired, and he asked me to take over the committee post during this pivotal time when the Sheriff of Wall Street was putting us under intense scrutiny. During the first meeting I led I was brought up to speed and was told that Grasso was entitled to deferred compensation totaling roughly $140 million. Grasso wanted to begin to claim that benefit while he was still serving as CEO.

It would not be an exaggeration to say that jaws dropped when we learned the size of the compensation package. I was stunned. We had no idea he was owed that much money in deferred compensation. The committee I had just been tapped to lead was torn by this information. A few members believed he deserved the money and had earned it under the rules of his contract. Others believed it was excessive and needed to be renegotiated. The consensus was that Grasso had done a very good job leading the NYSE, and he was well respected and had provided solid leadership. There were whispers and rumors that Grasso was under consideration by President George W. Bush for appointment as treasury secretary and also that he was being considered to head the US Securities and Exchange Commission, or SEC. The board members were in agreement that we wanted to keep Grasso at the NYSE, despite the storm of criticism that erupted when somebody leaked it to the media and it became a major story that symbolized the excess and corruption on Wall Street. Major investors weighed in with their opinions on the matter, including Bill Donaldson, former chairman of the NYSE and current head of the

SEC, who said that Grasso was acting within the rules of his compensation package and he had done nothing wrong.

The media ran multiple stories critical of the system and underscored the fact that the compensation committee included many leaders of NYSE-listed companies over which Grasso had regulatory authority as CEO. The inference in the coverage was that a fundamental conflict of interest existed. Spitzer charged Langone as head of the compensation committee in the lawsuit, which became a bitter and prolonged legal affair. Members of the board were deposed and we had to retain lawyers compensated by insurance to represent our own interests. I hired attorney William Wachtel to represent me in what became a long-running legal battle pitting Spitzer against Grasso, the Big Board CEO against the Sheriff of Wall Street. This was not what I had signed up for or expected my role to be as a board member. The controversy forced the board to decide whether we would give Grasso the full amount of deferred compensation he sought. To cloud the matter further, Grasso also was in line to receive an extra $48 million in compensation benefits in addition to the $140 million. This revelation made heads explode.

It was one of the most stressful and troubling tenures I have had on any board because it was a highly politicized and lengthy legal battle that stretched on for five years, beyond the term of Spitzer as attorney general and his election as governor in 2006. There was much finger-pointing and plenty of the blame game to go around. We did our due diligence as board members and sought out expert legal opinions. They determined that Grasso was indeed entitled to the $140 million he was owed in deferred compensation.

As the lawsuit dragged on and we were embroiled in an endless run of negative media coverage, the NYSE began to suffer and barely continued to function, and the board felt pressured to act. We took a vote and by a margin of thirteen to seven voted to terminate Grasso's employment. The board turned to me and asked me to serve as lead director. I voted to fire Grasso. I was now responsible for keeping the board functioning and focused on keeping the NYSE operating as the leading global exchange.

After Grasso's termination, we had to find an interim CEO quickly. Larry Fink, the chairman and CEO of BlackRock, which he cofounded with seven partners in 1988 and grew into a global leader in financial planning and investment management, was the person we sought out for advice. *Fortune* magazine named Fink one of the "World's Best CEOs" for fourteen consecutive years. Fink and his team grew BlackRock into the world's largest asset management company, with managed assets amounting to nearly $7.5 trillion in 2019. Initially, Fink supported Grasso but he eventually flipped and changed his opinion and did not feel that Grasso deserved the deferred compensation. Fink came to me with a suggestion to ask John Reed, the retired CEO of Citibank, to serve as interim CEO. John was the person who hired me originally at Citibank and by this time he was living quite comfortably and contentedly off the coast of France. A very good choice, it was agreed, and Fink called Reed. I called my old mentor John, as well. Double-teaming apparently worked and after some deliberation, John Reed accepted our offer to lead the NYSE as interim CEO. That gave the stock exchange instant credibility and a sense of stability, and it assured nervous investors that there was a steady hand on the tiller steering the Big Board through turbulent waters.

A month or two after he took the reins from Grasso, John had reestablished order and control, and I felt that things were going well, the stock exchange was on the right track, and I had provided a helpful contribution at a challenging time. I decided it was the right time to resign from the board. I felt relieved, since it had been the most difficult and stressful board assignment I had ever undertaken, including during the Tyco scandal that I helped the company weather. I was beginning to yearn for the peaceful and drama-free retirement I had envisioned.

The postscript to the Grasso scandal was anticlimactic. In 2008, following a costly and contentious legal battle that raged for more than four years, the New York State Supreme Court, Appellate Division, ruled that Grasso could keep the $139.5 million deferred compensation benefits he was paid and the court threw out the remaining claims against him and all other defendants, including Ken Langone. The 3-to-1 ruling lowered the curtain on one of the most embittered fights in Wall Street history.

The turbulent stock exchange experience did not dissuade me from lending my experience and skills to companies and causes I thought worthwhile. One significant public service effort I joined at this time was the New York State Public Higher Education Board. I was approached by Alan Lubin, the executive vice president of the New York State United Teachers union and a heralded leader in the fight for public education, civil rights, and working people across five decades. Alan was developing a coalition of labor and community organizations to support access to higher education, particularly at bargain-priced State University of New York and City University of New York colleges and universities. My commitment to an affordable public higher education, particularly for students of color and those from underprivileged backgrounds, was well known. I agreed to Alan's proposal that I serve as chairman for this newly created New York State Public Higher Education Board, which turned out to be an active and engaged consortium of fourteen different groups. We issued important reports, studies, and press releases, as well as lobbying on behalf of public higher education.

My involvement with the Public Higher Education Board was not the only voluntary public service assignment I accepted. Since leaving government service in 2002, until the present, I was always happy to offer assistance and share my expertise with friends, former constituents, officials with government agencies, and community organizations. Among other notable volunteer positions, I was co-chair of the Commission on Tax Reform and the Commission on Legislative, Judicial, and Executive Compensation. In addition, I served as a trustee of SUNY for twelve years. I was able to do this while I served at different times on nine corporate boards. I am presently serving on just one board for a financial services company, which originally was headquartered in Bermuda but has moved to London. During the coronavirus pandemic year, we held virtual board meetings and I did not have to travel to London. The compensation from boards provided living expenses and helped build a retirement fund, which made the volunteer work possible. I was recently invited to join another corporate board and one attractive benefit is that the company has a private suite at the Barclays Center in Brooklyn for Nets games. I have enjoyed watching the NBA throughout my life. Growing up in Boston, I became a devoted Celtics fan and it took some time to shift my allegiance to the New York Knicks after I moved to New York City. Lately, I have been very disappointed because the Knicks have been terrible for several years, although they are improved this season under new head coach Tom Thibodeau. I have come to embrace the Brooklyn Nets, a team that has three All-Stars in the lineup: Kevin Durant, Kyrie Irving, and James Harden. They have faced a series of injuries this season, but when that trio of superstars is in the lineup, the Nets have a very promising future and many consider them a playoff contender.

Playing and now watching basketball offers valuable lessons about life. As I have done throughout my career, I was not afraid to multitask, to try new things, to accept the reality of occasional failure and temporary disappointment, and to continue to challenge myself to grow and develop to my fullest potential. Doing so meant that I was always ready to seize opportunities when they presented themselves, as they did in this new phase of my postretirement career.

Chapter 19

State University of New York

My complicated relationship with Eliot Spitzer came into sharp focus during this period. I had supported Spitzer for attorney general in the 1998 campaign, his second try for the position, and he defeated Republican incumbent AG Dennis Vacco in a very close race. I also endorsed Spitzer for his second term as AG in 2002, and he easily won reelection against little-known Republican judge Dora Irizarry by a margin of more than two to one This was the same year I lost the gubernatorial race to George Pataki, who secured a third term.

After Pataki decided not to run for a fourth term in 2006, I supported Spitzer once again, this time for governor. Spitzer had supported my bid for governor four years before and we had become colleagues of a sort, and somewhat friendly. When Spitzer rolled to a landslide gubernatorial victory over Republican John Faso—with 69 percent of the vote, a record plurality in the history of New York gubernatorial races—we discussed my interest in the State University of New York Board of Trustees. We discussed it at some length and I believed I walked away with Governor-elect Spitzer's promise that he would appoint me chairman of the SUNY Board of Trustees. One month later, Spitzer informed me that he was appointing Carl Hayden, the former chancellor of the State Board of Regents, as chairman of the SUNY board. I was disappointed and it was also a reminder that politics is a tricky business that will break your heart and leave you discouraged—as I had learned on more than one occasion in my career. At the same time, I wanted to contribute and I felt that the SUNY board was a place where I could do that. I swallowed my pride and accepted the consolation prize, an appointment as a trustee, but not as chairman. Thus, I began my long-term commitment to SUNY with my being named a trustee in June 2006.

That was not the final time I would be disappointed in politics, as history repeated itself when I thought I had a promise from Governor David Paterson to be elevated to the chairman's role, but that also did not come to pass. It was not until Andrew Cuomo was elected that a governor actually honored his commitment when Governor Cuomo appointed me SUNY chairman on October 17, 2011. It took two disappointments and a third try, but I finally had the position where I felt I could be most effective as a leader of public higher education, by using all that I learned in my wide variety of public- and private-sector positions.

On the home front, Joyce had been named president of the Fashion Institute of Technology in 1998, FIT's sixth president, the first woman and first African American to lead the specialized college of art and design, business and technology. It is a big job. FIT serves 10,000 full- and part-time students, with a faculty and staff of more than 1,700.

At FIT, Joyce was a proven president who already had major successes by the time I joined the SUNY board. This presented a possible appearance of a conflict of interest since FIT was a SUNY school. I signed an agreement that stipulated I would not vote on any matters that came before the SUNY board that had to do with the governance of FIT and that I would recuse myself on all matters related to FIT. That satisfied everyone and made peace in our household. I'm proud to report we never had a problem and no issues arose, either internally or externally.

As SUNY board chairman, I maintained offices in Manhattan and Albany. Our country retreat, halfway between the two cities in Clinton Corners, Dutchess County, was a convenient stopover and made the frequent driving commutes less draining. I also spent a lot of time on the road visiting SUNY's sixty-four campuses and it was immediately clear that this unpaid position was a full-time job. The board appointments I maintained with private corporations supplemented our income and I also established a small financial services firm, Convent Capital, a financial services advisory firm that was a part-time side project after I concluded my position as comptroller of New York State in 2003.

I was interested in joining the SUNY board in large part because of its longstanding commitment to diversity and opportunity for minority students. Even though it was a position without compensation, I considered it an opportunity to give back and pay it forward for the mentors, Black ministers, and civic leaders who helped me gain access to achieving a college degree—which would not otherwise have been possible for my single mother or my family of limited means.

As a state senator and comptroller, I had interacted with SUNY officials on many occasions and found them to be terrific administrators committed to building a world-class system of public colleges and universities across New York. I was drawn to its history of inclusivity, which resonated strongly with me, as well as its legacy of excellence. SUNY is the nation's largest comprehensive public university system, with sixty-four schools that include research universities, liberal arts colleges, specialized and technical colleges, health science centers, medical schools, land grant colleges, and thirty community colleges. Today, SUNY enrolls roughly 1.3 million students, including online and part-time students, including 477,000 students enrolled in degree-granting programs served by 88,000 employees, and with a network of more than three million living alumni. SUNY was established in 1948, which was relatively late compared to other major states in the country. The delayed start was due to the fact that New York State had a large number of elite private colleges and universities and there was not any concerted pressure to create a public higher educational system. When it became clear that some of the private schools discriminated and excluded Jewish and minority students, the foundation was laid for the creation of SUNY. In 1931, there was an admissions scandal at a prominent private university after complaints surfaced from alumni that there were too many Jewish students being admitted. The director of admissions responded by sending a letter to alumni promising that he would never admit more than 10 percent Jewish students. This was reported in the press and it boiled over, causing an angry public backlash against the school and creating the environment that made it possible for SUNY to emerge two decades later. State legislators from all corners of the state formed the impetus for the loud call for a nondiscriminatory, open-to-all public university system for New York State. Governor Nelson Rockefeller made a major financial commitment of state funding to support SUNY, which began with twenty-nine unaffiliated colleges, eleven of which were teachers' colleges, including what is now the University at Albany. Another aspect that appealed to me was that the tuition was extremely modest and affordable, a fraction of the cost compared to private schools and even other state colleges and universities. By all measures, including outstanding outcomes, SUNY has always been a bargain.

One of the challenges SUNY faced was its choppy leadership, with a revolving door in the top post of chancellor with a series of short-term and interim leaders. SUNY finally gained the outstanding leadership it deserved and stability it needed when Clifton R. Wharton Jr. became chancellor of SUNY in 1978. He was the first Black person to head the largest university system in the nation. He previously held a series of influential positions where he was also the first Black to hold the post, including president of Michigan State University, a series of executive positions with the Rockefeller family philanthropies, and an appointment by President Gerald Ford as chairman of the board for the US Agency for International Development, or USAID.

I had a deep and abiding connection and friendship with Clifton Wharton, who became an important mentor and someone who encouraged me to join the SUNY board. He also grew up in Roxbury, Massachusetts, and I was a classmate of his younger brother, Richard Wharton.

During Dr. Wharton's nine years as chancellor of SUNY, through 1987, he was credited with improving the quality and flexibility of the complex and sprawling system's management, strengthening SUNY's research capacity and building and broadening the brand and benchmarks of SUNY across the board. His successor, Bruce Johnstone, served as chancellor from 1988 to 1994 and he was considered an effective administrator who extended Wharton's innovations and also provided strong continuity and stability in SUNY's leadership. Johnstone was the last chancellor who served for a block of years before a series of interims and high turnover in the position.

In 2008, after I joined the board, John J. O'Connor, who had served in a variety of administrative positions in Washington, became the de facto chancellor and essentially ran the SUNY system without the formal title, although he was secretary to the board and senior vice chancellor and president of the SUNY Research Foundation. We were in search mode once again for a new chancellor. A no-show job scandal broke in the news media involving Susan Bruno, daughter of the powerful Republican senate majority leader Joseph L. Bruno, who began working at the SUNY Research Foundation in 2003 in a newly created position that was never posted for applicants. The Research Foundation comes under the auspices of SUNY and manages grants awarded to SUNY professors for research projects awarded by federal, state, and private entities. Ms. Bruno was hired as assistant director of Foundation Relations for Legislation at an annual salary of $70,000. A year later, she was reassigned and allowed to work from home as special assistant to O'Connor, president of the Research Foundation. Ms. Bruno was charged with defrauding taxpayers for state services she did not perform in a lawsuit brought by the state attorney general.

This long-running scandal embroiled myself, members of the board, and the entire SUNY leadership for years. There were many layers of scandals consuming Albany in those years and I ended up exerting a lot of time, energy, and resources dealing with the corruption cases.

Former senate majority leader Joseph Bruno at one time the most powerful Republican politician in the state, resigned in 2008—the same year his daughter's scandal broke—after an FBI investigation led to his indictment on federal corruption charges.

At trial in 2009 Bruno the father was convicted of two counts of honest services fraud. The verdict was thrown out in 2010 when the US Supreme Court found the statute did not stand up to constitutional scrutiny. Federal prosecutors brought a second trial in 2014 and the former senate majority leader beat the rap on the corruption case a second time and was exonerated.

In Bruno's daughter's case, the attorney general's twenty-two-page complaint documented abuses of her no-show job. The case against Susan Bruno worked its way through the Board of Trustees. This was the state of affairs at SUNY in the first couple of years of my involvement on the board. As a result, there was added scrutiny of the SUNY Research

Foundation, which oversees more than $1 billion annually in research grants for SUNY institutions. Simultaneously, the state inspector general, Ellen N. Biben, and the state comptroller, Thomas F. DiNapoli, began their own inquiries and investigations into O'Connor and his leadership of the Research Foundation.

In June 2011, we as a board voted unanimously to accept O'Connor's resignation. SUNY's own internal investigation was conducted by an outside law firm at considerable expense and resulted in a scathing eighty-nine-page report. The report was critical of O'Connor's leadership and the New York State Joint Commission on Public Ethics, or JCOPE, charged him with violating state ethics rules in hiring Ms. Bruno. O'Connor denied any wrongdoing.

This was only one portion of a dark cloud of corruption and scandal that hung over Albany and never seemed to dissipate. In the midst of the corruption cases involving the two Brunos, a bombshell hit that overwhelmed all other scandals: the prostitution scandal of Eliot Spitzer, who was elected the fifty-fourth governor of New York until he resigned in disgrace on March 17, 2008, just fourteen months into his first term.

Spitzer chose my friend David Paterson as his lieutenant governor running mate in the 2006 gubernatorial campaign. David, of course, was the son of a political mentor of mine, Basil Paterson. David, who is legally blind, ended up winning the same Harlem senate seat that his father and I once held. I had great admiration for how David had overcome his disability and succeeded in what was essentially the family business. I have been quite open with David and others that I did not always agree or approve of his political calculus and felt that his acumen in politics was sometimes lacking. His agreement to run with Spitzer was such a decision. The Democrats were poised to take over control of the state senate in 2006 after decades of Republican control and David would have been assured the position of senate majority leader, the first time a Black senator had held that position. It carried tremendous power and accounted for one of the so-called "three men in the room" who hash out the state budget and all major Albany matters (the other two being the governor and assembly speaker). Many friends and political advisers questioned why David would choose the less-powerful lieutenant governor post over the almost-assured senate majority leader position. David could not be dissuaded. In his mind, he was playing a long game and his scenario was that US Senator Hillary Rodham Clinton would become president, which would then mean that Governor Spitzer would appoint her senate replacement and Spitzer would choose Paterson. That seemed to me and many others like magical thinking, but it was just David being David. He was nothing if not unconventional.

Of course, David had the opportunity to gloat when the Spitzer-Paterson ticket won in a landslide over Republican John Faso, Libertarian John Clifton, and other minor candidates with a whopping 69 percent of the vote. Theirs was a historic win, the largest margin of victory ever in a New York gubernatorial race.

Spitzer hit Albany like a force of nature after he was sworn in on January 1, 2007. The Sheriff of Wall Street became the tsunami of state government, swamping anything or anyone in his path with heavy-handed reform tactics. He pledged that he would "change the ethics of Albany" and he immediately ran into a recalcitrant legislature that asserted its state constitutional authority to fill executive vacancies. Legislators appointed and voted the approval of Assemblyman Thomas DiNapoli to replace State Comptroller Alan Hevesi, who resigned from office in December 2006 in yet another Albany scandal. Hevesi accepted a plea deal after he was caught unlawfully using state employees to chauffeur his wife, following his guilty plea on corruption charges in a "pay to play" scheme involving the New York State Pension Fund. Hevesi received a sentence of one to four years in state prison in April 2011. Of all the scandals, Hevesi's hit closest to home because we had held the same position. It pained me to learn throughout the case that Hevesi had illegally tampered with the state pension fund, which I had considered a sacrosanct trust of our state employee retirees as the sole trustee of their hard-earned pensions. One needed a scorecard to keep track of the quagmire of Albany scandals in that era. It was a depressing time to be in Albany, which I regularly visited for meetings of the SUNY board.

Spitzer doubled down after the legislature outmaneuvered him on the DiNapoli appointment, led by Assembly Speaker Sheldon Silver (also later convicted on corruption charges). I was part of a panel that Governor-elect Spitzer put together that included my predecessor as comptroller, Ned Regan, and former New York City Comptroller Harrison J. Goldin. We agreed to forward the name of Spitzer's choice and the panel's choice for state comptroller, New York City Finance Commissioner Martha Stark. The final vote in the legislature was 150 for DiNapoli and 56 for Stark. An enraged Spitzer showed up in the home districts of some Democratic assembly members who voted for DiNapoli and publicly chastised them— an unheard-of direct assault on the autonomy of elected lawmakers. This kind of gubernatorial overreach and confrontational approach would mark Spitzer's brief tenure and render toxic his relationship with legislators of both parties. According to media reports, Spitzer told Republican assembly minority leader Jim Tedisco: "Listen, I'm a fucking steamroller and I'll roll over you and anybody else."

The steamroller was revealed as Client No. 9: The *New York Times* broke the story on March 10, 2008, that Governor Spitzer had become a client of Emperors Club VIP, a high-priced escort service, had engaged in one- or two-hour sessions with $1,000-an-hour prostitutes, and had paid up to $80,000 for sex workers over several years, both as attorney general and governor. An investigation revealed that he had willfully lied to and evaded his State Police security detail to engage in these illicit trysts and other embarrassing details—such as Spitzer's penchant for wearing black dress socks while engaged in sexual activities with prostitutes—were splashed all over the New York City tabloids. Under threat of impeachment proceedings that legislators vowed to bring, Spitzer resigned on March 17, 2008, five days after a painfully awkward press conference where his ashen-faced wife, Silda Wall Spitzer, stood by his side as he promised to "dedicate some time to regain the trust of my family." The couple announced they would divorce at the end of 2013.

Spitzer's resignation meant that Lieutenant Governor David A. Paterson succeeded Spitzer and became the first Black person and the first legally blind person to serve as a governor in the United States. He greeted this historic moment with his signature humor. David never met a punch line he didn't like. He liked to start out speeches as governor by saying that he got to be governor because of a sexual encounter . . . and he wasn't even there.

In the wake of the series of Albany scandals, state government service also became a sullied career path and it made it very difficult to attract quality people to SUNY. The scattershot and disorganized pattern of the Paterson administration was a major hindrance when we opened a search for a new SUNY chancellor. This leadership position and the entire system depended on a governor who was focused and committed to higher education and who was willing to fully fund SUNY's needs even in difficult budget cycles. The chancellor candidates, who were highly credentialed leaders at acclaimed universities and university systems in other states, were wary of what they had observed of the interim Paterson administration. With so much uncertainty about Paterson's commitment and ongoing financial support of SUNY, several administrators identified by our search firm as potential chancellors did not wish to be considered for the opening.

The search dragged on and it was a demoralizing time. We were almost ready to declare it a failed search, when Nancy L. Zimpher surfaced as a possible chancellor candidate. At the time, Zimpher was president of the University of Cincinnati and previously served as chancellor of the University of Wisconsin–Milwaukee. She had a good reputation as a respected educator, an effective administrator, and a higher education leader who knew how to achieve success even in the deep recession that began in 2008.

As board members, we were thrilled when Zimpher accepted our offer and was sworn in as the twelfth chancellor of the State University of New York on June 1, 2009. She hit the ground running, marshaled resources, and quickly gained consensus on an excellent strategic plan she called "The Power of SUNY," which set priorities to drive economic growth and to have the most profound impact possible on the communities we serve throughout New York and around the world. Zimpher was an energetic presence, a dynamic speaker, and a hard-charging advocate for the "economic engine of opportunity" of SUNY. She was a national figure in higher education, frequently invited to speak at conferences, and she carried the SUNY message around the country and began removing the tarnish from Albany scandals and repairing damage to SUNY's brand. I was impressed with Nancy Zimpher's leadership. I felt strongly that she was the leader that we needed at that time.

After serving as a member of the Board of Trustees since June 2006 and giving an increasing number of unpaid hours to the role, I felt that I wanted to elevate my role now that the leadership had stabilized under Nancy Zimpher. I made it known that I was interested in being appointed chairman of the board and I got word directly to David. He referred the matter to his longtime trusted lieutenant and secretary to the governor, Charles J. O'Byrne, who held the highest and most powerful unelected position in state government. If you wanted or needed something out of David, you had to get through O'Byrne first. He started as Paterson's speechwriter in the state senate and was promoted to chief of staff when David served as lieutenant governor. The two men had a deep, trusting relationship because O'Byrne essentially became the one sighted person who handled everything visually and signed off on matters professional and personal for the legally blind Paterson. O'Byrne grew up in an Irish Catholic family in New York and was a Renaissance scholar at Columbia University, where he graduated summa cum laude. He later graduated from Columbia Law School and worked in corporate law at a Manhattan legal firm, becoming a close personal friend of the Kennedy family and its political dynasty. At thirty, O'Byrne felt called to the priesthood. He quit corporate law, spent twelve years as a Jesuit priest, and served as Harvard Law School's chaplain as well as a highly regarded teaching fellow at Harvard. As a priest, he presided at weddings and funerals of relatives of John F. Kennedy. O'Byrne quit the priesthood in 2002 under a cloud after he wrote a scandalous exposé for *Playboy* magazine. O'Byrne leveled explosive allegations about rampant homosexuality among ordained priests and predatory pedophile priests. O'Byrne, who is openly gay, left the Jesuit order and moved into political speechwriting, first working for Howard Dean's presidential campaign and later for David Paterson in the senate. He brought order and discipline to David's chaotic political operation and became the most valuable aide he ever had.

O'Byrne and I had a good discussion about SUNY and my interest in being appointed chairman. He listened carefully and was cordial, but in the end, he rejected me for the position because he was advising David to severe his ties with Harlem and those Black political organizations that had helped elect David, David's father, and myself. I was disappointed and angry but could not dissuade O'Byrne that this was a terrible strategy and it would backfire. I was so upset that I wrote my letter of resignation from the SUNY board and sent it to David directly. O'Byrne called to say David would not accept my resignation, he tried to do damage control, and he convinced me to continue to serve as a member of the board.

The media was tough on David, who dubbed him the "accidental governor" and it was clear that he leaned heavily on the skills of O'Byrne, who was called the governor's "gatekeeper" and "enforcer" and the one indispensable aide who kept the Paterson administration running.

It all came crashing down on O'Byrne, and also the governor, when O'Byrne resigned as secretary to the governor on October 24, 2008, after it was revealed that he had failed to pay taxes for five years and he owed almost $300,000 in back taxes. His lawyers attributed his actions to a unique addiction, "tax avoidance syndrome." It was refuted. O'Byrne became yet another scandal to pencil into the corruption scorecard of Albany, a very crowded tally.

The Paterson administration went into a tailspin and David began to lean on less qualified and barely competent staffers to run things. Veteran respected state political operative Larry Schwartz, brought in to replace O'Byrne, never meshed well with David's undisciplined style.

My relationship with David during his governorship was fairly remote. I did not meet with him regularly, but we had a couple of meetings and I called him from time to time. He did not seem interested in focusing on SUNY and its needs. I tried to stay in touch with him, but he seemed overwhelmed trying to run the office without O'Byrne at his side. Perhaps the most momentous decision in Paterson's governorship was filling New York's open US Senate seat after Hillary Clinton was appointed US Secretary of State by President Barack Obama in 2009. Under the New York state constitution, it fell to the governor to make the appointment and there was a lot of media speculation about whom David would choose. One name that rose to the surface was Caroline Kennedy, daughter of JFK, who had expressed interest, and Paterson seemed to flirt with making her his choice. Paterson wound up appointing Kirsten Gillibrand, an Albany native who was serving her second term in Congress and who had earned a reputation as a tough-talking Blue Dog Democrat in the House.

I was privy to some of the behind-the-scenes maneuvering and Gillibrand was strongly supported by New York's other senator, Chuck Schumer, a Democrat, as well as Republican power broker and former senator Al D'Amato, who was a personal friend of Gillibrand's father, Doug Rutnik, an Albany attorney. When Paterson installed Gillibrand as US Senator from New York at a hastily called and odd ceremony in the Empire State Plaza in Albany, many pundits were caught off guard.

David Paterson rightly gained national attention as the first Black governor in the history of New York State and he never really learned to capitalize on that. Moreover, without O'Byrne, I saw how he started depending on people who were not reliable or qualified. The most prominent example of this was his former driver and personal assistant, who became engulfed in a scandal stemming from allegations of domestic violence against his female partner, and reports surfaced that David allegedly tried to persuade the abused woman not to file charges. Of course, this is witness tampering. This all got blown up in the New York tabloids just as David was preparing for a reelection in 2010 that would give him his first full term as governor. Instead, Paterson read the polls and the harsh fallout of the scandals swirling around him and announced on February 26, 2010, that he would drop out of the race. It was the wise choice, since his tenure as governor had been very disappointing and the Obama administration and the White House itself signaled that it was opposed to David running for reelection.

Meanwhile, my former opponent, Attorney General Andrew Cuomo, who never failed to seize a political opportunity or to create one even if it did not clearly exist, swept into this unsettled terrain and a divided Black political caucus. Andrew jumped into the gubernatorial campaign and the media immediately tried to inject race into the matter. Reporters dredged up the 2002 gubernatorial campaign and Cuomo's primary challenge against my bid to become New York's first Black governor. I refused to take the bait, rejected the racial aspect, and reiterated publicly that I did not consider the 2010 gubernatorial campaign or the 2002 campaign a matter of Black against white. I had no desire to play the race card. I had never done so throughout my career and I wasn't about to start now. I did not make it a matter of skin color. The bottom line was that Andrew

Cuomo won a crushing victory over Republican Carl Paladino, whom the media portrayed as a crackpot—accurately so, in my estimation—and the final tally was 2.9 million votes for Cuomo and 1.5 million for Paladino. The huge plurality gave Cuomo a lot of momentum in his first term after he was sworn in as the fifty-sixth governor of New York on January 1, 2011. He appointed me to his transition team, which I appreciated, and I wasted no time in letting Andrew know I wanted to be appointed chairman of SUNY. Andrew agreed and appointed me as chairman of the State University of New York on October 17, 2011.

I was happy to work with Chancellor Nancy Zimpher, with whom I had a good relationship, but I also wanted to build a strong and independent board, which had not been the case for some time. One immediate need I saw was that we had to bolster the board with more medical expertise since our only member with medical experience was Dr. Marshall Lichtman from the University of Rochester Medical Center. The issues involving medical centers were very complex and the board was not prepared to deal with what would be required to make our case for additional funding for staff and resources at medical schools that were part of SUNY, particularly Downstate Medical Center in Brooklyn, whose financial situation was precarious when I became chairman. Downstate served mostly poor minority patients who had limited coverage or no insurance at all. The medical center also happened to be a major employer in the minority community; it was the only teaching hospital in Brooklyn and the main pathway to becoming a physician for Black doctors who trained at Downstate. It was losing millions of dollars each year because many patients were uninsured and the facility had not been receiving adequate reimbursement from New York State or the federal government in order to cover costs.

This effort to save Downstate brought my political career full circle because I had organized the demonstrations at Downstate in 1964 in order to protest a lack of hiring of minorities. We managed to win that battle and I got arrested in the process. I looked back on that episode as my political awakening of sorts. As a SUNY board, we were fighting a similar battle of racial inequity. A new challenge emerged. A private hospital with a long history of financial problems, Long Island College Hospital (LICH) was going to close in the Cobble Hill neighborhood of Brooklyn.

Under pressure from the powerful hospital employees' union, 1199 SEIU, which represented 1,400 employees at Long Island College Hospital, Paterson agreed to keep it open by having the state purchase LICH and connect it to Downstate in order to bring the combined new entity under the SUNY umbrella. Paterson approved this over the opposition of his health commissioner and budget director. Paterson wanted it, he was willing to pay for it, and we had no choice but to yield to the powerful forces at work.

The upshot was that soon there were two failing hospitals, LICH and Downstate, and this threatened the future of Downstate. It was a very turbulent period and the board maneuvered to get Downstate's president, John LaRosa, who had supported the merger, to resign in 2012. As his replacement, we hired John Williams, who had successfully run George Washington University Hospital in Washington, DC. Williams was a respected and decisive leader and he determined that the only way to save Downstate was to shut down LICH and to stem the draining of resources that amounted to tens of millions of dollars annually. Williams tried to shop LICH around, but nobody wanted to take it over and it became Cuomo's problem when he succeeded Paterson.

New York City's public advocate, Bill de Blasio, a former City Council member, altered the political dynamic when he jumped in on the issue and staged a demonstration at SUNY's New York City office demanding to keep LICH open. It was a play to raise attention for de Blasio's populist mayoral ambitions and he had himself arrested at the demonstration, hired a lawyer, and organized a grassroots community effort to stop the closure of LICH, a Cobble Hill institution. The LICH closure became a very emotional and heated saga that de Blasio exploited for his own political gains.

The lawyer for de Blasio moved the dispute to the Brooklyn Supreme Court. He asked the court to deny our request to the New York State Department of Health to close LICH, and to deny the department the power to close any hospital. Therefore, no hospital in the state could ever be closed.

The legal battle stirred up by de Blasio went on for more than a year, at considerable additional expense for SUNY, which we could ill afford to bear. We hired two lawyers, Ed Spiro and Frank Carone, and we fought this protracted lawsuit over the LICH closure. I tried to get Governor Cuomo involved, but he had a long relationship with the powerful SEIU 1199 healthcare workers union, a major campaign contributor to him. Andrew was not helpful and declined to get actively engaged as de Blasio continued to malign SUNY. It was a very difficult situation and a major and costly distraction for myself and the SUNY board, since the financial analysis made it clear that LICH was hemorrhaging money.

The Brooklyn legislators, with whom I had a good and longstanding relationship, aligned with myself and the SUNY board after we made the decision to save Downstate instead of letting two ailing hospitals both go under. The judge and the court finally agreed on a settlement process that created a vehicle whereby any entity could apply to take over operation of LICH as long as they continued to provide medical services. Whichever group put forth the best offer would be free to purchase LICH from SUNY.

As a board, we reviewed and thoroughly vetted the various offers and we settled on a group that agreed to pay $450 million for the hospital and that would give a portion of the property to NYU Medical Center to manage clinical medical services, while reserving the right to build housing on another portion of the property. After a contentious battle, the sale to Fortis Development Corporation was approved for $450 million. On paper, it looked like a win-win for the state, since Governor Paterson had paid $300 million in state funds for LICH. In my estimation, factoring in the legal costs, the bad publicity, and nasty politics, as well as entangling SUNY and its resources for years, the sale was not a net positive. I wished it had never happened. We did accomplish our main goal, however, which was to get out from under the LICH burden of heavy red ink.

The issue was still unresolved when de Blasio was elected the 109th mayor of New York City in 2014, in part because he attacked SUNY and said we intended to sacrifice LICH and sell it to make way for high-priced condominiums. This was a fabrication and a twisting of the truth. I met with the mayor, told him I was tired of his political grandstanding, and gave it to him straight: If he thought LICH was such an important facility,

I would give him the keys and he could operate it as a New York City hospital. He declined.

He knew from the beginning the truth of the matter and yet he kept the controversy afloat as a political gimmick to boost his mayoral chances. I don't believe he really cared about the outcome and he put his own personal interests above the interests of Brooklyn and New York State taxpayers. I came away with a very negative opinion of de Blasio. As the sale neared, he proved himself to be a disingenuous flip-flopper who said he knew LICH was not sustainable and he no longer supported it. The whole sordid political brouhaha was on de Blasio's hands and it was very damaging for the largely Black patients and staff of Downstate Medical Center. It is no secret that de Blasio and Cuomo have clashed repeatedly and there is no love lost between the two of them, but when it came to the LICH sale, they at least publicly projected a unified front.

It took the board some time to recover from what I considered an unnecessary trauma that de Blasio helped inflict upon SUNY. We licked our wounds and got back to the important work of increasing diversity among students, staff, and faculty across the SUNY system, which was a passion and personal goal for me and for which Chancellor Zimpher gave her full support. I was pleased with Zimpher's hiring of Alex Cartwright as provost, and he developed a major diversity strategy with SUNY's chief diversity officer, Theresa Miller. We had momentum and we were moving the needle on the very important objective of increasing diversity all across the system.

We established a significant and productive relationship with the University of West Indies, a university system with campuses in seven countries that were former British colonies that became known as British Overseas Territories. Several SUNY campuses, including Stony Brook, Downstate Medical Campus, University at Albany, and others collaborated with UWI campuses on research and other projects.

I developed a rewarding personal and professional relationship with the leader of UWI, Sir Hilary Beckles, a noted educator, economist, and historian of the sport of cricket in the Caribbean. He is also a leader of the reparative justice movement to secure reparations from former colonial powers. I was honored to receive an honorary degree from UWI in 2018 in recognition of my partnership with them—my tenth honorary degree.

After eight years of solid leadership, Nancy Zimpher stepped down as chancellor of SUNY in September 2017 after affording us the courtesy of giving us a full year's notice in advance of her departure so that we could find a suitable replacement.

I led the search committee and, frankly, it was easier with Governor Cuomo in charge than it had been with Governor Paterson. We had several excellent candidates interested in the position and the committee ended up selecting Dr. Kristina M. Johnson, who had a very impressive resume that included several patents in electrical and computer engineering, provost of Johns Hopkins University, and undersecretary of energy for the US Department of Energy for the Obama administration. She brought expertise and energy to the chancellor's position and she initiated key priorities, including advocacy for women in leadership in science and engineering roles, and an emphasis on women in STEM fields.

When Johnson was sworn in as the thirteenth chancellor of the State University of New York, I had been a SUNY board member for a full decade and chairman for six. I was starting to hear the voice of Vernon Jordan in my head about controlling my exit.

I had been through a roller coaster of challenges at SUNY and was proud of my calm, assured leadership of the board. Another achievement I was proud of, in addition to significant increases in diversity, was the expansion of SUNY's global presence. We had programs in three dozen foreign countries and I made it a priority to advance our connections and efforts in Cuba, the Dominican Republic, Haiti, and Caribbean nations because of the strong connection to New York City residents.

Near the end of my tenure at SUNY, we had to deal with a national issue, which presented the SUNY trustees with a major challenge and unexpected opportunity to make an important statement about sexual abuse and sexual harassment, women's empowerment, and the long struggle for equality during the height of the #MeToo movement. It also turned out to be a difficult situation for me, personally, and the outcome fractured a valued friendship.

Borrowing themes and practices from other social justice movements based upon shattering taboos and breaking silence, the #MeToo movement began trending on social media in 2006 after it was created by Tarana Burke, an activist and sexual harassment survivor. The movement's goal was to demonstrate solidarity and strength in numbers, especially among young and vulnerable women, by speaking out and demonstrating how many women had survived sexual assault and harassment, especially in the workplace. The collective effort was aimed at revealing previously concealed instances of sexual misconduct and holding abusers to account for their actions. As the #MeToo movement gained traction and momentum, credible allegations of sexual abuse and harassment led to criminal investigations, which set off a domino effect of empathy for the victims and severe repercussions for the abusers. For instance, one outcome was that colleges and universities began revoking honorary degrees for individuals both charged and convicted of sexual abuse and harassment crimes.

The first case that came to the attention of the SUNY board involved Harvey Weinstein, the prominent film producer, who received an honorary doctorate in humane letters from the University at Buffalo in 2000. Weinstein left the school before graduating in 1973 and had a bachelor of arts degree conferred on him in 2001 from the University at Buffalo after he earned experiential credits from Empire State College that fulfilled degree requirements. In the fall of 2017, after numerous women came forward with credible allegations of sexual abuse and his long history of admitted sexual misconduct came to light, University at Buffalo officials initiated a formal process, pursuant to the SUNY Board of Trustees policy, for the revocation of a SUNY honorary degree. Revocation is allowed if the recipient contradicts the spirit of the honorary degree, which recognizes persons of the highest character. On November 16, 2017, following a careful review, the SUNY Board of Trustees and the SUNY chancellor revoked Weinstein's SUNY honorary degree. It would not be the last such action we would take.

Six months later, in May 2018, the SUNY board voted to revoke honorary degrees given to Metropolitan Opera conductor and pianist James Levine and comedy star and actor Bill Cosby. Levine was awarded a Doctor of Fine Arts from SUNY Potsdam in 1996. He was fired by the Met in March 2018 amid a host of allegations of sexual misconduct, which he denied. Cosby was found guilty a week earlier of sexual assault and dozens of women accused him of similar acts in lengthy court proceedings. Cosby was awarded a Doctor of Humane Letters degree from the SUNY Fashion Institute of Technology in 2000, which Joyce, as FIT's president, had conferred. The matter was personal because I considered Cosby a friend and Joyce and I had socialized with him and his wife, Camille.

I first met Cosby in the 1980s through Edward Lewis, founder and publisher of *Essence* magazine, a highly successful publication targeted at a Black audience. Cosby later became a generous donor to my political campaigns for comptroller and governor. He made occasional appearances at my campaign events and his enormous popularity was helpful to my campaigns. Over time, we developed a friendship. During his years at Temple University, Cosby competed in track and was a supporter of track and field, particularly the Penn Relays, the oldest and largest track and field competition in the nation—hosted annually since 1895 by the University of Pennsylvania at Franklin Field in Philadelphia, Cosby's hometown.

Cosby was a familiar figure at the Penn Relays, a celebrity presence who mixed with runners on the field, commented on the races with the media, and mingled with fans. My friend Calvin Pressley and I had attended the Penn Relays for roughly thirty consecutive years and it was one of my favorite annual traditions. We connected with Cosby at the Penn Relays and Calvin and I went to dinner with him a few times after the competition, usually to his favorite Italian restaurant in South Philly. Joyce and I joined Cosby and his wife, Camille, at social events over the years. We met the Cosbys in the south of France, where they gathered with family and friends for a few weeks in the summer at the luxurious Cap d'Antibes Beach Hotel. We connected with the Cosbys there on a couple of occasions when we were in the area and we also dined with them at one of their favorite restaurants in Antibes, Restaurant Le Bacon, which featured Mediterranean seafood cuisine.

When the first news reports of allegations of sexual harassment and abuse surfaced against Cosby, I initially dismissed them because this was not the person I had come to know as a humanitarian and whom I considered a friend. I knew firsthand of his devotion to his family, his commitment to social issues, and his extremely generous philanthropy—

especially to HBCUs, or historically Black colleges and universities. A $20 million gift by Cosby and his wife, Camille, in 1988 to Spelman College, the elite Black women's college in Atlanta, was at the time the largest ever to a HBCU. As the accusations of sexual assault against the once-family-friendly comedian rose to number a dozen women, I had long stopped overlooking them. It was a surreal turn of events that forced many institutions, particularly HBCUs and other institutions who had been beneficiaries of Cosby's philanthropy, to part ways with the disgraced iconic entertainer. At the same time, some colleges did not immediately sever the relationship and maintained their ties to Cosby long after the allegations became public. The pressure became intense as the criminal cases against him progressed. In 2014, Cosby resigned as a trustee at his alma mater, Temple University, and as fundraising co-chair at the University of Massachusetts in the wake of the scandal. The only thing I could attribute his egregious criminal behavior to was some kind of sickness or addiction, but I would not condone it in any sense.

Since Joyce and FIT had bestowed an honorary degree on Cosby, it became a SUNY issue. SUNY was not alone, since Cosby had received nearly seventy honorary degrees over decades in recognition of his acclaimed career in acting and comedy.

There were additional complications. Our longtime friend, George Wein, the jazz impresario, produced the JVC Jazz Festival in New York City, including a concert at Carnegie Hall on June 21, 2006, that highlighted revered jazz musician and composer Dave Brubeck and also featured Bill Cosby as a commentator with comedy interludes. It was a sold-out crowd and Joyce had helped secure sponsorships from American Express and Barnes & Noble. Proceeds from the concert went to the FIT student scholarship fund.

The accelerating and troubling number of sexual abuse and sexual harassment charges and convictions against Weinstein, Levine, Cosby, and others, including popular television host Charlie Rose, brought to the forefront and into public scrutiny SUNY's process for both awarding and revoking an honorary degree. The process involves a recommendation for an honorary degree recipient made from a campus directly to the SUNY Board of Trustees. The board then reviews the recommendations and decides whether to approve or deny the recommendation. The revocation process is similar. In Rose's case, for instance, SUNY Oswego officials recommended to the SUNY board in January 2018 that it revoke Rose's 2014 Doctor of Humane Letters degree after eight women accused him of sexual misconduct and both CBS and PBS fired him in November 2017. The SUNY board approved SUNY Oswego's recommendation and Rose's honorary degree was revoked.

That is the procedure that FIT followed in April 2018, following Cosby's conviction on aggravated sexual assault charges. Following a college committee review, FIT recommended to the SUNY board that the honorary degree awarded to Cosby in 2000 be rescinded. FIT stated that Cosby's conviction "undermines the accomplishments that were cited for awarding the honorary degree and is injurious to the reputation of SUNY and the college. . . . Such behavior is inconsistent with the values embraced by FIT, as well as with those upheld by SUNY."

Joyce and I, as well as FIT officials and the SUNY board, agreed that this was a difficult but necessary decision.

At one point during this process, Cosby called me and we talked. I let him know a short time in advance of the announcement that his honorary degree was going to be revoked. He was not happy and it was an uncomfortable conversation, but he understood the rationale and had expected it. Notre Dame rescinded Cosby's 1990 honorary degree immediately following his conviction on sexual assault charges in April 2018, as did many other schools.

That was the last time I spoke with Bill Cosby. Our fractured friendship, which began in the 1980s, was finished. Cosby, who is eighty-four and nearly blind, was sentenced to three to ten years maximum in a state prison in Collegeville, Pennsylvania, after a jury convicted him of felony sexual assault of a Temple University employee in 2004. After Cosby served nearly three years of his sentence, Pennsylvania's highest court threw out the conviction and released Cosby from prison in June 2021 on a legal technicality that did not absolve him of guilt in the case.

I am still trying to process this troubling episode and my response to the matter. It called to mind what John Procope, the late publisher of the *Amsterdam News*, the Black newspaper based in Harlem, once told me in his blunt vernacular: "Sometimes you gotta do what you gotta do. And you gotta do what is right, regardless of the consequences." That is what Procope always strived to follow and a life lesson I have tried to emulate.

I was happy to conclude my twelve-year tenure as a SUNY trustee, which I considered a highly rewarding experience, at the end of June 2019 after making a smooth transition with Dr. Merryl Tisch, who had been vice chair and who was appointed by the governor to serve as chair.

In June 2020, right in the midst of the Coronavirus pandemic, Chancellor Johnson made the surprising announcement that she was leaving SUNY after less than three years, to become president of The Ohio State University, effective August 24, 2020.

This was unfortunate timing for SUNY and New York State, which had been the epicenter of the deadly COVID-19 outbreak in the spring of 2020. Both institutions were faced with catastrophic financial fallout from the pandemic and resulting shutdowns required to stem the spread of the deadly respiratory disease.

Several colleagues and associates tried to pull me back into the SUNY maelstrom brought about by Johnson's abrupt departure.

I had made my exit, I had controlled it in a refined and respectful manner, and I was ready to begin writing the chapter of my retirement.

Chapter 20

Retirement

On April 10, 2019, I announced my plans to retire as chairman of the Board of Trustees of the State University of New York through a press release distributed by SUNY officials with a dateline of New York City. I think Vernon Jordan would be proud of the way that I controlled my exit, because I undertook the announcement in a professional and transparent way with a long, deliberate lead time. Beginning in January 2019, I shared my plans with the SUNY board, my staff, the governor's office, and my family and friends. I said I would wrap up my projects before I concluded my twelve-year tenure, eight of those years as board chairman, on June 30, 2019. This was a six-month runway and I thought that was a fair amount of time to make a smooth transition. I also formed a committee to plan a retirement event as a way of thanking a wide array of mentors, colleagues, and friends who had helped me along the way.

The press release noted that I had overseen the installations of two chancellors and more than fifty university and college presidents. My leadership of the board was marked by a comprehensive expansion of SUNY's academic breadth, elevation of SUNY's national and international brand, and diversification of SUNY's senior administration and student body. I was known for an ardent advocacy of higher education, which led to substantial gains for SUNY students.

"I believe that it is time for me to pursue other interests and allow a new vision to take SUNY to even greater heights," I said. "I want to thank the governor, trustees, faculty, and New York's future leaders, our students, for their endless support as I have served in such a consequential office."

I called my service as SUNY board chairman "one of my greatest joys." I added, "It has been both rewarding and challenging to help direct the academic fates of our nation's brightest stars. Thanks to wonderful colleagues on the board and two outstanding chancellors, we have carried out this charge with unbridled commitment, integrity, innovation, and compassion."

I noted that I planned to teach a course at the University at Albany and to write a memoir covering five decades of public service. "SUNY has always been a beacon of light in New York State. Manning this lighthouse has been my deepest honor," I said.

"Chairman McCall has been a staunch advocate for the people—all people—throughout his esteemed career in public service," SUNY chancellor Kristina M. Johnson said. "We have been fortunate at SUNY to have his leadership, intellect, expertise and deep commitment for the students we serve while leading our Board of Trustees."

Following a summary of my professional and academic career, the press release noted that Dennis Mehiel, my lieutenant governor running mate and a longtime friend, and Lloyd Williams, one of my closest friends throughout my career and a trusted adviser, would co-chair a retirement event committee.

I had known Lloyd for five decades and he served as a campaign manager when I ran for the state senate in 1974. He was a great booster of Harlem and the founder of Harlem Week, an annual event to showcase arts, culture, and commerce in Harlem. Lloyd also serves as the president and CEO of the Greater Harlem Chamber of Commerce and he kept me connected to business people, political leaders, pastors, and regular folks in Harlem. Lloyd and I created a regular breakfast gathering we called the Harlem Think Tank and we met regularly at Sylvia's, a popular soul food restaurant in Harlem. We hashed out a lot of initiatives and strategy among political, business, and community leaders, all deeply committed to keeping Harlem a vibrant and prosperous center of Black opportunity, arts, and culture in New York. Lloyd and I were as close as brothers and our work to lift up Harlem in all ways has never ceased as long as we have known each other.

I picked a terrific lieutenant governor running mate in Dennis Mehiel, but better still, I was fortunate to build a lasting friendship with a wonderful man. Dennis ran a very successful manufacturing company that made boxes and packaging, and he was also active politically. The two of us collaborated on political fundraisers and other projects and he became chair of the influential Battery Park City Authority. Dennis and his wife, Karen, also owned a beautiful sailing yacht and they invited Joyce and me to join them on cruises through the Caribbean islands in winter and in summer months to the Greek Islands, Croatia, the Amalfi Coast of Italy, and to other spectacular seaside destinations. Their sailboat was 170 feet long and was operated by a crew of seven. Sailing with the Mehiels was restful, relaxing, and very special. They are warm, hospitable, and dear friends.

Dennis and Lloyd were helped tremendously by my wife, Joyce, who agreed to host the retirement event at her campus, SUNY's Fashion Institute of Technology in Manhattan. The co-chairs were ably assisted by Joyce's deputy, Jen LoTurco; my SUNY office assistant, Dulce Kontak; and Lloyd's assistant, Michelle Scott. Dennis and Lloyd put together a terrific committee that included Manhattan borough president Gale Brewer; former New York mayor David Dinkins; president of the NAACP New York State Conference Hazel Dukes; founder and CEO of Ichor Strategies Eric Eve; SUNY chancellor Dr. Kristina Johnson; former president of the Commission on Independent Colleges and Universities Abe Lackman; my daughter Marci McCall; state senator Kevin Parker of Brooklyn; former New York governor David Paterson; former congressman Charlie Rangel; former deputy director of State Operations Barry Sample; civil rights activist the Reverend Al Sharpton; public relations executive Ken Sunshine; SUNY chair Dr. Merryl H. Tisch; Tim Zagat; and SUNY chancellor emeritus Dr. Nancy Zimpher. My old Harlem newspaper, the *Amsterdam News*, described the party as "a galaxy of New York's political and business luminaries."

The June 27, 2019, retirement celebration, titled "A Legacy of Empowerment," which drew more than five hundred guests to the John E. Reeves Great Hall at FIT, was to reinforce your philanthropic efforts to provide scholarships for financially challenged students of color. This group of students had been the charitable focus of Joyce and my giving in recent years, since early in our lives we had received financial assistance that had allowed each of us to achieve our goals of a college education. Proceeds from the celebration, which included elegant gourmet food, and beverage and dessert stations, would also benefit the scholarship fund of Sigma Pi Phi, the first successful and oldest Greek organization for Blacks. It was established in Philadelphia in 1904, an exclusive national professional fraternity limited to five thousand members, with chapters known as member boules, or a council of noblemen. It was founded by two doctors, a dentist, and pharmacist in an era when Black professionals were not allowed to join or participate in professional and cultural organizations organized by whites. Fighting discrimination and racial prejudice was a core principle of the organization, which has 140 chapters across the United States, England, and the Bahamas. Notable past members have included W. E. B. Du Bois, the Reverend Martin Luther King Jr., Arthur Ashe, civil rights leader Andrew Young, and a mentor of mine, Vernon Jordan. I was inducted in 1976 into the New York chapter, Zeta Boule, which Du Bois established in 1912. I have been very active in the organization over the past twenty years and I have developed scholarships for financially needy students and provided mentoring and career guidance to high school students in Harlem. I am proud to be a member of an organization of prominent Black men that provides leadership and service on social issues such as urban housing, racial injustice, and other challenges facing Black America.

At my retirement party, I reconnected with former colleagues and friends from across the spectrum of my fifty years of public service and private business positions. I posed for dozens of photos and had the sensation of my whole life flashing before me. It was a feeling of warmth and satisfaction and gratitude, especially when I heard countless stories from successful professionals I had mentored or assisted when they were just starting out in their careers. It felt good to know I had been such a positive influence on the lives of many, particularly young people of color.

Most importantly, the retirement celebration raised $130,000 for a scholarship fund to provide support for McCall Scholars, a select group of high-achieving Black high school students from Harlem who will receive financial assistance and mentoring. I was humbled and grateful to learn toward the end of the event that Dr. Kristina Johnson, the SUNY chancellor, had personally matched that amount and therefore the total raised was doubled to $260,000. I expressed deep gratitude for Kristina's unexpected and generous commitment to the McCall Scholars program.

There were wonderful tributes as part of the formal program, which was emceed by the very funny and entertaining David Paterson, who displayed the wit and timing of a stand-up comic. My daughter, Marci, welcomed guests on behalf of the McCall family. David Dinkins and Charlie Rangel offered brief remarks that were warm and personal. Dennis and Lloyd each had a page in the printed program to share a few words about our enduring friendships, professional and personal. Lloyd called me "a man for all seasons" and also noted, "Carl could not have accomplished as much if it were not for the amazing partnership that he has with his wife, Dr. Joyce Brown." You got that right, Lloyd.

Dr. Merryl Tisch, my vice chair and successor as chair of the SUNY Board of Trustees, offered a very gracious note in the program. "I am so fortunate to have seen your integrity, wisdom and kind heart firsthand as we worked together to take SUNY to new heights," she wrote.

Governor Andrew M. Cuomo also sent a formal citation that chronicled my life and career, particularly my accomplishments as chairman of the SUNY Board of Trustees. It called me "an outstanding leader in public service to New York State and its people, displaying commitment, passion, and a vision for the future . . . in which his hard work, dedication, and civic-minded spirit have produced a noteworthy and lasting record of success." I have never been one to get a swelled head or let my ego get the better of me, but trust me, it is slightly disorienting to be the recipient of so much concentrated praise—a bit like attending one's own funeral, I imagined.

The most eloquent and touching remarks during the entire evening, according to myself and the guests, came from my beloved wife. "Let's be clear: In my family we do not celebrate the end of anything," Joyce began. "It is always the beginning of the next chapter, the next challenge, the next opportunity. And that is what we are celebrating tonight."

Joyce highlighted the theme that reverberated throughout that evening's celebration. "The theme is service—service and the transformative power—certainly of education, but the power of reaching back, lifting up, and making sure there is a legacy for the next generation to build on. The McCall Scholars are a fitting tribute to all that the past fifty-five years have been about. Because the instinct to make a difference in the world and more specifically in the lives of those not seen at first glance . . . those desperate for a chance—just a chance—to prove what they can do—*that* instinct: that is what fuels Carl McCall. It is innate; it is unwavering; it is authentic."

Joyce added, "Carl has certainly known challenge. He knew that to change his circumstances and to have a voice and a chance to excel and be recognized, he would need a path and some helping hands along the way. He was fortunate to find mentors. And somehow, deeply embedded in his faith and belief he formed a silent vow to never forget how he got here from there."

She quoted Jesse Owens, who said, "We all have dreams. But in order to make dreams come into reality, it takes an awful lot of determination, dedication, self-discipline, and effort."

"Carl's great determination, dedication, self-discipline, and efforts have helped him realize his dream. It was a dream not about the trappings of positions, but rather about the pathways the positions could provide. I have had the privilege of being part of this journey for the past thirty-six years. I always smile when I think of our marriage. Who would have thought that Roxbury and Harlem, where I was raised—Harold Street and Convent Avenue—would be the intersection for those with the determination, the intellect, and the commitment to excel."

Joyce's speech was met with warm, sustained applause. She offered beautiful and heartfelt remarks and she captured my life's focus very well. Nobody knows me as well as Joyce and I am so grateful for the incalculable ways she has enriched my life. Following a video that included more testimonials and a lovely visual chronicle of my career, I stepped up to the podium to offer my honoree remarks. Joyce was a tough act to follow and she had already said everything that I wanted to say, and more eloquently than I could have done. I chose to keep my remarks very brief and simply to thank my family, friends, and colleagues who had put together such a wonderful retirement celebration and, especially, I thanked all the generous donors who made the evening a $260,000 statement on behalf of financially needy, high-achieving high school students in Harlem who would become McCall Scholars and would be given the support and resources necessary to pursue their dream of higher education—as Joyce and I had done.

I also mentioned what I had in mind for postretirement projects: to write a memoir about public service, to assist McCall Scholars, and to teach a college course on how public education is influenced by politics, social justice, and race. I got right to work on that next chapter, not only because I had stated those goals publicly, but because I am not one to sit still or enjoy a life of idleness. I prefer to be active and engaged on issues that matter.

I didn't have to look far for material on the course I was preparing. Dennis and Lloyd and the retirement planning committee had explored a naming opportunity on my behalf of a state or SUNY building. They noted that there is a glaring absence of names of women, Blacks, and minorities on SUNY and state buildings and they floated the idea of rectifying that by naming a building after me. They found one precedent. Governor Andrew Cuomo renamed Harlem's Riverbank State Park in 2017 for my friend and colleague, longtime assembly member and former chair of the New York Democratic Party Herman "Denny" Farrell Jr. Upon his retirement at age eighty-five, after forty-two years as the most powerful Black lawmaker of his generation, the Harlem park was named for Farrell. The governor also announced completion of a $25 million pedestrian bridge also named after Farrell that allowed access to the park at West 151st Street. As noted in media accounts, the plan to name the park for Farrell was part of an agreement that also named the new Tappan Zee Bridge for Cuomo's father, Governor Mario M. Cuomo.

My retirement committee co-chairs focused on the New York State Comptroller's Office Building at 110 State Street in downtown Albany, which I had financed and built under my tenure—while earning the derisive nickname "Taj McCall" by the media for misrepresentations of its "extravagance." Again, I want to stress that the co-chairs kept me apprised of their efforts, but this was entirely the committee's idea, and while I supported what they were trying to do, I was not engineering their actions. They approached Andrew Cuomo about naming the SUNY Administration Building after me as a possibility.

Later that summer of 2019, after the June retirement party, I got busy on my promised projects. I began interview sessions with author Paul Grondahl, director of the New York State Writers Institute at the University at Albany and an award-winning *Times Union* journalist. I had known Paul for twenty years or so, ever since he wrote a full-length profile on Joyce and myself as a power couple for the *Times Union*. I liked his writing style and heard good things about him from colleagues in Albany, and I was pleased he agreed to collaborate with me on the memoir. Jim Malatras, then president of the Rockefeller Institute of Government and currently chancellor of the State University of New York, helped put together the project and named me an author-in-residence at the Rockefeller Institute, a historic building in the heart of Albany across from Washington Park, where Paul and I spent many hours conducting interviews in a comfortable office that Jim provided for me.

"Chairman McCall has had an extraordinary career and his memoir will serve as required reading for those looking to enter public service," Malatras said in a press release, which also mentioned that he was naming me to the Rockefeller Institute's board of advisers to provide strategic advice and direction as the institute continues its groundbreaking public policy research.

"I am honored that Carl McCall asked me to work with him on his memoir. He has a remarkable story to share and I look forward to helping him tell it," Grondahl said in the release.

My first discussion on teaching a course was with UAlbany president Havidán Rodríguez, who supported the idea, and we began to make plans for me to teach in Albany in the fall of 2019. The more I considered the requirement of a regular weekly commute to Albany that I had just left behind, the more I wanted to reassess that issue. I had made that drive to Albany hundreds of times, but I did not relish having to do it each week while nursing a bad back.

Havidán and the other academic administrators at UAlbany were understanding of my change of plans and, instead, I began a discussion with a highly respected CUNY leader, Jennifer J. Raab, president of Hunter

College. I decided that, rather than a long commute to Albany, I would instead teach at a great public college located a short cab or subway ride across Manhattan at a City University of New York institution. President Raab and her staff worked out a wonderful opportunity and named me the Hunter College Roosevelt House Leader in Residence for the 2019–2020 academic year.

In Hunter's press release about my appointment, President Raab said: "His wealth of knowledge will be a huge benefit to our entire Hunter community, adding to our Roosevelt House programs and public policy courses. This is a tremendous opportunity to learn from his vast expertise."

I also reconnected with an old political colleague, Harold Holzer, whom I had known since he worked as an economic development aide to Governor Mario M. Cuomo, from 1984 to 1992. A renowned historian and Lincoln scholar, Holzer spent twenty-six years at the Metropolitan Museum in New York as senior vice president for public affairs. In 2015, he was named director of the Roosevelt House at Hunter College on East 65th Street—the historic former presidential home of Franklin and Eleanor Roosevelt, a double townhouse where the president's mother, Sara Delano Roosevelt, also lived. Holzer said: "Carl exemplifies the traditions we reflect at Roosevelt House: FDR's commitment to public service and public policy, and Eleanor's decisive impact on the field of human rights."

Harold was gracious and helpful as I prepared my syllabus and began developing the course at Hunter. For the fall semester, I participated in forums and programs at Roosevelt House on the topic of leadership and taught the course in the spring semester for twenty-two students, fifteen of whom were in the graduate program. I taught the class with assistance from Sigmund C. Shipp, a Black scholar on race relations and associate professor who directs the undergraduate urban studies program; Assistant Professor Catherine Voulgarides; and Professor Joseph P. Viteritti, chair of the Urban Planning and Policy Department. I had the students read and discuss essential texts by renowned Black authors W. E. B. Du Bois, Frederick Douglass, Richard Wright, Derrick Bell, James Baldwin, and Ta-Nehisi Coates.

For my lectures, I focused on integration in education and we analyzed data on the benefits of racial integration, while also reading reports and studies on the fact that New York City remains one of the most segregated public school systems in the country. It amounts to a caste system that can be traced to opposition by affluent white stakeholders who controlled the levers of political power through wealth and privilege. I also focused on the charter school movement, which I was involved with because SUNY authorized charter schools. Several of the undergraduates in the course had attended charter schools and a few of the graduate students had taught in charter schools, which made for a lively class discussion. The consensus among both the undergraduate and graduate students in the class was that charter schools had a negative impact on them and left a less-than-desirable impression—the reality, in their experience, being far inferior to the marketing claims.

I also got a call from the Governor's Office in early January that he was making a special request for me to attend Andrew Cuomo's tenth State of the State Address in Albany. This annual tradition kicks off the legislative session and brings together all 213 members of the New York State Legislature, as well as state commissioners, leading state officials, and former lawmakers and VIPs. It draws several hundred politicos, a virtual *Who's Who* of state government past and present. The governor's staff would not tell me exactly why I was extended this special invitation, but I figured I should be there, and I accepted.

The governor's theme of his address was to advance a bold agenda to continue New York's role as the progressive capital of the nation. Near the beginning of his speech, he paused to honor "two great public servants," longtime state senator Betty Little, who was retiring after thirty years representing the North Country, and myself. He called me "a true trailblazer who was the first African American to be elected to statewide office in this state. A statesman who served our country as ambassador to the United Nations, a public servant to the State of New York for fifty years as a state senator, comptroller, and most recently chairman of the SUNY Board of Trustees—Carl McCall. We're going to miss you. Let's show him our appreciation. Carl McCall also whooped me in a race for governor."

That last line caught me by surprise and seemed to me to be ad-libbed and off script. It drew a murmur and a few muffled laughs. I broke into a grin. It was the first time I had heard Andrew acknowledge our political primary battle all those years ago. I appreciated his kind and generous words and especially the candor of his afterthought. It made the trip to Albany all the sweeter.

There seemed to be a slow warming in the relations between Andrew and myself, which I would describe as a cross between aloofness and indifference. Some weeks later, one of his senior aides reached out to me to offer another plaudit. It caught me off guard, since I figured the State of the State shout-out was the end of it. But the governor's aide indicated that Andrew wanted to name the SUNY System Administration Building in downtown Albany after me. This time, I was speechless. The aide indicated that the governor would make the announcement as part of a major reception at the Executive Mansion in February during the 2020 Black, Puerto Rican, Hispanic & Asian Legislative Caucus in Albany. I was sworn to secrecy and found the whole thing very surprising.

Andrew Cuomo was gracious and said kind things about me at the reception in the governor's mansion. "He was the first African American elected statewide when he became comptroller of the State of New York. The first African American as chair of the SUNY Board of Trustees. Carl McCall broke the trail and in breaking the trail he bore the scars of the thorns and the obstacles in his way. But he cleared the path for all who followed: Governor David Paterson, Senate Majority Leader Andrea Stewart-Cousins, Speaker Carl Heastie, Attorney General Tish James. Carl McCall went first and he showed the way forward."

He also said kind things about Joyce and my daughter Marci and led the crowd in a round of applause for them.

And then Andrew paused, took a deep breath, and added this. "On a personal note, Carl taught me a great lesson in the governor's race in 2002 in the primary I ran against him and he knocked me right on my rear end. I tell my daughters you can learn more from defeat than from success. Well, I had a master's course in that campaign. So, I want to thank Carl, a belated thank you. It doesn't feel good to get knocked on your heinie, but you can learn from it and he did that for me."

The governor continued, "Today, it's my privilege to honor Carl McCall in the best way the State of New York can. The State of New York has a beautiful and historic building, the SUNY Education Building, right at the bottom of the hill, with the most historic and beautiful architecture of any building that the state has. And we're going to name that building for Carl McCall."

I responded to the governor's remarks by thanking him and highlighting the positive developments in New York State. "He's delivered a progressive agenda and it works by bringing people together," I said. "He has reformed the criminal justice system and it no longer leaves out poor people and look at what he's doing for diversity throughout this state."

I expressed gratitude for my family and colleagues. "My wife Joyce is my partner. I can't do anything without her. I don't even try," I said. "My daughter Marci and all the people who have been there helping me every day like Jen Mero, Jen LoTurco, and also Steve Greenberg and Barry Sample, and all the folks who helped me move through all the issues we face here in New York. I'm so grateful to have had an opportunity to have been a part of SUNY, the largest and best public higher education system in the country. The best!"

I also praised the vital work and growth of the Black, Puerto Rican, Hispanic & Asian Legislative Caucus. "I was a member of the caucus back in the day when there were five or six of us. Look how it's grown today. The caucus used to be sort of a protest group. They used to go after the leaders and urged them to do the right thing. Now all the leaders are part of the caucus. Things in Albany have really changed."

I mentioned the achievements of New York's dynamic Black political leaders, including Latrice Walker, Carl Heastie, Andrea Stewart-Cousins, Letitia James, and Rodneyse Bichotte.

"You know, I came from Boston but I was really nurtured in Harlem," I added. "That's where I was adopted by Percy Sutton, David Dinkins, Basil Paterson, Charlie Rangel. They were my leaders. They made it possible for a lot of us to do things and they said to me you've got to be part of this leadership group to try and provide opportunity for others. So, that's what I've done. I've tried to make sure that if I'm in a position, I'm going to perform in such a way that anybody who looks like me who comes after me, people will believe that they too can succeed."

I concluded by thanking Governor Andrew Cuomo and Governor Mario Cuomo, who appointed me a state commissioner. It was an emotional moment, especially when I saw a brass nameplate with H. Carl McCall SUNY Building engraved on it.

I had a spring in my step after this wonderful event on February 14, but my excitement came crashing down in mid-March when the deadly global novel coronavirus pandemic, a highly contagious respiratory disease, forced the shutdown of New York City, the state, the nation, and the world.

Fortunately, the faculty, staff, and students at Hunter College pivoted quickly to an online remote learning mode after COVID-19 protocols forced the shutdown of in-person, on-campus classes. The situation for Joyce was the same at FIT, as it was across the SUNY system and at colleges and universities across the country. With help from Harold Holzer and the Hunter co-teaching professors, we were able to complete the course and keep students engaged. I found that I didn't mind shifting to a virtual classroom and conducting my lectures and discussions via Zoom. While Joyce and I were sheltering in place in our Manhattan apartment, I quickly grasped the severity and deadly seriousness of COVID-19, particularly because my age and my medical condition put me into a very high-risk category. I took all necessary precautions and quarantined in the apartment.

Thankfully, I was receiving treatment from a terrific team of oncology specialists at Memorial Sloan Kettering Cancer Center, one of the world's finest cancer research and treatment facilities, conveniently located in Manhattan. I was also being treated with a promising medication and I learned an immediate lesson on the crushing cost of drugs, and appreciated the good fortune that I had the benefit of excellent medical insurance as a state retiree. The drug I had been prescribed cost $12,000 per month, which was covered by my state insurance plan and Medicare. Imagine if I did not have quality health insurance. It would be an impossible annual cost and it reminded me about the fragility of so many New Yorkers without health insurance—including homeless people, low-wage employees, gig workers, and young adults whose employers do not cover health insurance.

It was clear to me, as well as any rational and informed person— perhaps with the exception of then-president Donald Trump and his administration—that COVID-19 was a deadly and highly contagious virus and extreme measures were required. It was terribly painful to read newspapers and watch cable TV each night and see the number of infected Americans climb past seven million and the terrifying death toll in excess of five hundred thousand. I was in the heart of the epicenter of the pandemic and it became increasingly clear that, given my high-risk factors, I had to escape the high-density, high-infection landscape of Manhattan and relocate to a safer locale.

Fortunately, Joyce and I had owned for the past twenty years a weekend home in Dutchess County, about ninety minutes from our Manhattan apartment, chosen because it was equidistant between New York City and Albany. As comptroller, I could easily shuttle between my two offices in Albany and Manhattan, where my duties required me to be each week. I could stay at our country house in between the cities to make the commute more tolerable. Given the fact that both Hunter and FIT were in lockdown and devoid of students, faculty, and staff anyway, it made it easy for Joyce and me to relocate to Dutchess County—where she could carry out her presidential duties and I could teach over the internet. That is what we did.

I was grateful for the bucolic setting and wide-open spaces of Dutchess County. Although we do not ride, we were in the heart of the rolling hills of horse country. We also had installed an in-ground pool in our yard, which provided exercise and back pain relief. Things like shopping and going to restaurants certainly were not as convenient in Dutchess County, but New York City was in quarantine lockdown mode anyway. We settled in and managed to be productive and calm, while greatly reducing our chances of COVID-19 exposure amid the sparsely populated countryside. I continued to offer my assistance at SUNY and was called to serve as a sounding board, given the budgetary and programming challenges of the pandemic.

Joyce was able also to pivot quickly to a virtual format and to make our country home her remote office for running FIT. During the workday, I did not get much chance to spend time with Joyce because she was in constant Zoom meetings due to COVID-related issues with her staff. She faced enormous challenges of keeping her faculty and students safe while shifting to remote learning. At the same time, she also confronted dire financial fallout that the pandemic created because of a precipitous drop in revenue amid looming catastrophic deficits for New York State. Despite all the challenges, chaos, and fear in the wake of the deadly pandemic,

Joyce managed to create a viable operation that would have FIT up and running on a remote learning hybrid model for the remainder of the spring semester and the impending summer and fall semesters. Her leadership and consensus-building style proved crucial in dealing with the crisis and creating a rapid response so efficiently.

And then came the horrifying eight-minute, forty-six-second video that the world witnessed of the May 25, 2020, murder of George Floyd, a handcuffed and unarmed forty-six-year-old Black man. He died in the custody of Minneapolis police after a white officer pressed his knee on Floyd's neck and ignored his repeated pleas of "I can't breathe." The explosive footage recorded by a bystander was widely shared on social media and incited large protests against police brutality and systemic racism in Minneapolis and more than 150 American cities, as well as dozens more worldwide, over the summer and into the fall.

The community outrage over Floyd's killing sparked an FBI civil rights investigation and an internal review by the Minneapolis Police Department, which led to the firing and arrest of the officer, Derek Chauvin, who pinned his knee on Floyd's neck. The three other officers, who also were white and who watched Chauvin without intervening as he squeezed the life out of Floyd, were fired from their jobs.

Joyce and I watched the video of the George Floyd killing in horror and it had an enormous impact that shocked the world, spurred demonstrations globally, and had a galvanizing effect on forcing a racial reckoning after centuries of racial inequality and oppression against Blacks in the United States and beyond. At the same time, President Donald Trump continued to display a complete lack of empathy or leadership ability to try to calm the escalating protests, some of which included property destruction and riot-control tactics by police that included firing tear gas, flash-bang explosions, and water cannons to try to disperse the protesters. We were reminded of the grace and oratorical skills that former president Barack Obama brought to the White House and how skillfully he deployed all his talents in order to reassure and calm a bitterly divided citizenry during times of strife and disunity during his presidency. By contrast, Trump succeeded in business and politics by disruption and rancor. Trump used his bully pulpit as president to back the police unequivocally and to drive home a campaign platform urging law and order rather than to express empathy to the family of George Floyd and other Black victims of racism and lethal police violence.

I was particularly outraged when Trump ordered National Guard troops and United States Park Police to use tear gas, batons, and shields to push back protesters in the nation's capital who were demonstrating against police brutality late on a Monday afternoon on June 1. Trump ordered the aggressive police tactics so he could walk from the White House through Lafayette Park to the nearby St. John's Church for a photo opportunity to display that he kept his law-and-order promises. Trump was joined by Attorney General William Barr, Trump's daughter Ivanka and her husband, Jared Kushner, and other administration officials. Trump stopped briefly to hold up a Bible in front of the church and to say: "We have the greatest country in the world. Keep it nice and safe." Trump held the Bible awkwardly, as if it were a prop, simply so the media could photograph him. He did not pray or quote a Bible verse that might have tried to bring comfort or calm to the fraught moment. Trump's actions were denounced immediately by clergy.

"I was outraged that he felt that he had the license to do that, and that he would abuse our sacred symbols and our sacred space in that way," said the Right Reverend Mariann Edgar Budde, Episcopal Bishop of Washington, with oversight responsibilities for the church.

As an ordained minister, I was personally affronted by Trump's despicable and opportunistic photo op and I completely agreed with the Right Reverend Budde that Trump's action violated the sacred text at a sacred space.

The eruption of racial unrest and demonstrations that the killing of George Floyd touched off made me think deeply about my own experience with racial injustice in my life. I have described instances of prejudice and discrimination I faced growing up in Roxbury, during my time in the army, and other instances of racial insensitivity throughout my life. Fortunately, I was never the victim of police violence, but that was perhaps because I was raised by a strong-willed mother who was savvy to the long history of oppression against Blacks because of her family's experiences in the Deep South. That is why they migrated to Massachusetts, to escape the injustice of Jim Crow laws and the South's infrastructure of systemic racism. I consciously avoided encounters with police and never put myself in a situation where white officers could, for no apparent reason, inflict physical harm on me as a Black man. But I knew it happened and was far more common than reported. Friends, family members, and colleagues shared numerous stories of being harmed by racist police tactics. I had a sense of good fortune and privilege—on account of my Ivy League degree, military veteran status, and being an ordained minister—and I was blessed never to have been victimized by police brutality. But I prayed, and pray, for those Blacks and people of color who are.

My accepting nature and perhaps naive assumptions that as a Black man I was not vulnerable to such police violence were challenged by the case of Amadou Diallo, a twenty-three-year-old Guinean immigrant living in the Bronx. In the early morning on February 4, 1999, Diallo was fatally shot by four New York City Police Department plainclothes officers. The officers, who were all white, fired a total of forty-one shots at the unarmed Black man. Diallo was struck nineteen times while entering his apartment. The cops claimed that they thought Diallo was a lookout for reputed drug dealers in the area, and they also later said he matched the description of a rapist whose attacks occurred a year earlier. The officers said that Diallo did not heed a command to stop and show his hands. When Diallo reached into his jacket, they said they assumed he had a gun and they fired. A witness testified at the trial that the cops shot without warning. It was later revealed that Diallo pulled a wallet from his coat and that he did not possess a weapon.

A Bronx grand jury indicted the four officers on charges of second-degree murder and reckless endangerment. In December of that same year, 1999, a court ordered a change of venue to Albany because of extensive pretrial publicity. The trial against the four police officers was moved to the capital city, in theory, so that the cops could get a fair trial after the killing touched off a wave of protests and outrage in New York City against police brutality, racial profiling, and excessive use of force. I was serving as state comptroller in Albany at the time and I followed the trial closely. After two days of deliberation, a jury in Albany acquitted the four police officers of all charges.

I was stunned as a public official. As a Black man, I was outraged. The Diallo trial was what I considered to be a miscarriage of justice. This travesty resulted from our country's deep strain of racial inequality, and it was a tipping point for me. My interpretation after close reading of the trial evidence and the Diallo verdict was that the white police officers were looking for a Black man, they found a Black man, and they killed him. It made me feel vulnerable. Even as the state's first Black official elected to statewide office, I had no more protection or inoculation against racism and police violence than this unfortunate Guinean immigrant had. Perhaps for the first time in my life, I felt at risk and it suddenly sunk in that I could be a target simply because of the color of my skin. I understood that I, too, could be a victim of police violence if I happened to find myself in the wrong place at the wrong time. I felt that I had to do something as a Black man, with a platform as large as comptroller of the state of New York. I was compelled to act.

I decided to join the demonstrations in front of Police Plaza in Manhattan, where protesters continued to express their anger at the racial injustice of the acquittal of Amadou Diallo's killers and the barbarity of the forty-one shots. I agreed to join a high-profile act of civil disobedience with former New York City mayor Ed Koch and Bronx borough president Fernando "Freddy" Ferrer, along with other public officials. Unfortunately, Koch, who had confirmed his participation, became ill that morning while exercising and was a last-minute cancellation. But Freddy and I and others were arrested, along with several other demonstrators. We ended up spending most of the day in jail in a holding cell before our paperwork was processed and we were released. I felt that I was making a very visible and conscious stand against the outcome of the Diallo trial and raising my voice against racial injustice. It was something that had hit me in the gut and I felt compelled to do. It harkened back to 1964, when I took a stand and was arrested alongside my three closest friends—Leon Watts, Jim McGraw, and Calvin Pressley—as well as a group of prominent Brooklyn ministers and about two hundred other protesters during a demonstration at the construction site for a new Downstate Medical Center Hospital in Brooklyn after hospital administrators refused to hire minority construction workers.

The acquittal of the four white cops who riddled Mr. Diallo's defenseless Black body with nineteen hits out of a barrage of forty-one bullets—followed by a promotion to sergeant for one of the cops—was a grotesque and racist abuse of power and it struck me to the core of my racial identity. I felt like I had come full-circle from my days at the Brooklyn hospital civil disobedience to confront racial discrimination and support grassroots efforts that I undertook on behalf of poor, voiceless residents who did not have the platform and the resources that I had been blessed to possess.

It was in that context that I began to feel drawn to pay closer attention and get involved with the Black Lives Matter movement and support the flood of protests and demonstrations following George Floyd's killing by Minneapolis police in the spring of 2020.

I also understood that this was about far more than SUNY practices and policies. I have long understood that systemic racism is embedded in American history and particularly in New York State politics, which I experienced firsthand. I also do not want to be accused of reverse racism, although I do support affirmative action and other efforts to level a playing field that has long been tilted away from Blacks, Indigenous, and People of Color, or BIPOC, which is a new iteration for inclusivity that I have adopted. I believe that the BIPOC community deserves to be given special attention at this moment of racial reckoning, but I also firmly believe that all lives matter and that it is a demonstrable truth of American life that white lives receive privilege and Black lives are discriminated against. I particularly like how this issue is framed in a quote from Ta-Nehisi Coates, an acclaimed Black journalist and author of the number one *New York Times* bestselling book *Between the World and Me*. The quote from Ta-Nehisi Coates that so well encapsulates the centuries-old issue of white supremacy for me is this: "To be black in America is to be plundered. To be white is to execute and benefit from it."

I have long been drawn to the philosophy of nonviolence and the brilliant mind of the Reverend Dr. Martin Luther King Jr. I particularly feel this quote from Dr. King provides a nuanced view on racial justice that speaks to my own beliefs and sense of hopefulness: "I refuse to accept the view that mankind is so tragically bound to the starless midnight of racism and war that the bright daybreak of peace and brotherhood can never become a reality . . . I believe that unarmed truth and unconditional love will have the final word."

I also have been drawn to the quote often mistakenly attributed to King: "The arc of the moral universe is long, but it bends toward justice." President Barack Obama helped to popularize that quote and loved it so much he had it woven into a rug in the Oval Office. It became a rallying cry for those who practiced progressive politics and Obama cited it frequently to temper the fact that, even though he was the first Black president elected in American history, his election was just one more step along the long road toward a just society. Rarely was the source discussed, but history records that King paraphrased and compressed a portion of a sermon delivered in 1853 by the abolitionist minister the Reverend Theodore Parker, a Unitarian pastor in the Boston area who was also an influential reformer and transcendentalist. Parker delivered these lines in that sermon: "I do not pretend to understand the moral universe. The arc is a long one. My eye reaches but little ways. I cannot calculate the curve and complete the figure by experience of sight. I can divine it by conscience. And from what I see I am sure it bends toward justice."

As a minister myself, I can appreciate Reverend Parker's elegant prose, but I also think that Dr. King's phrasing is much more succinct, highly quotable, and packs a much more powerful punch.

While all the disruption of the Black Lives Matter movement and protests against systemic racism were escalating in response to George Floyd's murder and the number of deaths from COVID-19 was also beginning to spike and become a full-blown global health crisis, I received a surprise phone call from SUNY chancellor Kristina Johnson in June. Kristina had been very helpful and kind during my transition into retirement and extremely generous in matching a six-figure sum raised at my retirement dinner for scholarships for needy students of color. But this call caught me completely off guard. Kristina told me she had just returned from Columbus, Ohio, and she had accepted the position of president of The Ohio State University. I listened in stunned silence. She would become just the sixteenth president in the history of Ohio State, which was founded in 1870. She explained that this was an extraordinary offer that she could not refuse, a professional opportunity that fulfilled both personal and career goals. She had deep family roots in Ohio. Her grandfather graduated from Ohio State, played football there, and met his future wife on the Columbus campus.

Also, Ohio State is widely considered one of the most prestigious schools in America and most recently ranked number fifty-three in the 2021 edition of "Best Colleges" among national universities. With nearly fifty thousand undergraduate students, highly ranked graduate programs, and a College of Medicine on its sprawling campus—not to mention the prestige of the Ohio State Buckeyes' numerous national championships in football and other sports in the Big Ten Conference—Kristina said she had accepted this prestigious position. She also confided in me that she was particularly drawn to Ohio State's single campus, as opposed to SUNY's sixty-four-campus system, which she found very challenging to manage. She also had expressed early concerns to me about how political the SUNY chancellor position was. Although we had tried to explain this to her during the interview process, she had not grasped how interlocked the operation of SUNY was with political realities and the influence and control of Governor Andrew Cuomo until she actually arrived in Albany and started doing the job.

The announcement was made by The Ohio State University on June 3 and Dr. Johnson was scheduled to begin her new position in Columbus on August 24. SUNY barely had time to absorb the shock before pivoting to fill-the-position mode. We were in the midst of a global health emergency and the losses were staggering by every measure, certainly in terms of deaths and hospitalizations, but also in catastrophic economic damage. New York State was facing an estimated budget deficit of roughly $15 billion as a result of the COVID-19 business shutdown and loss of tax revenue. As a result, the entire SUNY system was facing dire consequences after the Cuomo administration signaled that the sixty-four-campus system should anticipate reductions in state assistance of at least 20 percent. At this moment of the worst crisis to hit the state in decades and perhaps in the past century, Dr. Johnson chose to move on and SUNY was faced with trying to negotiate an unprecedented crisis without a chancellor at the helm. It was very unfortunate timing and I told Kristina that.

Fortunately, Robert Megna, SUNY's senior vice chancellor and chief operating officer, a first-rate administrator whom I respected, agreed to serve as interim chancellor. I have known Bob for many years and he has served three decades in public service, including a stint as senior vice president for finance and administration at Stony Brook University, executive director of the New York State Thruway Authority and the New York State Canal Corporation, as well as budget director for the New York State Division of the Budget.

And throughout all this upheaval and stress at SUNY, the Black Lives Matter protests continued, sometimes in violent clashes between demonstrators and police. I was firmly on the side of the demonstrators and believed deeply in the right of civil disobedience, nonviolent protests, the rights of free speech and to assemble, and that all Americans had a constitutional right to protest without being harmed or injured. I have found in my experience that most protesters are peaceful, but in the case of Black Lives Matter, some outside groups who intended to create disruption and havoc gave a bad name to the protesters who were going about their demonstrations in the proper way. One element I did not fully understand and could not support is the movement's call to "defund the police." I rejected that idea as misinformed and overly simplistic and idealistic. I feel that we do need, as a society, trained police officers who are sworn to protect and serve the people in their communities and who take an oath to do so. If there are some racist officers who do not live up to that oath and who commit acts of police brutality and use excessive force or shoot and kill unarmed Black people, I believe they should be charged and prosecuted to the fullest extent of the law. That would show the community a serious effort to weed out corruption and bad behavior and it would also deter other bad cops. Rather than defund the police, I would support efforts to reform the police. I think much can be changed in the ways police departments go about policing, but I want well-trained officers to respectfully protect us and transfer some of their other responsibilities, such as dealing with mental health crises, to other agencies.

As the novel coronavirus pandemic escalated throughout the summer and into the fall, I regularly watched Governor Andrew Cuomo's press briefings as he tried to mitigate the initial terrible and deadly spike of COVID-19 deaths in New York City, Long Island, and Westchester County—which became ground zero in America's response to the pandemic. Cuomo and his outstanding team of state government experts on the state's interagency task force did an excellent job of putting in place stringent lockdowns and protocols to combat the spread of COVID-19—although the high number of infections and deaths in nursing homes remained a dark cloud over Cuomo's otherwise successful strategies and demonstrable success.

Given the fact that the state was in the midst of a singular public health emergency and the state legislature had essentially gone into hiatus during the widespread quarantine that shut down businesses across the state, Cuomo ruled with unprecedented and unchecked authority. The governor was given carte blanche in terms of issuing executive orders without the usual checks and balances of the legislative branch. Some began to bristle at Cuomo's unilateral decisions—including bar and restaurant owners, movie theater operators, and managers of gyms—that threatened their livelihoods with a lockdown that extended for many months while their businesses teetered on the edge of bankruptcy. Critics began calling Cuomo the "King of New York," which was the title of a penetrating and critical profile by Nick Paumgarten in the *New Yorker* magazine in October.

Even though I was enjoying retirement and engaged in meaningful pursuits teaching at Hunter, working on this memoir, and fishing for bass in the lake at our country retreat, I was called back by my former colleagues at SUNY to help them recover after the unexpected departure of Chancellor Johnson and the resulting confusion and leadership vacuum. The news had not yet sunk in when Larry Schwartz, a longtime loyalist and top aide to Governor Andrew Cuomo, spoke to Capitol reporters and began actively promoting SUNY Empire State College president Jim Malatras as the next chancellor of SUNY. Schwartz went so far as to urge the SUNY Board of Trustees to forgo a nationwide search and to give the job to Malatras posthaste, and without the usual process of hiring a high-profile executive search firm due to the extraordinary immediate challenges created by the unprecedented novel coronavirus pandemic.

What Schwartz did not need to say was that he was serving as Andrew's messenger and he had signaled to the SUNY trustees and to the press and all New Yorkers that Malatras was his guy and he wanted his guy installed as SUNY's next chancellor. This raised eyebrows, ruffled feathers, and caused something of a crisis for my colleagues on the SUNY board, where I had dedicated twelve years of my service. My email inbox and my phone began pinging with entreaties of concern and calls for assistance. I thought I was done with SUNY. I was retired. The requests for help kept coming. The dedicated administrators and staff of SUNY felt like a second family to me. I could not turn my back during their time of turmoil. I was drawn, reluctantly, back into the periphery of the maelstrom.

Personally, I had come to know and respect Malatras, who was smart, ambitious, hard-working, and very well connected politically. He also earned all three of his degrees—bachelor's, master's, and doctorate in political science—from UAlbany, a SUNY school. That fact was a plus in my mind. He had become a trusted and loyal aide to Andrew Cuomo as executive director of legislative affairs and state policy when Cuomo was attorney general. As governor, Cuomo appointed Malatras to his New NY Education Reform Commission. I had also seen Malatras in action when he served as chief of staff for Chancellor Nancy Zimpher for one year, beginning in 2013, where I observed he was relentless and had sharp elbows.

Cuomo appointed Malatras to one of the governor's most demanding positions, director of state operations, where he made the machinery of the Empire State run day to day and also advised the governor on policy development. Cuomo had promoted Malatras up the rungs of state government for his loyalty, tenacity, and acumen. I also crossed paths with Malatras when he served as president of the Rockefeller Institute of Government in Albany and later as the fifth president of SUNY Empire State College. His rapid rise was both earned and expected. Moving up to chancellor of the entire SUNY system was the biggest leap yet of his career and some felt he needed a few more academic postings to earn his higher ed stripes.

After Schwartz's public campaigning and Cuomo's not-so-subtle thumb on the scale, the ascension to chancellor seemed a fait accompli for Malatras. The backstage maneuvering put the SUNY Board of Trustees in an impossible position—a virtual checkmate. How could the eighteen trustees—fifteen of whom are appointed by the governor, who controls

SUNY's financial support—defy Cuomo and go against his pick of Malatras. The board sought my counsel and I said that Malatras had exceptional ability and he was qualified. I noted that, given Malatras's deep connection to Cuomo, he might be in the best position to get the governor to deliver on his promises to support SUNY despite the yawning budget gap caused by the coronavirus pandemic. Maybe having Cuomo's inside guy as chancellor would be the best thing for SUNY in the long run. I argued that from my perspective Malatras, who was on the governor's COVID-19 task force, would be in a unique position to advocate for SUNY with looming budget cuts due to the pandemic.

There was modest pushback and some resistance to Malatras voiced by the three board members who represented the SUNY faculty and students, but they were not the leaders or most powerful voices among the trustees. I spoke with Dr. Merryl H. Tisch, the chair and my successor. She is a pragmatist and she, too, came to accept the fact that Malatras had the qualifications and connections to do the job.

In the end, I supported Jim Malatras as the fourteenth chancellor of SUNY and so did the board. He was sworn in on August 21, 2020, and he was immediately thrown into the tumult brought about by spikes in COVID-19 cases on some SUNY campuses that were traced to large off-campus parties with crowds of students drinking and partying without face masks and without social distancing. This was an unprecedented situation from the outside, including his appointment without a search process, and Malatras earned his stripes by taking the helm of the SUNY ship in turbulent seas and an uncharted course.

I welcomed Jim Malatras as the new chancellor and wished him luck. I knew that he would need it.

"This is a long way from Roxbury," my collaborator, Paul Grondahl, told me when he came to visit Joyce and me at our Clinton Corners retreat in September.

"Yes, it is," I said. "My forty acres and a pool."

We spoke that afternoon about the long journey I had made out of poverty, raised by a single mother on welfare after my father left us, and on to an Ivy League education at Dartmouth and a long and productive career in both public service and the corporate world.

Our rural retreat is halfway between Albany and New York City, which have been the two touchstones of my career. I love being in the country. Joyce tolerates it. She is an urbanite to the core. You can take the girl out of Harlem, but you can't take Harlem out of the girl.

Meanwhile, we are delighted to note that Joyce's dogged determination and management skills have overcome financial and bureaucratic obstacles with the city and state. A state-of-the-art FIT academic building, the first academic addition to the campus in more than forty years, is under construction and slated for completion in the fall of 2023.

We enjoy entertaining our friends here on weekend getaways from the city, or visits from my daughter Marci or Joyce's nieces. We do not have grandchildren.

As the end of 2021 approaches, I am encouraged by the new political leadership that will be guiding the city and state.

Eric Adams will be the mayor of New York City, an ex-cop and a probusiness moderate who has pledged to curb the rising crime rate and challenge the ascending progressive-socialist coalition in the city. I endorsed Adams in the Democratic primary and I agreed to join an advisory group he formed to address the city's economic recovery.

In an astonishing reversal of fortune, Kathy Hochul is our governor and she brings a refreshing change in leadership style. She has not been inside on the Cuomo leadership team. As lieutenant governor, she traveled the state, promoting the governor's agenda, making contacts, and impressing people with her work ethic and earnest commitment to public service.

Andrew demonstrated remarkable leadership during the darkest days of the pandemic. His focus and hopeful, reassuring personal messages at his daily press briefing attracted national attention. He was controlling a determined response, in contrast to President Trump, who was lying about the seriousness of the pandemic and had no plan to defeat coronavirus.

Devastating allegations of sexual misconduct, falsification of the number of reported coronavirus deaths in nursing homes, and using state employees and staff to write a book about leadership that netted Andrew $5 million all came crashing down on him. Andrew denied all of it and asked Attorney General Letitia James to investigate. The allegations elicited calls for Andrew's resignation and impeachment by both Republican and Democratic elected officials.

The attorney general's investigation was conducted by two independent lawyers retained by James. Their report identified eleven women, several of whom were state employees, whose claims of sexual harassment and misconduct were deemed credible and were corroborated by investigators. The report accelerated demands for the governor to resign, and at that point even President Joe Biden joined the chorus calling for Cuomo to step down.

On August 10, 2021, Andrew Cuomo announced that he would resign as governor of New York on August 24. It was a spectacular fall from his powerful post. His aggressive and often combative governance style, which he claims was necessary to get anything done in New York, left him with no friends or allies. He leaves a complicated and contradictory legacy.

The collateral damage from Cuomo's undoing continued to destroy careers of those who had become enmeshed in the toxic culture created and fostered by the disgraced governor. Embattled SUNY chancellor Jim Malatras, a longtime Cuomo confidant and trusted adviser, announced his resignation on December 9, 2021. Malatras had faced a barrage of criticism and a rising chorus for his resignation after media reports detailed his berating of female staffers and disparaging on social media of one of the women who leveled sexual misconduct allegations against Cuomo. In addition, the governor's brother, Chris Cuomo, a prime-time star on CNN, was fired that same month by the network after new information surfaced about the extent to which the broadcast journalist assisted the defense of his brother against sexual misconduct charges. There were other, less high-profile resignations and firings in the wake of the Cuomo scandal. I came to view the implosion of Andrew Cuomo's political career and so many of those close to him as a kind of train wreck: hard to turn away from, and grim in the number of lives destroyed by the ongoing derailings. I took no pleasure in observing the wreckage.

I am content to grow old here at our rural retreat, puttering around the acres with Joyce, who enjoys gardening. I feel like a country squire in Clinton Corners and I have the time and space to reflect on all the things I have done and what I have learned, which I have tried to put into this memoir.

Joyce does not like to fish, but Matt, our wonderful caretaker, joins me in a pontoon boat outfitted with an electric motor. We glide noiselessly over the placid water, casting with jigs, fishing in silence. One evening this summer, we caught two dozen bass between us in two hours. Matt built a lovely dock with benches and Joyce and I like to go there at sunset and sometimes to raise a glass of wine to our good fortune.

Fishing helps me feel connected to the natural world. It clears my mind and allows me not to focus solely on human problems, at least for a time. Fishing is a kind of meditation for me, almost a prayer, and it keeps me in touch with deeper levels of my consciousness.

When I am out fishing on our lake, I am reminded that I surely am a long way from Roxbury. I am deeply grateful for my life, which has been truly blessed and highly favored. Amen.

Acknowledgments

I wish to thank Paul Grondahl, who was my dedicated collaborator in this effort. As the director of the New York State Writers Institute at the University at Albany, following a distinguished career at the Albany *Times Union* spent covering New York state's political and cultural activities, Paul brought a unique set of skills and experiences to guide me. I am grateful for his friendship and assistance.

I am grateful to Barbara Jariri, who provided valuable and essential staff support during my tenure as New York State Comptroller. She interrupted her retirement to assist in producing this book. I could not have completed this without her.

In addition to her many skills, my wife Joyce was a terrific editor, and an inspiration for this project as she has been in all of my endeavors.

James Peltz and Diane Ganeles are superb professionals who made my experience with SUNY Press a rewarding one. I thank them for assisting me and for their leadership promoting the State University of New York through SUNY Press.

I also want to commemorate and dedicate this book to my mother, Caroleasa, who taught me the importance of a quality education and made sacrifices to ensure that I achieved that goal.

I want to dedicate this book also to Joyce, my wife and partner, whose advice and actions keep me hopeful and grateful for what we can accomplish together.

I include in my dedication Marci, my daughter. I am proud of her professional growth and her commitment to social activism.

Also, I dedicate this book to my sisters Judith, Inez, Audrey, Edythe, and Cheryl, my earliest and most enduring friends and steadfast supporters. I remember also my aunts Inez, Hazel, and Eunice, who taught me the meaning and value of family by their example.

Some are no longer with me, but my memories of them are everlasting. These are the women who loved me, inspired me, supported me, and enriched my life. This book would not have been possible without them and I am deeply grateful to each of them.

Index